The Empty Schoolhouse

⅋

NUMBER SIXTY-EIGHT:
*The Centennial Series of the
Association of Former Students,
Texas A&M University*

The Empty

Schoolhouse

Memories of
One-Room
Texas Schools

COLLECTED AND
EDITED BY
LUTHER BRYAN CLEGG

Texas A&M University Press
College Station

The paper used in this book meets the minimum requirements
of the American National Standard for Permanence
of Paper for Printed Library Materials, Z39.48-1984.
Binding materials have been chosen for durability.

Library of Congress Cataloging-in-Publication Data

Clegg, Luther B.
    The empty schoolhouse : memories of one-room Texas schools / collected
and edited by Luther Bryan Clegg. — 1st ed.
        p.   cm. — (The centennial series of the Association of Former
Students, Texas A&M University ; no. 68)
    Includes bibliographical references (p.) and index.
    ISBN 0-89096-749-0 (alk. paper)
    1. Teachers—Texas—Interviews. 2. Students—Texas—Interviews.
3. Rural schools—Texas—History—20th century—Case studies.
4. Education, Rural—Texas—History—20th century—Case studies. I. Title.
II. Series.
LA2315.T4C54   1997   96-52977
                                                                CIP

In memory of my mother,
Narcissa Poteet Clegg,
1902–84

Teaching is something to enjoy twice. You enjoy the days with your pupils; then when you are old, you are filled with pleasant memories that make your life happy as you quietly piece quilts to fill the hours.

— Ina Dingus Cowan, 1906–91

Contents

✌ PART I ✌

Ain't Nothin' There Now But a Cistern Full of Rattlesnakes: Recollections of Pupils

---

⁓ PART II ⁓

If I Had Another Life to Live, I'd Teach Again:
Recollections of Teachers

Illustrations

Preface

In 1984, I returned to my boyhood home in Longhorn Valley, located on a bend of the Double Mountain Fork of the Brazos River. My mother was dying of cancer, and I was struggling to bring purpose and meaning to the experience.

I shuffled along the dirt road that climbs to the hills south of the house where I was born, and puffing my way to the top of the bluffs, I studied the panorama before me. Hawks floated lazily above my head, but nothing moved in the valley below. All was eerily silent. Scanning the horizon, I could scarcely make out the outline of a rock foundation that once supported a two-room cabin on the banks of the little creek that flowed eastward. Shadows from the hills to the west shrouded a jumble of decaying lumber, the gaunt remains of an abandoned homestead.

I looked across to the north, hoping for visible signs of life. There were none. Clumps of purple iris that had escaped into the wild marked the sites of the eight or so houses that once crouched under the bluffs and along the banks of the river. I turned to the east and searched vainly for some vestige of the three houses that earlier stood, sturdy and stalwart, among the cottonwood trees. In the entire area, where smoke from a dozen or more chimneys had once drifted upward over the bluffs, a lone house remained, a stark reminder of the life that previously bustled in this valley.

Missing from the landscape also were the three schoolhouses that distinguished their communities in the early years of the century. County Line School, sometimes one room, sometimes two, had stood to my right; across the river, a few miles away, Riverdale School had sat among the cedar breaks; down the road, near the cemetery, Cottonwood Flat School had flourished. Like the hundreds of rural schools scattered across Texas in the years before consolidation, little remained to mark their existence—a few scattered rocks, a rusty tin can or two, and the crumbling rims of water cisterns.

That afternoon, the river valley and its environs were virtually devoid of human life. Wild animals—turkeys, deer, bobwhites, skunks, and rattlesnakes—and a few shorthorn cattle had usurped the settlers of the late 1880s; they had replaced the farmers and ranchers who built their homes and raised their families in these communities. Gone were the chickens scratching in the red dirt, the wash flapping on the clothesline, the path leading to the outhouse. Gone, too, were the children carrying slop to the pigs, the women bending over their "rub boards," and the men planting their fields to corn. Gone? When did they leave and why did they go? Where were they now? How did it happen that a place vibrantly alive a few decades ago could now resemble the country cemetery?

I thought of my mother who had grown up, married, and lived to old age among these hills and cedar brakes. When she was no longer alive, what would we remember? What were some of the things she had told us? Searching my memory, vignettes arose: children getting in trouble for playing hooky on April Fool's Day; Aunt Blanche, eccentric but lively at age eighty, skipping down the road to visit a neighbor; Lila Foote riding a train west to marry a man she had never met; Miss Florence in her dame's cap trying to instill culture into a group of recalcitrant, rambunctious boys.

In the distance a car honked; my wife was growing impatient. I knew that soon I must come down from these bluffs, yet I was reluctant to leave the memories of the afternoon. Was there a way to preserve for my children and my children's children an understanding of how our forebears lived? Could I make them aware of what it was like to attend school where every grade from one through eight was clustered in one room; to eat without complaint a steady diet of biscuits, fried meat, and sorghum because that was what one had; to sleep with four in the bed, two at the head, two at the foot, because your home had two beds and Ma, Pa, and the baby slept in one? Could they be made to envision life not only without radios, television, computers, and hair spray but also without automobiles, electricity, running water, and penicillin?

I could feel a project stirring within me. I knew what I was going to do: I would provide through first-person accounts—through the eyes of those who experienced it—a record of life in "the olden days," and thus preserve for posterity a sense of its singularity and uniqueness.

∞ Before the coming of the automobile, community life revolved around the school. It was the center of educational, social, political, and religious activity. It was here children were taught to read and cipher, couples were united in marriage, funerals were preached, and Friday night socials were held. It appeared that one way to preserve the history of an area was to record the oral histories of the people who attended its schools. Thus, I came to the nucleus of my project: to interview those persons who were associated with one- and two-room schools and record their histories for the purpose of obtaining firsthand accounts of rural life. In order to limit the scope of the project, I decided to concentrate on locales in central West Texas, roughly the areas between Fort Worth and Odessa and the Hill Country and Amarillo. I limited the years of my study to approximately the first half of the twentieth century.

I began my research by looking at historical and sociological data related to the locales and time period of my study. I found that most West Texas counties were settled between the years 1880 and 1900, and rural counties peaked in population around 1930. One example is Fisher County, located about sixty miles northwest of Abilene. The rise and fall of its population is typical of many counties in rural Texas. The U.S. Bureau of the Census reported only 136 people living in the county in 1880. During the next ten years, the population increased more than twenty-fold to 2,996. Soon, hundreds of settlers were pouring into the county, and by 1910 the population had swelled to 12,596. The population rose steadily over the next two decades until it peaked at 13,563 in 1930.

The Depression and World War II were responsible for some families' leaving the county, and by 1950 the population dropped slightly to approximately 11,000. However, it was not until the 1960s and 1970s that a mass exodus to urban areas occurred. The county's population dropped to less than 5,000 by 1990, most of whom now reside within two towns. Many of the families who continue to operate farms no longer live on their land. They have become "gentleman farmers," overseeing the production of their crops by means of the farm-to-market roads that crisscross the county.

As more people moved into and settled an area, more and more schools were necessary. Because of the limitations associated with transportation, schools were generally established within thirty-six square miles. With the coming of automobiles and mechanization, these small districts were no longer necessary, and the move toward consolidation began.

An extensive county-by-county report on the adequacy of public schools was prepared by the Texas State Board of Education in 1936. This report, entitled *Texas Statewide School Adequacy Survey,* listed the names and school populations of common and independent school districts and made specific recommendations for reorganization and consolidation. Within ten years of the survey's recommendations, consolidation had swept across Texas. By 1950, the small one- and two-teacher schools in Texas had ceased to exist except in remote, out-of-the-way places.

In order to successfully preserve portions of the history from this earlier era, I needed support from my university. In 1986, I was granted leave of absence from Texas Christian University and began a search for teachers who taught and pupils who attended one- and two-teacher schools. I was fortunate to have numerous contacts in Fisher County among friends and relatives with whom to begin my research. As my project broadened, it spread across much of West Texas, from the Hill Country to Pecos County, from Lubbock into the Panhandle. In 1994, I was given a second leave of absence to complete my research and prepare this manuscript.

I interviewed a total of seventy-seven persons, some of whom had both attended and taught in rural schools. The oldest respondent was born in 1890, the youngest in 1934. Of the interviewees, fifty were female and twenty-seven were male. (The accounts of some interviewees are not contained in this volume.)

The selections by Stella Gipson Polk in chapters 7, 9, and 10 are similar to material that appears in her book *For All Those Pupils Whose*

Lives Touched Mine. (At the time of my interview with Stella in 1986, she gave to me her manuscript to use in whatever way I found helpful. Recognizing the merit of her writing, I took the manuscript to TCU Press. They advised me to send it to Texas A&M University Press, and it was published by them in 1989.)

I have transcribed the interviews verbatim, editing only for clarification. In some stories, I have changed names to protect individuals from possible embarrassment. I want the reader to hear the voices as they were spoken to me. In order to retain the speech patterns, I have attempted to spell words as they were spoken. It is my hope that the reader will be spellbound as was I upon hearing these reminiscences and will view them as preserving a part of our educational heritage.

Since I began my research, more than a third of the interviewees have died. It is obvious the memory of this era is rapidly passing, and the preservation of its history must be immediate.

ᴥ I am deeply indebted to the persons I interviewed; they gave eagerly and generously of their time to further my research. Without their cooperation, much of the history of an era would have been lost.

I am grateful to TCU for its support of this project. Additionally, my work was greatly enhanced by the assistance of Susan Ford Carr in preparing the photographs and by the generosity of Frances Clegg Ferris for sharing with me the interviews she conducted in 1983 with our mother, Narcissa Poteet Clegg.

Introduction

Throughout its history, the species *Homo sapiens* has desired to pass to its offspring the knowledge it deemed important. In primitive eras children were taught skills that promoted survival. As societies became more sophisticated, the body of knowledge that was passed to succeeding generations became more complex. It was no longer sufficient to teach boys the means of providing food and shelter and girls the ways of homemaking and child rearing. They also needed the ability to store and access information, that is, to read and to write. It became important to preserve the collective knowledge of the group: the history, values, and function of the society as well as mathematical and scientific discoveries. Because the task was too enormous for each family, groups pooled resources. Hence, the birth of the school.

As one looks at the history of education in the United States, it is evident that schools reflect, and have always reflected, the society and times in which they operate. For example, the religious fervor of the Puritans resulted in reading being taught for the purpose of understanding the Bible. Formal education was reserved for those preparing for the ministry. As the colonies grew, an increasingly diverse population saw need for broader opportunities. Four types of schools evolved: the dame school, the town school, the Latin grammar school, and the college.[1] Soon after the end of the American Revolution, with the establishment of our nation, the idea developed that a democratic government in a democratic society necessitates that the majority of the people be literate, hence, the birth of the common school with its primary goal of promoting literacy.

The rise and fall of the rural school mimicked the rise and fall of the nation's population patterns. As settlers migrated westward in larger and larger numbers, schools were established to accommodate increased populations. These rural one- and two-room schools in West Texas were distinguished by certain characteristics.

The population of the school was largely homogeneous. The limitations of transportation decreed that school districts be quite small, usually thirty-six square miles. The families within this radius were neighbors, often related, who not only shared a common school but also often worshiped at a common church, pursued common goals, and were beset by common problems, such as grasshoppers, drought, hail, and epidemics. There was little ethnic, economic, or employment diversity.

The length of the school year was variable and was affected by sundry factors. School began in the fall when crops were harvested and ended in the spring when it was time to plant, as it was accepted that children were needed at home to assist with farming. The calendar was always flexible and was based on money available. If the money ran out after four months, then there was only a four-month school term. If an adverse problem arose, such as a teacher's leaving or becoming ill within the school term, school might be terminated for the remainder of the year. An epidemic within the community usually closed the doors for the duration of the illness. Thus, school was in session when conditions allowed. In 1910, the average length of the school term in rural schools in Texas was 117 days compared to 160 days in nonrural schools.[2]

The trustees of the school were given large powers of control. They were usually three men (always men) respected by the community, who had the responsibility of making all decisions related to the school. They hired and fired teachers, set the school calendar, made arrangements for supplies, such as fuel and water, settled moral issues, and often lent a hand in disciplining and punishing pupils. One account relates that trustees assessed the number of squares of toilet tissue each child should use in a day! As they were the ultimate authority, a teacher must please them not only in punctuality, methodology, and classroom management but also in the length of one's skirt, or the length of one's beard, and in the "moral rectitude" that one exhibited.

The curriculum reflected the values of a rural society. There was strong emphasis on the basics, with little time devoted to creativity, art, music, hygiene, or even physical education outside noon recess. For example, trustees looked askance at an applicant who offered to teach tap dancing. These rural parents were men and women attempting to wrestle a living from an austere and sometimes hostile environment, and they desired for their children a no-frills education. Emphasis was placed on reading, spelling, handwriting, and arithmetic. History, geography, and science were regarded as less important and were taught when time allowed.

There was freedom to engage in Christian instruction, including daily prayer and Bible reading. Religious exercises were performed with the blessings of the school board. When the community was primarily of one religious faith, trustees deemed it not only appropriate but also important for the teacher to instill religious principles in the children. Likewise, practices or tenets that might be at odds with community standards were not permitted entrance into the schools. There was no mention by those interviewed of teachers exploring means of making the occasional dissident or nonconformist feel comfortable during Bible reading or prayer.

Teachers were expected to control students and were allowed extraordinary freedom in punishing them. The right to maintain order and, indeed, the responsibility for assuring children exhibited appropriate behavior were given by the parents to the teacher. It was rare for parents to complain or question the wisdom of the teacher in disciplining pupils. While some of the punishments described in these accounts were excessive and inhumane, the use of corporal punishment is best understood in the light of mores of the day. "Spare the rod and spoil the child" was an oft-repeated adage. Fathers were known for their use of the razor strap—"for the child's own good," of course, and many mothers gave their children healthy doses of "peach tree tea," administered by switching the legs of a naughty child with a peach tree limb. Children were sent to school with the admonition to the teacher "You make him behave." It is not surprising that children were punished by being spanked; it is startling, however, that the punishments often went beyond spankings to beatings—and that there was no ensuing outcry of horror and outrage from the parents and community.

Despite the aura of nostalgia that surrounds the one-room schools, there were distinct limitations to their effectiveness.

Teacher training was minimal, especially when compared to today's standards but also when examined in light of nonrural schools. Certification included three levels of certificates: third grade, second grade, and first grade, with first grade certification being the highest level. A permanent certificate was granted upon completion of the study of specified pedagogy and a bachelor's degree. Teachers in rural schools fell far behind their urban counterparts in advanced levels of certification. For example, in 1909–10 only 32 percent of teachers in rural schools held first grade and permanent certificates compared to 78 percent of nonrural teachers.[3]

A teacher had to be a generalist since he or she must teach all subjects in all grade levels. In nonrural schools, larger school populations meant teachers could specialize and teach only one grade level, or in some instances, one discipline.

Pupils were given little individual attention from the teacher. Although a teacher was listening to recitation most of the school day, each child's recitation time was limited. This resulted in time spent in boredom, daydreams, or mischief. Exceptions might occur if enrollment was small.

There was no means of controlling the pupil-teacher ratio. The teacher was expected to teach all who appeared at the ringing of the bell. It was left to the discretion of the trustees to decide when to enlarge a school and add an additional teacher. Even then, enrollment might be large. Ina Cowan speaks of 108 pupils in a two-teacher school in Haskell County.

Facilities were limited and often woefully inadequate.

Prior to 1918, when legislation was enacted providing for free textbooks, poor farm children who could not afford to purchase texts simply did without. Library books and supplemental reading materials were virtually nonexistent. For example, in Texas schools in 1908–1909, the average expenditure for library materials in rural schools was nine cents per capita; in nonrural schools, the expenditure was eighty-five cents per capita.[4]

No provisions were made for education beyond the seventh or

eighth grade. If one desired a high school diploma, it necessitated leaving home and boarding in the village or town to complete one's schooling.

School districts made no provisions for children with special needs, such as learning disabilities or physical impairments. All efforts to provide for these children were left to the teachers.

The lack of compulsory attendance laws enabled parents to keep children home to help with farm chores. Consequently, a large percentage of pupils dropped out of school before completing seventh grade.

Children walked long distances to school and were subject to the vagaries of weather and to the harshness of terrain. Clothing and footwear were often inadequate for the conditions.

In spite of the limitations inherent within small rural schools, there was much that educators in subsequent decades would come to admire and seek to incorporate into the large urban schools.

Rural schoolteachers typified old-fashioned, enduring qualities that are still viable today. Although ill prepared professionally (and there are grim tales of inadequacy, such as Miss Florence in her dame's cap), they were, as a group, hardworking, generous, concerned pedagogues who wanted to give their pupils a chance at success. Working within a small community in which they knew each pupil well, where they had easy access to parents, and where all community resources were readily available, they fostered a family-like atmosphere that was to be envied by urban counterparts in later decades.

These rural teachers saw their task as "lifting up" their students to try harder, see farther. They motivated them with praise, encouragement, awards, and an occasional unexpected treat. Although their districts largely ignored the special needs of impaired children, individual teachers tell of making provisions for handicapped pupils long before inclusion became a topic tossed about in educational circles. In Boyer's book, *The Basic School,* he gives the teacher's task as "reaching every student rather than covering the curriculum, connecting to all learners rather than merely offering education."[5] It would seem many rural teachers were intrinsically aware of this decades ago.

The one-room school has served as a prototype for the nongraded or multiage classroom used in many of today's schools. The theory behind the nongraded school is that students, regardless of age or achievement level, can progress through designated subject material at a speed and on a level appropriate to their ability. Hence, third-year pupils may take a fourth year if necessary in order to complete the material expected of a third-grader. This practice was universally employed in the one-room school. Children continued to read from a reader for as long as was necessary to complete it, whether through one, two, or more school terms. A fourth-year student might be in a fifth-grade reader, a third-grade speller, and a fourth-grade arithmetic text.

The rural one-room schools served as the embryonic stage of student-centered instruction. Cuban in *How Teachers Taught* defines student-centered instruction as dividing the class into small groups and letting individuals work independently as opposed to a teacher teaching the entire class as a unit.[6] The pattern of instruction in one-room schools involved the teacher calling one group of pupils to the recitation bench while the remainder of students worked on various assigned tasks in small groups or independently. Student-centered instruction was more clearly defined and considerably enhanced by later reformers attempting to move methodology away from teacher-centered instruction, but its rudimentary stages were found in rural classrooms.

The open-concept schools prevalent in the 1970s were also loosely patterned after the one-room school. Although much larger than their earlier cousins, open-concept schools sought to bring children of a variety of ages and abilities together for the purpose of instruction. Team teaching was a widely touted adjunct to the open-concept school, intending to use the strengths of two or more teachers for the enhancement of instruction. One interviewee, when comparing her early experiences of teaching in a one-room school with her later years, said, "When they started talking about team teaching in Fort Worth in the sixties and seventies, I said, 'Mercy goodness! That's what I started with, you might say, team teaching.'" Several teachers, especially those who taught in a two-room school with a colleague, told of combining classes for instruction, planning programs that involved both groups, and bringing the pupils together for Friday afternoon activities. Often teachers helped each other when one had expertise the other did not. For example, Stella Gipson Polk taught the younger children and her sister Jennie taught the older children. Polk states, "Only Jennie couldn't teach algebra." The three boys taking algebra came to Stella's room for their math lessons.

While the pedagogical jargon varied, early teachers utilized good teaching practices long before they became the "innovations" of modern education. Lizzie Underwood tells of a teacher who employed cooperative learning techniques as early as 1910. If the teacher asked a question to which a child did not know the answer, the child could ask someone else. "That would give you a chance, don't you see? She said that a-way each of us would learn faster than we would otherwise. We should learn from each other."

An additional innovation practiced by teachers in one-room schools was peer tutoring. Lack of time often necessitated this, as the teacher was unable to listen to all lessons each day and would pick one of the best pupils from the top grades to assist with the younger children. Enough mention was made of this practice to assume it was common. This technique is similar to that used today in many classrooms, particularly where multiage grouping is practiced, but in others as well. For example, fifth-graders might read to first-graders, or sixth-graders might present a class-written play to third-grade children.

In summary, the one-room school was a reflection of its time, the means by which a community could teach curricula, values, and mores it deemed important. Although beset by limitations, it was a noble effort to provide instruction for the young, exhibiting practices and concepts that later educators admired and sought to emulate.

While the rural schools have disappeared, this preserves memories of pupils and teachers who experienced them. By recording these oral histories, it is hoped they will provide insight into the history of education.

Notes

1. Edward J. Power, *Main Currents in the History of Education*, 433.
2. Milam C. Rowold, "The Texas Rural Schools Revisited, 1900–1929" (Ph.D. diss., University of Texas at Austin, 1983), 46.
3. Rowold, 42.
4. Rowold, 60.
5. Ernest L. Boyer, *The Basic School: A Community for Learning*, 43.
6. Larry Cuban, *How Teachers Taught: Constancy and Change in American Classrooms, 1880–1990*, 132.

Ain't Nothin' There Now But a Cistern Full of Rattlesnakes

RECOLLECTIONS OF PUPILS

The dozens of oral histories collected for this project had amazingly similar content regardless of age or gender of the storyteller, location of the school, or whether the narrator was a teacher or a student. Small, rural one- and two-teacher schools in West Texas were very much alike during the first half of the twentieth century. The size of the classes may have varied, but the instruction and daily operations conducted by the teacher followed predictable patterns.

In effective schools, instruction and recitation were regularly conducted, children were treated with respect and dignity, and discipline was stern but consistent. In schools with less effective teachers, instruction was often nonexistent, some of the boys were viewed as agents of the devil, and punishment, although frequently administered with a "steel rod and an iron fist," failed to maintain order or affect learning.

While these oral histories share much in common, they are made individual by what the narrators choose to tell. As each tale is distilled through the eyes of its teller, it becomes a unique reflection of one person's experiences. Some are witty, some poignant, some mundane, but collectively they give a fascinating view of what it was like to attend school "back then."

An interesting observation of this research is that few of the stories contain details or specifics of instruction, how learning took place, for example. Most children learned to read and to "figure," but rarely did an interviewee remember the cognitive processes involved or whether the learning was the result of a teacher or his or her parents or if it "just happened." They were much more likely to remember the good times at recess, what they took for lunch, or traumatic events related to punishment.

In part I, individuals who were students in rural schools in West Texas remember and recount their experiences.

CHAPTER ONE

❧

They Built a New Schoolhouse, and Oh, It Was Modern

BUILDINGS, FACILITIES, AND SCHOOL ORGANIZATION

Once a community determined its need for a school, four factors were important in its establishment. The most important was location—where should the school be sited in relation to the houses in the community? Farm children had chores to complete before school began at nine o'clock. They had to eat, dress, and then walk or ride a horse to school. It was felt children should not be required to travel more than three or four miles, or approximately an hour's distance, if possible.

In order to assure the school was accessible to all children, most rural school districts were approximately thiry-six square miles, barring other factors, such as rivers, hills, or rugged terrain. A district of this size would enable the furthermost family living in the community to be within a reasonable distance of the school.

Once the location of the school was determined, other factors came into play: availability of water, fuel for heating, and what to do about bathroom facilities. In West Texas, the most difficult of these considerations to solve was adequate drinking water. A well, cistern, or some other means of storing water had to be constructed. Access to firewood or other sources of fuel also had to be considered because the drafty, uninsulated schoolhouses were difficult to keep warm in the cold windy months. Two outdoor toilets, or outhouses as they were called, were constructed at appropriate locations, always facing in opposite directions, allowing privacy for both sexes.

All of these factors were only part of the school trustees' responsibilities. They were the first steps in providing an educational environment for children. Hiring teachers and running the school would come later.

There Was a Sign That Said "No Spitting on the Floor"
NARCISSA CLEGG

I started to school in 1909, and in that school year, February 20th, the old schoolhouse burned down on Sunday night, February 20, 1910. The Methodists had church service that afternoon in the schoolhouse, and the weather was warm enough that they didn't have any fire in the stove. Folks talked about it later. Some of them remembered leaning against the stove while they talked.

That night, though, John Lay and May Adair got married at my uncle's house, which was less than a mile from the school. They had their families there. There were a lot of boys there, too. And right afterwards, they found out that the schoolhouse had burned. People wondered and talked about it a lot then, but they didn't know for years and years what really happened. Some of the men told. One man, and I'd rather not say who, said that was the meanest thing he ever did. He said he and two other boys burnt the schoolhouse down. He said they went there and set it afire. They didn't mean to burn it down at all, but it got out of hand, so of course, they went off and left it.

They rebuilt the schoolhouse right straight! It burned on February 20, 1910, and they got busy right quick. I understood they were planning to build a new schoolhouse anyway. So right straight, they hired carpenters. There were four men who worked on it. We were there for a church service under a brush arbor, and the schoolhouse was already almost ready to be entered, and I remember seeing the men around it.

So school was out only a month. On March 20th, we entered school again. It was a beautiful white house, painted all white on the outside, green around the windows, nice good windows with wire over them, with a rostrum, new desks, a new teacher's desk, a nice closet that we put our books in on Friday, and other things, many blackboards—a beautiful place. The desks were factory made, double. Two pupils sat in each desk. The old school had desks like that too, but they were old. Of course, the recitation bench was long, but it was homemade. The recitation bench was where we went up to have our lessons. We sat on the bench and stood up when the teacher called us. If we needed to go to the board, then we went and worked on the board, but when the teacher was taking and giving us lessons, we sat down. We had from one to seven or eight grades. If the teacher had a first grade certificate, she could teach through the eighth grade. If she had a second grade certificate, she could only teach through the seventh grade.

On March 20th, when school opened, our teacher, Miss Mattie, talked to us and told us what a beautiful house we had, and we must keep it clean. And I remember, someone had written—I think it was Ed Acker, for he could write well—up right at the ceiling. There was a little sign that said "No Smoking." Another one said "No Spitting on the Floor," and as far as I know, they stayed there as long as I went to school. We took care of the cleaning of the house by two girls' sweeping each day at noon. They had a big girl and a little girl to do the sweeping. My first year I swept it with an older girl named Hattie. She was the big girl, and I was the little girl.

We started school in the new schoolhouse on March 20th, and it ran to May 20th. But we didn't have an exhibition or anything. We just had a last day of school with all of us together.

My Dad Gave the Land for the New School

IRA HESTER

My dad gave the land for the Mid School, which was half a mile north of where we lived. Then when they decided to move the school and add to it, my dad gave more land in the northeast corner of our home place, which was a half mile from where we lived. When they moved Mid and added to it, they called it New Mid. I attended school at Mid my first year. The school was heated with a coal stove, with a jacket around it, you know. And usually the teacher or the principal would get there early and start the fire, or he would appoint some big boy to get there early and build the fire. They would get the coal from the gin; that's where they sold it. There were not a lot of trees around, not really in that area, just sandy land, no trees. So they had to have coal or there wouldn't be a fire.

Of course, all the county had dirt roads, and usually when we'd get out of school or be going to school, there'd be four or six in a group. I can recall one time two boys got in a fight, and this one boy whammed the other boy over the head with his dinner bucket. Some fights broke out occasionally between some of the students.

Several times school was turned out because of sickness. Scarlet fever was the most common cause. During cotton picking season, of course (back then we picked cotton, we didn't pull) they would turn out school for so many weeks. We were always told when we got out of school to come on home because we had a job to do.

They Built a Two-Room Schoolhouse, and Oh, It Was Modern

CLYDE HODGES

After the first year I went to school, they built a two-room schoolhouse. Oh, it was modern! We had single desks to sit in and had a table here and a place over there to set your bottle of ink, and it had a drawer to pull out here to keep the books in. It was up-to-date. It was modern!

You go in the room and you had a coat closet on each side, one for the boys, and one for the girls. You put your coat in there and hat or cap, whatever you wore. It was up-to-date—had two teachers. When we had two rooms, we had about forty in each room. One teacher would teach [grades] up so high, and the other one would go on up. The higher ones would be in one room, and the lower ones in the other.

Hobbs Was the Birthplace of the Consolidated School in Texas

BUDDY BURNETT

This is a typical story of the "nomadic" schoolhouse. It was not uncommon for a school building to be moved two, three, or even four times in its history on the way to eventual consolidation with a larger district. Sometimes the name of the school changed with the move, other times it remained the same. Moves were necessitated by changes in population within an area. The small box-frame buildings could be placed on wooden skids and, with the use of several teams of horses, dragged from place to place.

Old Hobbs School was originally called Chicken Foot and was

located near the Hobbs Gin where the Willingham's farm is. When Hobbs started it [the school] was in about three different places. It was first north of the old Hobbs store. They used to call it Red Town. Then the school was moved later on up west of Barton Willingham's house. There was some conflict about the school, and the Willinghams and old man Baird split apart. Mr. Baird gave the land up here—located about three or four miles west of present Hobbs School—to build a school. It was called the Baird School. He said as long as it was used for a school the land would be given for that purpose. If it ever ceased to be a school then the land returned to him or his heirs. The Hobbs school moved then east of the gin, about two hundred yards away on Buffalo Creek.

There were lots of tenants here then. A 160-acre farm was considered a big farm. When the drought of 1917 came, farms were hit hard. Back then families harvested their own crops. When 1918 came, it hadn't rained drop one. People stayed until about April. They couldn't even get seed in the ground, so they had to leave out. They left here like an exodus going back where there was some moisture.

In 1918, there was no school at Baird because so many people moved out. Papa went over to talk to them and tried to get them to leave the school where it was. Papa believed the people would be back and there would be students eventually. He stated how it was— that when it ceased to be a school it reverted to Mr. Baird, and that's how the records was. He was strictly in the right according to the stipulation. Some of the people went to Hobbs, some to Dallas. This left us in a spot. Grady was too far to go to. Camp Springs was about three or four miles from us. The Baird School was only three-quarters of a mile, but it was closed so we went to Camp Springs. I went to school two years at Camp Springs. I was too young to go to Baird. I didn't start until I was nearly eight years old.

Then some of the men got to talking and decided they should build them a nice school. Times were progressive. This would be in the 1920s. People were beginning to come back after the drought. In 1919 they had a wonderful crop.

J. W. Hale, the county superintendent, envisioned a school in the rural area like the city school. These small schools only went to the seventh or eighth grade. If you wanted to go to high school you had to go into town. The men got together with Mr. Hale to build

7

an eleven-year high school in this area. There was a large number of students in the area. An election was called, but prior to that, they had to have an act of the state legislature in order to create the consolidated school where they could assess and collect taxes. The district would be independent.

Hobbs was the birthplace of the consolidated school in Texas and perhaps in all the United States. It was made up of Grady, Hobbs, Dallas, and old Baird. It was moved to its present location to make it more centrally located. When it came up for a name, Jackson Willingham said they won't consolidate unless it is called Hobbs. The plans started in about 1922. I don't remember the date when the election was. They started building in 1923. I believe 1925 was the first year they had school there. My father was elected sheriff of Fisher County, and we moved to Roby. He was on the original school board but had to resign when he was elected sheriff.

Mr. Guy E. Casey was the principal at Camp Springs and was elected the first superintendent of Hobbs. They had a teacherage back near the old lunchroom. I believe Hobbs had some of the first school buses, also. They had old Model T Fords. The kids called them chicken coops.

If once in a school term your basketball team got to go over to the neighboring school, that was a big deal. It was like going to a state meet.

They Moved It over on the Hill and Called It Bunker Hill

FRED BROWN

We had a school over at Grayson. It was only named Grayson for three years. Then they moved it over on the hill, and that's when they named it Bunker Hill. They moved it with block and tackle by mule teams. You see, the block and tackle was like a gear shift in a truck. The more times you lay the block, the more power you have. It took them four or five days to move that house a mile—a little over a mile. They'd have to hook on and pull a little ways, and then the teams would have to go back and hook on again. Every time they'd go forward after they hooked on, it moved it a little ways about the length of this house. This was in 1925.

They Would Usually Wait until the Cotton Was out to Start School

JOSIE BAIRD

We moved to Kent County from Mills County in 1916, when I was ten years old. My sister Delilah and I attended school at Riverdale for two years. She was two years younger than I. The first year I was there, the teacher was Miss Leona. There were fifteen or twenty students that year.

School was about six months long then. They would usually wait until the cotton was out to start school. The trustees would get together and check with the people around to see when they [the children] would be through picking cotton. Then they would start going to school. It was very much local control. They settled on the teacher's salary according to how much money they had. The teacher could take the job or not.

After two years, we moved back over to the north near Double Mountains to where Harmony School was later. At that time it was called Perkel School. It was a one-room school too. At Riverdale, I had been accelerated in school, so they put me in the sixth grade when we started to school over at Perkel. That almost ruined me for being studious. There was nobody else in the sixth grade. When a teacher just has one pupil in a grade, it's very easy to pass him by and work with the ones that need working with. I sat there and daydreamed a good deal of the time. Instead of letting me go on and read my own history and let me write answers like teachers would do now, I just had to wait. I had United States history again because it was easier for me to have it with the other class than for the teacher to hear my lessons. So I skipped Texas history in grade school.

The next year, World War I was going strong and the way they did then, they cut out all the money they could for the war effort. So they cut the schools down. Our little ol' school over here at Riverdale ran just three months.

There Were Two Children to a Desk

ROBERT MARTINEZ

I went one month in 1917 to Riverdale School. I was five years old and we rode in a buggy through sand about eight miles. We all went.

9

There was Fred and Mary and Frances and Joe and Manuel and myself. I am the seventh child. When I was going to Riverdale, I didn't know what was going on. I was five, you know. There were two children to a desk. I was so short, you know, five years old, my feet was about that much from the floor. I remember the teacher told a girl by the name of Retha, the only Mexican besides us—she knew English, but none of the rest of us did—the teacher would tell her to tell me not to swing my feet and kick the front desk. She said I was making too much noise. That teacher would get me and sit me in her lap and tie my shoes. We just went one month. It was too hard. Just too far. Then we didn't go anymore until about 1925. That's when they built the Harmony School.

Between 1917 and 1924 my father hired a tutor for us. During that time we didn't go to school because, as I said, it was just too far. My father hired this teacher from San Antonio. She was Mexican and stayed with us around six or seven months. I know how to read and write Spanish because of her. In our home we spoke nothing but Spanish. I learned English in 1925 when I went to school. I didn't know a word. It was rough because it was just "wee-wee-wee-wee." It was too fast.

The Ceiling Was Covered with Paper Wads

CLYDE HODGES

I went to Pound School, out southwest of De Leon about six miles. I was seven years old. I was born in 1900 and started to school in 1907. Couldn't go to school then 'til you was seven years old. We lived about a mile and a half from the school, south of the school. We either walked through the woods or would go around the road. It was nearer through the woods. The first school I went to was a single room. I guess we would have seventy-five kids and one teacher. Just one teacher. It was just taught up to the seventh grade. And back then, ever' county had a county superintendent and he'd visit schools, you know, during the school year. As many schools as there was out over the county, he wouldn't get to visit but about once a year, you know, there were so many to go to.

We used to have a big ol' pot-bellied stove up towards the front—burned wood—and we had just long wooden benches to sit on. Four, five, or six of us kids sat on a bench, you know. Lots of kids went to school then. The benches had backs to them. You just had to sit there with your books in your lap or hand or the best way you could. And the ceiling—I'm not lying to you now—the ceiling was covered with paper wads. That was done before I started. The boys would chew up paper and throw 'em up and hit the ceiling, and the ceiling was solid with paper wads. Kids would chew 'em up and throw them up on the ceiling.

There Was Forty-Nine Students and One Teacher

CONNIE HAYTER TUTT

In 1886 my mother's family came to Fisher County. The first year they were here, they lived with her father. My mother's aunt, Eugenia Martin Hanks, came from Louisiana. Her husband died and she came to live with her father. She taught the first Hobbs School in 1886 or 1887, I don't remember which. It was located on Buffalo Creek and was called Buffalo at that time. I remember my mother telling about that school—she and her older sister went to that school. The first school was in a tent—a canvas tent. In a few years they bought

Old Hobbs School in the early 1900s. The young woman on the extreme right is the teacher for this group of forty-nine pupils. Note the dozen or more young men in the back row who appear to be larger and older than she. Courtesy Fannie Willingham Albert

a one-room house in Roby and moved it out there, and then they had a house. Of course, they had church services there too.

My sister started to school at Buffalo School and so did my mother, but by the time I started it was named Hobbs. I have a picture of the first school that was called Hobbs. There was one teacher and look how many kids she had. . . . There were forty-nine students and one teacher. The teacher was Florence Middleton.

The school was moved several times. . . . On the third move, they called the school Hobbs instead of Buffalo. The reason it was called Hobbs was because my grandfather Martin volunteered to carry the mail for six months so we could get a post office established. He carried it free for six months. He and the postmaster at Roby sent in names for a post office. My grandfather sent in the name Shiloh, I think, or some Bible name. Mr. Patterson was the postmaster at Roby and he sent in Hobbs, his middle name. And so the postal officials selected the name Hobbs for the new post office, so the school was changed to that too.

When I left the little two-room school at Hobbs, I had to go into Rotan to high school. It was fifteen miles away, so of course, I had to board in town. It was lonesome until after you got acquainted. It was fifteen miles to Rotan and that was a long way. In my first years we had to go in a wagon, but while I was still in school we bought our first automobile. In the later years we had a car but it was still too far to go back and forth.

My father came to Texas from Tennessee in 1892, and he taught school three years after he came here. Beginning in 1893, he taught at County Line, and Grady, and the Dallas community for three years. He was paid twenty-five dollars a month for his teaching. He took turns living with the families of his pupils, staying with each family for two weeks at a time. Life was a serious business in those days. You didn't get married because you were in love. You got married when conditions got right. He married my mother in 1896. The wedding was in the home of her parents, and my father came to the wedding riding a horse and leading another one to carry his bride home on. Their first home was in an abandoned schoolhouse named Bush on the banks of the Clear Fork.

Each Student Had to Furnish Their Own Plate and Silverware

JUANITA VINSON

In 1940, I attended first grade in a two-room school called Oak Grove. Oak Grove School was located a few miles north or northwest from Caddo, Texas, between Caddo and the Possum Kingdom Lake about twenty miles or so east of Breckenridge. Oak Grove was in pretty rugged country. We had hills all the way around, not up close, but all the way around. It was like we were setting in a bowl. Anyway, one time we heard a panther scream back over there on the hill, back behind the barn. Daddy got to answering that thing. And that panther came clean down to the barn. It like to have scared Mama to death, and we headed back to the house in a hurry.

The things that stand out in my memory about Oak Grove School was that it was taught by a husband and wife and that they were very nice and good to the children. The wife taught the younger children, and her husband served as principal as well as teaching the older students. A lady in the community fixed lunch for the school and each student had to furnish their own plate, silverware, and cup. These were kept at the school until the end of the school year. The lunches cost ten cents each, and the best I can remember they were very good meals.

Another thing I remember about the Oak Grove School, the people in the community used the school building to make mattresses in. I think the government furnished the cotton and maybe the ticking also, and the people in the community who needed the mattresses all worked together to make them.

He Brought a Slide Projector That Run on Batteries

JAMES P. CLEGG

Over at our school we had no electric lights. There was no electricity out there until after the building was tore down. There was all windows on the north and all on the south. All windows. There was no windows on the east or west. There was a door on the west. I think at the east end was where the teacher's desk sat. I think there was a door up there too.

I remember one year Mr. Dalton, the county superintendent, came out to school. He brought a slide projector that run on batteries. That is the only one I ever saw that run on a battery. He brought a battery and set it down and hooked it up and showed some slides. That's the first and last I've ever seen.

The School Was Just a Big Ol' Room

WILLIAM I. POTEET

The school was just a big ol' room, about sixteen or maybe twenty feet wide by thirty feet long. The desks were double desks. The boys sat on the left-hand side and the girls on the right-hand side. I sat off towards the front with someone, some friend. We sat according to age or class. We were called up for recitation by the teacher. Each class would come up front and sit on a long bench—a wooden bench, homemade. We'd either read or do whatever the lesson was. If it was arithmetic we went to the board. The teacher would give out a problem, and we'd work it on the board. That's the way it was in those times. If we weren't doing recitation, we'd be studying—studying for our lessons. There'd be about five or six of us in each class. In all, there would be about forty kids in the room, thirty-five to forty, with just one teacher, all the time. I never went to a two-teacher school, except the last year or two I was there.

Every Friday afternoon after the last recess, the teacher would stop any schoolteaching, and we'd have something like a little program. We'd choose sides and we'd go to the board with problems or with spelling or something like that. And whichever side would win, we'd have a big time together. We did have literary societies once in a while and would have a public gathering and a program. Somebody would give a recitation and maybe a few songs, a little play, or skit.

"You're Too Little to Be in the Second Reader"

HENRY T. POTEET

There were three trustees and my Uncle Jeff was one of them. I'd gone to school one year, and that was supposed to pass me to the second reader, second grade. Uncle Jeff was the trustee that had the books sent out from the county superintendent's office. His house was on the way, halfway between our house and the schoolhouse. So he had the books at his house to give out to the kids that lived south of the schoolhouse. Probably someone else had the ones to give out to the kids who lived to the north. I had already gone from the *Primer* to the *First Reader* in the first year, and I was ready for the *Second Reader*.

We stopped at Uncle Jeff's to get our books, and he looked at me after looking at the older boys, and he says, "Henry, what grade are you in?"

I said, "Second."

He said, "You're too little to take the second. Here!" He gave me a *First Reader* and I stayed in that reader, as far as I know, for that entire year. I was in high second, but I had to take that *First Reader* and stay in it a year because he thought I was too little. Talk about authoritarian. The trustees could do about anything they wanted to.

It Was the Teacher's Job to Build a Fire Every Morning

Teachers in rural schools were expected to perform many onerous tasks outside their responsibilities for instruction. Building and maintaining the fire was one of these chores. It was the teacher's responsibility to see that the fire was built early in the morning, for the building had to be warm when the pupils arrived. The stove, of course, had to be tended throughout the day.

Fortunately, it was not the teacher's responsibility to secure the wood. Wood was hauled to the school by a trustee or a local farmer or rancher who either volunteered or was paid for the service. This usually included cutting the wood into stove-length sticks. However, in some cases, the wood was piled near the school, and it was left to the older boys or a male teacher to cut it into usable chunks.

We Had a Big Cast-Iron Stove with a Jacket around It

BUDDY BURNETT

We had a big cast-iron stove with a jacket around it. The stove was inside the jacket so there was less danger of kids getting burned. The jacket cleared the floor about six inches and was about five feet high. A door in the jacket opened up and then the door to the stove would open to allow you to put coal or wood in. It was the teacher's job to build a fire every morning. Usually we had coal because it would last longer. We'd go down in the pasture and get kindling to start the fire.

We Used the Stove for a Trash Basket

LEO E. CLEGG

There used to be some meanness goin' on in the schoolhouse. We used the stove for a trash basket. Boys would take .22 shells and wrap 'em up in paper. So they would throw 'em in the stove wrapped up in that paper good and heavy. Then whoever done it would be readin' a book actin' like nothin' was goin' on and d'rectly there would be an explosion. That shell would go off. The one that done it would look up like he never knew what was goin' on. I don't remember if I ever did that or not.

You know there's fifty shells in a box, and one feller put a whole box full in the stove once. There was the awfulest smoke and shootin', you never heard the like. Somebody put in four or five .32 pistol shells in there once. Them caps would jump up in the air and hit the top of the stove. I guess it was dangerous, but it was a big ol' heavy stove about four foot long. Heavy iron. Smoke was just boilin' out.

That's Probably What Caused the Fire

BESSIE CLEVELAND

The teachers always had to build the fire every day. The teacher would have to see that the boys had brought in enough coal and kindling for the next day. When my mother was going to school at Pleasant Valley, they burned wood. When I started, we were burning coal, and later on they burned kerosene. One of the school buildings burned because of kerosene. There was a glass holder or tank for the kerosene with a valve on top to regulate the flow. When the tank was filled up, you'd have to turn it upside down to put it back in its place in the stove. If you wasn't careful you'd spill it. It would splash when you turned that tank over. And they also used oil to oil the floors. That's probably what caused the fire.

The Teacher Had Used the Stove for the Restroom

NARCISSA CLEGG

We had a teacher named Karl Richards [name changed]. It was in 1913, and I don't know if I should tell you this or not. Anyway, the kids didn't like him. Our family had scarlet fever, and we were out of school at the time, but we were told later what happened. One morning the kids all went to school, but at recess they picked up their dinner buckets and left. They went over the hill east of the schoolhouse. They stayed all day. They would go every once in a while and see the teacher standing out looking around, but they didn't come in.

So the next day, the trustees went to the county seat and met with the county superintendent, Mr. W. C. Martin, and he came out with the trustees and talked to Mr. Richards. Mr. Martin said, "Karl, you've got to do better than this." I don't know what the accusation was that the trustees made against him. But anyway, they fired him. He had been a good schoolteacher years before, they said.

We learned that, at some time before, he had been in the hospital and had surgery, and somebody said that he had got on dope from all the medicine he had to take. I do know he sat there with a pasty face and would pay no attention to what went on. I got along with him all right. I learned. But the kids did what they pleased, most generally.

I asked a friend years later what was the straw that broke the camel's back that made them run off from school that day. She said, when they all went out at recess time, the first thing they did was go over the hill, which was our way of going to the restroom. Mr. Richards was supposed to go, too. But he didn't. When they got through with their playtime, and he called them back in, he shut the door, and they said the stove smelled terrible. They knew what he had done. He had used the stove for the restroom! He had urinated in it! It was hot, and of course it would smell, and they knew what had happened. They just ran off and the trustees fired him.

We Didn't Even Have an Outdoor Toilet

The outhouse, or privy, was a necessity in rural homes before indoor plumbing, and trustees of most schools provided outdoor toilets for the children. It was a rare school that failed to have two small buildings, one for the girls and one for the boys, usually on opposite sides of the school grounds, a hundred feet or so from the school building.

Toilets were usually constructed of wood, about twenty-five square feet and six or seven feet tall. The roof was a shed type, higher in the front and sloping downward in the back. Generally, there were two holes in each toilet so it could accommodate more than one child at a time. However, depending upon the size of the school, the toilet may have had more than the customary two holes; sometimes they were "three- or four-holers."

Toilet paper for the outhouses was not a problem. They were equipped with the same materials that were available in the outhouses at home: catalogs—usually Sears, Roebuck or Montgomery Ward. Pages were torn from the catalog as needed. When a catalog was used up, someone in the community would have a spare to send to school. Sometimes newspapers were used. However, they were rarer as subscriptions to newspapers cost money. Catalogs were free. Some students spoke of using whatever was available—corncobs, leaves, or sticks.

Many tales were told about problems at the outhouse. For example, most outhouses had two latches, one on the inside to keep someone from barging in unexpectedly, and one on the outside to keep the door closed when the toilet was not in use. Often, a prankster would sneak up to the toilet while it was occupied and latch the door from the outside, locking the unsuspecting victim inside.

If the terrain surrounding the school was unusually rough with cedar breaks, hills, or canyons nearby, the trustees might view it unnecessary to waste taxpayers monies on such luxuries as outhouses when so many private places were available. This is what happened at County Line School during the early part of the century. It was decided the girls would go east, down in the canyon, and the boys would go west, over the hill into the cedar breaks. Usually there were no problems with this arrangement because, with an effective teacher, anyone caught in the wrong place at the wrong time was in deep trouble. However, the strict code of modesty broke down completely when there was a weak and ineffective teacher.

There Was No Toilet Paper
So They Used Catalogs or Whatever

BUDDY BURNETT

There was a toilet for the boys and one for the girls. The girls was a four-holer and the boys had a three-holer. There was no privacy.

You just sat elbow to elbow. The boys' was off up here on the hill, and back down here was the girls'. Each toilet had a wing [extension] that came out from it about four or five feet, maybe six, and then came across the front about eight feet. The access was turned farther away from the school so there would be no vision from the schoolhouse whatever. There was no door on the toilet. There was no toilet paper, so they used catalogs or whatever. They didn't ever know what toilet tissue was.

The Girls Would Sneak up over the Hill and Peek at the Boys

GRACE PHILLIPS

We didn't have a privy for a long time. Finally we had a three-holer. Before a revival, men would bring ashes and put [them] in the privy to keep down the smell and flies. Before we got an outhouse at school, the girls would go down the little canyon on the east and the boys would go over the hill to the west. The north end of the hill slanted down. We could act like we were going down this little canyon and sneak right back up over the road and peek at the boys. The greatest revelation to us was that the boys could stand up to go. I had five brothers but they went behind the barn and the girls went behind the hen house. That was the difference.

We finally got modern at home and got a toilet. That was right before a revival. That's when we made home improvements, right before a revival, because we always kept the preachers at our house. We'd have a new water bucket and a new wash pan, and Mother usually got a new chamber, a pot, you know. She called it a chamber. The preacher was coming. The chamber had a lid if you bought a good chamber. It took several dozen eggs to get a good chamber.

I Couldn't Unbutton My Underwear by Myself

JO BLACKSHEAR

I started school when I was five and went part of the year out at Wright School over in Stonewall County. We had an outdoor toilet and that's the only thing we had. You had to raise your hand if you wanted to go the bathroom. It was two fingers if you wanted to go to the bathroom and one finger if you wanted a drink of water. If you wanted to go to the bathroom, you had to take a buddy, because in the wintertime you couldn't get undone by yourself because you had to have your underwear unbuttoned, you see. And when you're little, you certainly couldn't button yourself back up. We didn't have elastic or anything like that.

Our underwear had a flap in the back that came down. There were three or four buttons at the top around the waist that held the flap up. Then we had our little cotton stockings buttoned onto the underwear. It was a big operation. Somebody had to help you get buttoned up. Every time we had to be excused, I remember the teacher sending us in pairs so we could help each other with our buttons. I don't remember about the boys, but the teacher always sent us girls to the outhouse as a team. We had to have help, or we'd be in trouble.

I Just Whammed Him over the Head with My Dinner Bucket

NARCISSA CLEGG

Henrietta [all names changed] was seventeen, and I was fourteen. One day at recess we went to use the bathroom. The girls' side was the sinkhole side and the boys went down there in the canyon. There was a big hill between them. We went over there at recess. Down by the sinkhole there was a drop-off before it went in the canyon where we would usually go. Well, we all got down there and pulled up our dresses and sat down. We looked up over the hill and there was Vaughn and Roger standing there looking at us. Of course, we all jumped up.

Henrietta said, "Now, the teacher ought to know this. But it wouldn't do for us older girls to tell him." She said, "Faith, you go tell him." Faith was the youngest in school and, besides, Vaughn and Roger were her older brothers. She was in the first grade.

She said, "No, I can't. My brothers will whip me."

Henrietta and I both said, "Well, we'll protect you." So she went to the house and told Mr. Hill.

Mr. Hill called Vaughn and Roger out and talked to them, and he told Vaughn, "Now, I'll not punish you. You just let that alone, and don't do that anymore. Don't say a word about it. Let it alone."

Sure enough, when school turned out and we were going toward home, Vaughn and Roger jumped on Faith. So Henrietta and I jumped in. We'd said we would protect her. I don't remember what went on or was said, but anyway, Vaughn talked sassy to me. I had my dinner bucket in my hand, and I just whammed him over the head with it. Of course, my dinner bucket was empty. It didn't hurt him a bit. As far as I know it stopped the fight.

I don't remember if anything else went on. But anyway we went on home.

We never heard any more about it until the next morning when we went back to school. When recess time came, Mr. Hill said, "I want everybody who went up that south road to stay in." So we stayed in, and he said, "Now, what was that ruckus about?" We were close enough to school that he could have heard, so I guess he did. Anyway, Henrietta spoke up and told him it was about what had happened yesterday afternoon. She told him how Vaughn and Roger were going to whip Faith, and we were protecting her. She told him that I had hit Vaughn over the head with my dinner bucket. Mr. Hill never said a word to me.

He said, "Now Vaughn, I told you to let that alone, and not do a thing about it. Now I've got to punish you." He called him up and gave him a whipping right in front of us.

A Boy Would Hold up His Two Fingers to Be Excused

IRA HESTER

A funny thing that always tickled me was when a boy would hold up his two fingers to be excused. We'd go out to the outhouse. We just had these outhouses with men and boys back over here and women's a little closer to the school. And you could look out at the guys out in the outhouse, and you could see smoke billowing out. They were smoking cigarettes. You could always figure out who the smoker was. I know when I was a kid growing up, cedar bark was what I smoked the most—cedar bark. Sometimes I smoked cotton leaves, and I've smoked ground coffee. Cedar bark tasted bitter, but you didn't inhale it.

We Had a Common Water Bucket

Providing drinking water was a difficult chore for the trustees. They usually chose one of two solutions. Either the children brought water from home or trustees provided some type of storage container for holding water. In some schools, a large barrel was placed in the corner of the schoolroom, and the water was replenished periodically by someone in the community who hauled water from his cistern or stock tank.

A more common means of providing drinking water was from a cistern, a large jug-shaped hole dug in the ground and plastered to hold water. The cistern was filled with rainwater channeled from the roof by means of gutters. This method was not always successful, however, because there could be long periods of drought. Also, the small area of the schoolhouse roof did not always provide an adequate supply of water. When there was not enough, hauling water was necessary. Unfortunately, the only available water might come from a rancher's stock tank where water was put into barrels and transported to the cistern. It didn't matter that this same water was used for cows and horses who waded into the water to drink.

In addition to impure water, a further health hazard was the community drinking cup. A common dipper was regularly used in schools in the years before hygiene and sanitation became a concern. Amazingly, few of those interviewed reported deaths or illnesses related to drinking water.

This Was to "Purify" the Water!

INA DINGUS COWAN

The water situation was a problem in the homes as well as at school. No one had plumbing in those days. Eastern Haskell County is not a place where water can be found underground. The only water available is tank water. The tanks are also used by the livestock. Our tanks are what some folks call ponds. Strange as it may seem, there was very little illness in our area and never any epidemics except measles or whooping cough. The school had to have water, so a cistern was dug and cemented. Water was hauled from tanks and poured through a filter and into the cistern. The filter was filled with charcoal—homemade by the nearby farmers. This was to "purify" the water!

The larger boys drew the water from the well with a bucket and rope attached to a pulley. They brought the water into the hallway and poured it into a large zinc container. It was a ten-gallon size or larger and had a hydrant. All the children had some type of cup. Some were made of aluminum rings with a little bottom on them. They'd stretch the cup out. When you were finished with it, it had a little lid you'd put on it, and you'd squish it back down. Most all the children had those. They took them to school and brought them back. Back and forth. You carried them with your lunch. Sometimes the school would have tin cups and they'd put the child's name on them, and they were hanging by the water fountain. They'd pour water in the fountain. Some families shared one cup. Also at home they drank from a common dipper.

Children were taught to fold a paper cup, which worked in case of an emergency. For a drinking cup we'd take a sheet of notebook paper and fold it a certain way, and it would hold water. Our first-grade teacher showed us how to do it. We'd take this little cup, usually out of notebook paper and catch a drink of water.

Often a Rat Would Get in the Cistern

JIM POTEET

We always filled up the school cistern in the fall before school started. We'd take barrels and fill them up at the stock tank. We'd use tank water and fill up four or five barrels and bring 'em to the school and pour 'em into the cistern. The schoolhouse was usually too small to catch much rainwater and then, too, I don't think they had gutters on the schoolhouse. Anyway, that's the way they'd do. They just hauled water from the stock tank. Me and Jack, we'd haul the water. Of course they'd pay us for it. One time we brought up the water to the school and it wasn't but about a week or so that [the] water was so bad we had to go dip it all out of that cistern and haul more water. It was terrible. I imagine it was a dry year and the tank was low and it was alkaline, and it just got worse as time went on.

Quite often a rat or mouse would get in the cistern. They would drown, then you had to draw them out. We'd go ahead and drink the water. When you hauled the water from the stock tank, there was probably an old dead cow laying not far from when you was getting the water anyway. My Uncle Jeff always put some lime in his cistern. He had the best water in the country. He had the clearest, prettiest water. I guess that helped purify it, I don't know. He thought it did.

We Had a Windmill for Drinking Water
BUDDY BURNETT

At Camp Springs they had a windmill for drinking water because the underground water there was good. They ran water down to the school with two faucets outside the building. Prior to that they had a bucket of water and everybody brought their drinking cups. Later they had little folding cups. When they piped that water down to the school, that was a big deal.

Some of the Men up and Hauled Water in a Barrel
LEWIS H. CLEGG

Before the schoolhouse burned, we didn't have any cistern then. Uncle Jeff and some of the men up and hauled water in a barrel and put it in the school. We drank out of that barrel, all drinking from the same tin cup. One day, the older boys went out and got their hands full of hackberries. When they went to get a drink, and when they dipped the little tin cup in there, they turned those things loose. When they all got through drinking, that barrel was full of hackberries. The teacher tried her best to find out who did it, but nobody told. The whole bunch was in to it. Ever' last one of 'em.

We Had a Common Water Bucket
WALTER CLEVELAND

We had a common water bucket. Nobody ever thought a thing about it. Ever'body drank out of that same cup or dipper. Then we went to having school inspections. After that we had to use a paper cup—at least while the inspector was there. The inspector would come maybe twice a year. The inspector would be the county superintendent. He'd watch for things like that.

We drew our water out of the cistern. Sometimes we'd find things in the cistern. Snakes and rats and mice. We'd get 'em out, you know, and just keep drinking the water. They'd usually die in there, and

24

they'd just let the water bucket down there and chug it up and down and pick 'em up in the bucket. They'd pour a little coal oil [kerosene] in it sometimes to kill the wiggle tails. They'd pour just a little bit to kinda form a film over the water to kill the wiggle tails.

Water Was Pouring out of That Jar onto My Leg and into My Shoe

JOE NORTON

When I was a boy going to school, the trustees decided it was better for each family to provide their own drinking water rather than to dig a cistern. My older brother always carried the dinner bucket for us four children, but it was my job to carry the water. I'd usually bring it in a half-gallon fruit jar. No matter how cold it was, we always went to school unless it was blowing snow or driving rain. Then we'd get to stay home.

One morning it was unusually cold. We had to walk about two miles to school and I was lugging this half-gallon jar by a wire bale around its lid. Just before we got to school, I felt a cold wet sensation coming down my leg. I looked down and saw water pouring out the side of that jar onto my leg and into my shoe. What had happened was that the jar had partially frozen, which caused it to break. Fortunately, the teacher had a roaring fire in the stove when we got there and some extra drinking water to get us through the day.

I knew it was cold that morning, but I sure had a time convincing my parents of what really happened. I don't think they ever did believe me. They thought that I hit the jug on a rock and broke it. Maybe so, but I still believe it froze and broke.

CHAPTER TWO

✧

We Walked to School Because It Was Too Cold to Take the Horses

PREPARATION, TRANSPORTATION, AND WEATHER

School "took up" at nine o'clock, but preparation for the day began hours earlier. There were numerous outside chores to do—cows to milk, chickens and hogs to feed, and horses to water. Inside activities included making bread, cooking breakfast, and fixing lunches, and the children had to be washed and dressed for school.

Children who lived some distance from school often were forced to leave home before sunup. The walk might take an hour or longer. Riding a horse or driving a buggy or hack required less time for travel, but the extra time needed to tend the animals negated the advantage.

Weather was always a factor. The school calendar was usually from late November until May—when cold and stormy weather brought unpleasant traveling conditions, often over rugged terrain. The warm, sunny days of spring tempted children to dillydally along the way—a time for play and friendship or perhaps scuffles and fights. As Naomi Mayfield stated, "It's a wonder we ever got to school!" Occurrences between home and school, regardless of the time of year, were often kept from the adults. Some of these stories reveal a touch of devilment, but they also show children coping with adverse, even harsh, conditions with the exuberance of childhood. Whether all these events happened as told is unimportant. What is important is that, in recording them, the storyteller is preserving a slice of life from an era that has disappeared.

My Mother Had Six Children to Get Ready for School

FANNIE WILLINGHAM ALBERT

We carried our own lunch. Mama always fixed us individual lunches. She would have four boxes if she had four children in school at one time. She'd set them down on the table and fill them up that morning. Ever' feller had his own. She didn't want any fussing over the lunches. We had our own individual box or little bucket.

My hair was braided and my mother had to do that each morning. My mother was a busy woman. She had six children, got them ready for school, braided my hair, and fixed our lunches. She was a busy woman. My daddy didn't help about getting us ready for school. He had milking to do, and he counted and tended the sheep.

We all had to help. The boys had chores to do outside, and when I was older, my job was to make biscuits. I guess I burnt myself out on biscuits. I never make them anymore. Never! *Never!* But that was my job to get up and make the biscuits. We had a wooden bowl or tray that I made them in. I'd start with a bowl of flour, make a hole in the flour, and pour in milk and shortening and baking powder. We used sour milk. I'd put in both soda and baking powder,

The children, with their lunch buckets and book satchels are ready for the three-mile walk to school. This photograph was taken in front of the home of Barton and Bobbie Willingham, 1906. Children from left to right: Buddy, cousin Archie, Baby Olin, Abbie, and Fannie. Courtesy Fannie W. Albert and Abbie W. Martin

more baking powder than soda. Just very little soda. I'd start stirring that around until I got the consistency I wanted. Then I'd roll it out. Whatever flour I had left over, I'd put back in the bin for the next time.

My daddy bought flour in fifty pound sacks, and he bought one every week. It took that much. We couldn't go to town and buy a loaf of bread. When we didn't go to school, we'd make corn bread at lunch. I made it about the same way I did biscuits. I make it now just like I did then. I did put an egg in corn bread. Every morning was biscuits and at noon was corn bread. Sometimes we'd have biscuits and corn bread both at lunch. It depended on the other menu. There was no such thing as having anything else but biscuits for breakfast. For supper we usually started all over again. Sometimes we'd have leftovers, but you had to add something to it. I didn't make the bread at supper. Mama usually made the bread at supper, but at breakfast it was my job to get up and make the bread.

Us Boys Would Feed the Hogs

LEO E. CLEGG

School took up at nine o'clock. It took us about an hour or so to walk to school because it was three miles. We'd have to be leaving the house by about daylight. We'd get up about five o'clock in the mornin' and milk the cows and feed the hogs. In the wintertime when they wasn't using too many teams of horses and mules, we'd go in a hack.

We'd do all the chores first and then eat breakfast. Us boys would feed the hogs. We did our water pumpin' at night. Papa usually helped cook, and he'd have a fire goin' there in the kitchen. He'd cook meat, ham and such, so we'd have plenty to make a sandwich. He'd cook eggs and make coffee, and some of the girls would make biscuits. They'd make a big pan of biscuits, because we didn't have any light bread ["store bought" bread, i.e., a pound loaf made with yeast and usually sliced, as opposed to homemade biscuits and corn bread; having been "blown up" with yeast, it was lighter in texture than baking powder bread] for sandwiches. We'd pick out some of the best pieces of meat to make sandwiches out of, and we'd eat the rest of it for breakfast. My dad had a warmin' closet on the stove where he'd keep the meat warm. While my dad was doin' that, my mother would get the little kids dressed for school.

My mother sent off somewhere and got dried fruit in flat boxes. There was twenty-five pounds in a box. She got a box of dried apples and dried peaches and one of apricots and one of raisins, about 125 pounds in all, and they'd put them in big lard cans. My mother would cook a great big stewer of dried fruit whenever she cooked at the noon hour. We'd have it for dinner and supper, and the next mornin' we'd have a lot left over, and my mother would make fried pies out of that fruit.

My Job Was to Get up and Go Milk the Cow

H. GOVAN

When I was a boy going to school, I'd walk to school. I was working for some white people. My job was to get up and go there to milk the cow, strain the milk, eat my breakfast, and get ready to go to school. Maybe I'd have to churn—used to have to churn a little. Then I'd wash the clothes and beat the rug, mow the yard, or work in the garden. Always had plenty for me to do. I think I got two dollars a week, or maybe it was two dollars and a half a week.

My daddy told me this, he said, "You give me that money so when you need some trousers or some socks or shoes, I'll have it to buy, 'cause if I give it to you, you ain't gonna do nothing but buy candy with it."

He was right. I never did think nothing of it after he told me that.

Dad Was Supposed to Comb Our Hair

NAOMI A. MAYFIELD

There was seven of us kids and five going to school then. Everybody would try to get ready at once. Dad was supposed to comb our hair.

He always fixed mine the same way, back like that with bangs. That was his job to comb [the] kids' hair and get us off to school. We carried our lunch in a syrup bucket usually. We'd take biscuits with maybe a little nutmeg and sugar in one. You'd butter the biscuit and sprinkle sugar on it and then a little nutmeg. That was kinda like a cake. It was sweet. Then we'd take maybe a boiled egg and a biscuit with sausage in it or pork of some sort. We didn't have beef, and I don't remember taking chicken to school. It was mostly pork.

Mother Did All Our Sewing

INA DINGUS COWAN

When I was a girl, when we went to school, my mother would make us maybe three dresses. We'd wear them over and over. We wouldn't have a fresh dress every day. If a dress had red on it, I liked it. Mother did all our sewing. Merle and I were so near the same age, and Mother made our clothes exactly alike, and everybody thought we were twins. The way this happened, Merle was very easy on her clothes, and I was just as rough as could be. So when we got new clothes, I got her old ones. I got her old ones so that would finish me out to where these new ones would last closer to hers. There was four of us girls and Mama dressed the older two alike and the other two alike, just because it was easier. It's easier to make them alike because you didn't have to have as many patterns. When children would get home, they would have to take off their school clothes. Parents would teach children to hang up their clothes and wear them back.

I Had a Saddle and a Pretty Little Bridle

EVA WALL SINGLETON

I went every day on my horse, but many of the other kids walked to school. Mrs. Rose had a younger boy—he was about two years older than I was—that got to go to school some, and my father asked him to teach me to ride. He rode in the saddle, and I rode behind him until I learned to ride. The children teased me because I'd put my arms around him to hold on. He was embarrassed so he began to walk beside me and I rode the horse. I had a little saddle, a pretty little bridle. All the roads were dirt roads. When it rained, we just rode through the mud. When it was cold, I wore little leggings. Mother and Daddy put leggings on me. They'd button them up and I had a little raincoat and a toboggan cap, and there I went to school, rain or shine, rain or shine.

Later I went to school in Keller. It was a little bigger and was more like a little town, even though it was still small. There was a bank there where my Daddy banked. My father would send money for me to deposit in the bank, pinned inside my coat. After school, I'd stop by the bank and deposit it. Keller was about five miles from our house and I rode a horse every day. There was a shed there to keep the horses in when we got to school.

When I got home, I always took off my school clothes because I had to do chores at home. I think I had one dress for each day of the week, but I still had to be careful because we wouldn't be washing them all the time. I'd change them back and forth. I always had a Sunday dress and a hat and patent leather shoes. They were just for Sunday.

I Still Remember How We Went to School Like It Was Yesterday

CLIFFORD CLEGG

I started to County Line in 1917. I was 7 or 8 years old. I was the teacher's pet because I was the only guy in my class. She wouldn't make me work.

We went to school in a hack unless the river was up, and we walked then. I still remember how it was when we walked. It was about three miles. We went south of the house to the mouth of Sugar Loaf Creek, climbed up on the south side by way of an old cow trail to the top of the bluff. When we got on top we followed a trail up to the edge of the old Hughes tank and turned straight east toward Little Rough Creek. We followed a ridge down toward the creek until we got to an old road that sloped down into the creek, crossed the creek, and went up the bank to the Adair road. Then we followed the road on up to the school.

Many times, though, instead of going east to the Adair road, we'd turned south and follow what we called Indian Ridge. It was a sharp ridge that on one side dropped straight off into the creek, and on the other sloped down toward the creek. There was a bend at that point where the creek turned north for a ways, then turned sharp back south, making a tight S curve. From there we climbed up to the top of the south side of the creek, and went right on to the school-house. The climb on the south side of the creek, when we went that way, was not too steep. It sloped up gradually to the top of the bluffs. I still remember how we went to school like it was yesterday.

I Walked Two and a Half Miles from Our Little Farmhouse

VIRGINIA HAYES

I remember my first day of school very well. I am amused now, for parents wouldn't think of sending their children off to school alone on the first day. They take them and enroll them themselves. I walked two and a half miles from our little farmhouse, and I recall there was a railroad that went parallel to the highway. I walked down the railroad track. As I was going—I can even remember what I thought about—I thought, now, when I get there, the teacher is going to ask me my name. She's going to want to know how to spell it, and I guess I'll have to tell her my whole name. My name was Dorthy, D O R T H Y, Virginia. But I went by Virginia, not Dorthy. So I thought, I think Dorthy is very plain, so when I get to school, I'm going to tell her I spell my name D O R O T H Y. So I spelled it that way all through school and have only recently changed it back to the way it's on my birth certificate. My grandmother named me, and that's just the way she spelled it on the birth certificate.

I learned to read before I started to school. My mother was sixteen when she married, and I was born when she was eighteen. For a while, before we moved to the farm, we lived in town. Mother joined the library for me, and I recall she would take me to the library. We would come home with a stack of books until, by the time we moved to the country, I had read all the books in the children's section of the library.

There Was a Great Big Snake Right in the Trail

LIZZIE UNDERWOOD

When we went to school, we had to walk. One of our neighbors, the Grays, had a big ol' tank where we had to cross the canyon. Daddy

[had] taken some long cottonwood poles and put 'em across the canyon. On top of the poles he put cedar and put dirt on the cedar like a bridge so we wouldn't have to go down in the canyon. Then we went on by the Grays and turned down toward the schoolhouse and had to cross a canyon down there.

One morning early in the spring, it was getting late and the kids was in a hurry, and Frank Gray had caught a big ol' bull snake. He put some tobacco sacks on its head and tied 'em so it couldn't see. We passed by the Gray place and headed down the canyon between their house and school. We headed down that canyon and was nearly to the top, and there was that great big snake—it was the biggest snake I ever saw— right in the trail. The kids nearly knocked each other down gettin' back down the hill. We had to go up the creek to get around it. The teacher got after us for being late, and we told her what had happened. So Mr. Gray found it out, and that evening when Frank got in from school, his daddy had his quirt, standin' there waitin' for him.

When my brothers Jim and Vernon was about ten or twelve years old, they never did have to wear shoes. Daddy went to Sweetwater, and he brought 'em back some of the prettiest little high-top shoes that laced up partway and buckled on up the rest. He brought both of 'em back a pair just alike to wear to school. They didn't like 'em. They didn't want to wear shoes. They went barefooted; cold or hot—they went barefooted. So one morning between our house and school over on the other side of the canyon, they sat down and pulled their shoes off and tied 'em to a mesquite tree and left 'em there. It started gettin' cold that day, and when we left the schoolhouse it had started snowin'. There was snow on the ground. We started back toward home and looked up and there was Daddy. He'd come after us. If it was bad weather or snow or somethin', he'd come after us in a buggy. We had an old horse called Roan, and he'd get in that buggy and he'd come after us.

Well, he come after us and Jim and Vernon didn't have their shoes on. He said, "Boys, what happened to your shoes?" They said, "We didn't want to get 'em messed up so we hung 'em in a tree."

33

He said, "Next time, don't leave 'em in a tree, leave 'em at the house." He didn't whip 'em for it.

Vernon was seven or eight years old before he ever did wear britches. He wore dresses. He was a pretty good-sized little boy and would still go to school with a dress on. Kids didn't laugh at him because he said he didn't like britches.

It's a Wonder We Ever Got to School

NAOMI A. MAYFIELD

I went to a country school for two years. It must have been about 1925. I went to the fourth grade there, and we moved away in the fifth grade. We walked to school except when it rained and the river came down. Then we went in a hack or on a horse with some of the neighbor kids. On the way to and from school we'd eat anything we could find a-growing. There was a blue weed that had little brownish potatoes on the roots that we'd find sticking out on the side of the canyon, especially after a rain. We called them hog taters. They were about the size of an almond and had a sweet nutty taste to them. In the spring we'd stop and hunt cactus berries. They grew on little flat cactus—these little red berries; they really looked more like little red peppers, growing out of the center. They tasted mighty good when you could find enough of them at one time. We picked algerita berries, too. They grew on hollylike bushes, and when they were ripe they'd turn red. We'd chew mesquite wax that was the sap from the mesquite trees, and then there was a white gum we'd chew that came from a shittim tree. It was more like a chewing gum. It's a wonder we ever got to school.

Kids Were Tougher Than They Are Now

CLYDE HODGES

Going to school each morning, on the road I traveled, there'd be about eight or ten of us kids together—all the conversations going on, boys and girls, you know. There was three at our house, then four at Bob Harris's and two cousins of mine. There'd be about eight to ten of us come up that road together. They didn't start school then until nine o'clock, and they didn't turn out until four. We'd leave home about eight, and we'd get over there in plenty of time. Give us plenty of time to get there. In cold weather, we would want to get there extra early so we'd get warm, you know, before school started.

We didn't have to milk or do chores before we went to school. We never did have to do that. We didn't have to do no milking. Mom and Dad done it. Oh, sometimes we might have to bring in a little extra wood before we'd leave, but not much.

If it was really cold we'd just wrap up because we had to face the wind going to school. We had our backs to it going home from school. But I tell you what, kids were tougher than they are now. They were used to it. Toughened up to it. They had warm clothes then, and most of the clothes was homemade.

Jimmy Was Last Because He Had to Open the Gates

JUNA REYNOLDS

In rural areas, public roads were the exception rather than the rule. The farther one lived from town, the more likely one's path would meander through private farms, fields, and pastures. What this meant, of course, was fences. By the early 1900s barbed wire (called "bob wire" by West Texans) was in common use, and most farms and pastures were fenced to keep livestock either in or out. As a result, gates were placed across roads, creating barriers for the animals but providing travelers access from one property to another. On the way to school, there might be numerous gates to contend with: "We opened gates all the way."

Sometimes we would walk to school because it would be so cold they didn't want the horses to be out in the open. It wasn't too cold for us to go to school, but it was too cold for us to take the horses. I remember one time we walked home from school and a norther had come in. It was snowing something terrible. I had gotten way behind because I was just five years old. The bigger kids all got home before I did, and my dad came back looking for me.

When we rode on the horse, old Daisy, we had a special place for everybody. I rode up front and held on to the saddle horn. My Aunt Nita rode next and drove. She was always in charge of things. My Sister Loretta rode behind Nita and held on to her. And my Uncle Jimmy was last because he had to open the gates. There must have been a dozen gates between home and school. Jimmy would

Betty Jean Murphree arrives at County Line School, Fisher County, on her mule, 1937. Children often rode a horse or mule to school, sometimes two, three, or four astride. Also pictured are the teacher, Aline Darden Northrup, and fellow pupils, Delia Hardin (right) and Juna Reynolds. Courtesy Luther Bryan Clegg

slide off the back of old Daisy, open the gate, and then get back on. Sometimes the gates would be so close together that Nita would make Jimmy stay off and walk to the next gate.

"I Wish You Little Devils Would Stay Off of My Gate"

JAMES P. CLEGG

When we went on a horse or rode in a hack, we had to open lots of gates. I don't remember how many, but it must have been a half dozen or so. Some of them was hard to open, but if they had a stick around the pole to use for a lever, it wasn't too bad. When my brothers, Wallace and Willard, was going to school, the gates that one of our neighbors made was the hardest to open there ever was. Man, he made them hard! What we used to do—I've done it, and Wallace and Willard used to do it—if you couldn't open 'em, you'd get in the middle of the gate, and jump up and down on the wire to loosen it up. It'd stretch the gate, and it'd be easier to open and shut.

One day our neighbor come along and said, "I wish you little devils would stay off of my gate."

Wallace said, "I wish you big devils would make one that we could open."

When we went on a horse, my sister would be the driver. She was bossier. I'd slide off the horse and open the gates. We'd wear our corduroys and sometimes a sweater. But we didn't have a windbreaker. Man, that wind against you would get so cold! I don't remember what all we wore, but whatever it was, it wasn't enough. That wind would go right through it. Your feet would get so cold, it was pitiful.

The Buggy Was Just a-Flyin', I Mean Just a-Bouncin'
DELIA HARDIN

We went to school in the buggy, I guess it was really a hack because it had two seats. A buggy had one seat and a hack had two. When we'd get to school, we'd unharness the horses so they wouldn't have to stand there all day. We had ol' Pete, a mule that was just lazy as the dickens, and an old horse that was with him.

One time at the end of the day, we was getting ready to come home. Dorothy Mae Robinson and I harnessed the horses and hooked 'em up to the hack. My sister Dot never would harness the horses or help in anyway. Dot and Betty Jean sat up in the hack and wouldn't get out and help us. The rest of the kids was walking on. So we got to the hill ready to go down, and the brake was wore out on the hack, so we'd have to lock the wheel.

We said, "We harnessed the team, y'all lock the wheel."

Betty Jean and Dot said, "We're not lockin' it."

We said, "We're not either." So I said, "Gitup!" Down the hill we went. You know, the traces, when the hack runs up on the horses, they get unhooked. There we were, wildly goin' down the hill. Dot and Betty Jean jumped out the back, and there's me and Dorothy Mae hanging on for dear life. We got to the bottom and the hack just went running out there and just rolled over. And the horses just went crazy.

Another time my older sister Mary told a boy going to school with us named Clyde, "This old Pete mule is so lazy he'll hardly go." So she said to Clyde, "Cut us one of those big ol' long mesquite limbs." They were about that big, just straight up and

37

down. There was a thicket of 'em. So he's cutting the thorns off and got most of 'em off, and finally Mary said, "Leave 'em on, Clyde."

Clyde said, "These thorns?"

She said, "Yes." So she said, "Everybody get set. We're going home." So she whopped old Pete with the switch. When she did, the switch jerked out of her hand some way and went down between the traces and the mule. Ever' time ol' Pete would take a step, it'd slap him in the side with those thorns. Well, away he went, just a-runnin', and of course, the old horse with him would run ever' time anyway.

We went down the hill there to the river. The buggy was just a-flyin', I mean just a-bouncin'. We was slingin' kids out right and left. Dot was sittin' up there hollerin', "Hit 'em again, Mary. Hit 'em again." And we went down the hill, and it was a pretty big hill, and Mary circled 'em down the river and she took 'em about a mile. The switch fell out going down the river. Just Mary and my brother R. L. and Dot was all that was left in there. All the little kids was out, Nita and all of us. They got the hack circled back, and R. L. walked in front of 'em and I walked on one side and we led 'em through the cedar breaks.

Ol' Pete tried to run all the way home. When we got home, he got calmed down some, but he was still just sawin' at the bits, tryin' to go. Daddy was fixin' to go haul wood and said, "What's the matter?"

We said, "Old Pete run away."

Daddy said, "Old Pete run away?" He was just dumbfounded. Daddy got out and unhooked his mules, and he said, "Just hook Pete on here, and I'll see if I can run him down." Poor old Pete had ever' right to run. Daddy hooked him up to the wagon and whipped him with the lines and run him down the road to the river and hauled wood.

I said, "Poor ol' thing." But we didn't tell what really happened.

That Horse Reared up and Fell Back on 'Em

THELMA BURK

Sometimes we rode to school on horseback. One time we had a horse who would rear up and fall back. If you tied her up, she'd just kill herself trying to get loose. Mary and R. L. were riding her to school. You couldn't ride her up a steep hill or she'd do the same thing. There was a real steep hill at the bottom of the Adair place, and the other kids dared them to ride the horse up it. Kids are not going to pass up a dare, so they went up it and got nearly to the top. That horse reared up and fell back on 'em. They all rolled back down the hill, and the horse rolled back on top of 'em. It's a wonder it hadn't of killed 'em.

We carried our lunch in a soda or baking powder box. It was kind of square with two little bails. It looked a lot like some of the lunch boxes today. I had to ride with Mary because this little horse acted up. Daddy told Mary not to put me up on the horse until she got on the horse because it might run away with me. We had raised the horse from a colt, and it was spoiled rotten. Of course, Mary didn't pay any attention to what Daddy said. One morning she put me up behind the saddle and handed me the dinner bucket and reached up to get a hold of the saddle horn. When she did, the horse broke to run. He drug her down the road a little ways because she had a hold of the reins. I was just holding on, of course. Mama was hollering "Turn loose, turn loose!" and when I did, boy, off I come!

I Went along as a Bodyguard for My Sister

DONO DARDEN

A "blue norther" is a term used in West Texas for a severe winter storm. Its approach is foretold by a heavy bank of dark clouds in the northwest. Soon after the clouds first appear, a sharp, biting wind howls into the area, bringing dust and chill and often blowing snow. A norther might be nothing more than cold, blowing wind, but a blue norther is fierce—something to be reckoned with!

We first moved to this part of the country from Ellis County. We moved over close to Hitson and Afton in Fisher County, and that was before there were any public roads. When you went to town, you opened gates all the way. The only public road went from Rotan to Hamlin. The rest of the way you was opening gates, through people's farms and ranches, one after the other.

I started to school over at Hitson before I was six years old. My sister's three years older than I was. She had to go to school. Well, we went through a big pasture where there was longhorn cattle. And

I carried rocks to chunk the cattle. They would look at us and shake their heads, and Dad told us not to run from 'em—to chunk 'em. The cows would start toward us and would shake their heads. There wasn't any trees to climb if we got in trouble—no trees out over there around Hitson. So I loaded my pockets down with rocks, and I went along for protection. I started in January and I lacked about two and a half months being six years old. I went along as a body-guard for my sister.

One time a blue norther blew up, and we didn't have suitable clothes. Teacher turned us out earlier than my father expected us to get turned out. So we had to face a blue norther going home, and we got so cold. When we crawled under a fence on the way home, my sister couldn't get up. I was too little and too cold, so I couldn't help her up. I had to go off and leave her. Now that was frontier times! My father went and found her, picked her up, and carried her home. *Now that was frontier times for you!*

That's When My Heels Both Froze

LEWIS H. CLEGG

When we changed schools and went to Riverdale, one of the men over there was determined he was going to run us off. He was mad because we was going over there. He was just that kind of a guy. He wouldn't even let us go through his pasture. Made us go around the fence, down the lane. Said, "You're knocking the steeples out of my fence." We wasn't doing no such a-thing. I tell you what I did. I'd take a big rock about that big, and I'd throw it, and it'd hit a post right in the middle. If it was just the least bit rotten, I'd just break it in two. I bet you a nickel I broke fifty posts with rocks. I did that. That's how mean I was. I don't blame him for not wanting me around.

I was the oldest and I kinda took care of the brood. I remember having to leave real early. It's a long ways over there, and in part of the winter it was dark. You never seen the sun come up until you got across the first river down there. And it'd be cold. *Real cold!* By the time we'd get across that sand, my little sister Bertie would be a-cryin' with her feet. We'd get in the cedar breaks, and I'd build up a fire and warm up her feet. And by the time I got to the next place

40

where we had to cross the river again, the sun was up, and it wouldn't be quite so cold.

Once we was caught in a real blizzard coming from school. Jess Greene had just married Addie Bostick, and he come up there in a buggy after Addie's sister Ethel. And he carried Bertie home too. That just left my brother Jack and me and we struck out. We never thought about having any extra clothes on except just a jacket. That's all. That's all we had. We struck out down through that brush, and when we got to Bostick's we was just about half froze. We stopped out there at the barn and got behind the barn. The wind was pushing. We warmed up a little bit and made it across the river, and that's when my heels both froze. I didn't go to school the next day because my feet was too sore.

Time We Got Home, We Was Crying Because We Was So Cold

DOROTHY HEAD

I started to school in 1930. We rode horses to school mostly when I was smaller. But when I got older we walked a lot. When it rained, we had to go through the hills. I remember how cold it was. One time we was riding a horse, and I didn't hold on when we went up the riverbank. Whoever was in front driving the horse said, "Hold on!"

I said, "I'm not going to. I'm not going to hold on." I wasn't holding on to anybody and my sister Thelma was behind me holding on to me. When the horse went up the bank of the river, Thelma and me slid off his back—fell off in the water. And it was freezing, and Thelma was screaming at me. We got to school and the teacher got our shoes off and put us behind the stove 'til we dried off.

I remember one time it snowed and we walked home from school. We was walking then. Daddy came in the car to get us, but the teacher turned us out early. Time we got home we was crying because we was so cold. The snow just got worse and worse before we got home. I remember Mother made us put our hands in cold water because our hands were so cold. We wanted 'em in warm water, but she wouldn't let us. She even got some snow and rubbed on our hands. It was *very* cold. We was facing that north wind. It was about three miles and took us more than an hour. We had on dresses, but we had on long brown stockings over our long underwear. Then we had supporters that came up and hooked onto our underwear, and they'd bind me so I'd let 'em down. I know they didn't look neat, but I didn't care. They were binding me.

I didn't have a store dress until I was grown. I wore hand-me-downs. Two sisters older, you know. I never had a coat that was *mine,* like bought for me, until I was sixteen. It was exciting. A brown coat. We bought it at H. L. Davis Department Store. Brand new coat. *My very own.*

He Tied His Clothes on Top of His Head and Swum across the River

MOLLIE HUDNALL

When we was going over to Riverdale, if the river was up we couldn't go. We went to school once, and it hadn't rained down at home, but it rained up above and the river had come down. We got to the river, but nobody went across but my brother Jack. He swum across. He tied his clothes on top of his head and swum across and went on to school. I don't know what he told the teacher about why he came and the rest of us didn't.

I Remember Well the Blizzard of 1918

NARCISSA CLEGG

I remember well the blizzard of 1918. It was the tenth of January. We went to school that morning. It was what I'd call a pretty nice winter day. I had on, of course, all the coat I had, and I had on a cap. When we went to school that morning, the sun was shining. I don't know if there was ever any cloud in the north that showed a storm was coming. I don't remember. There usually was. Of course, we had no radio. We got to school before nine o'clock and right afterwards here come that thing. Oh, the whole sky just clouded over, and it went to snowing, and the wind was a-blowing. Whee, it just snowed and it snowed, and it was so cold it could freeze the horns off a billy goat. *It was just terrible!*

It went on that way all day. I know it was a blizzard for it got a lot of snow on the ground, and the wind would come and blow that snow in the air so you couldn't see. It didn't seem to be coming out of the sky, but coming off the ground, blowing like that. And *cold, it was just terrible!*

Arby and Ruby Gough came wearing their bonnets. Somehow or other Mr. Gough and his son Carl got the car started and come around the hill and got their children, or they would have frozen to death, sure enough. We all went home. I know Miss Sydney was our teacher, and she was boarding at Aunt Lindy's. We started home. Everybody that went up our way had caps except Vernon Helms. He had on a hat. Before we got very far, Miss Sydney noticed that Vernon's ears were freezing. She happened to have a big silk handkerchief in her pocket. She got it out and tied it over his ears under his hat. That's the way he got home without his ears freezing.

Annabelle Hudnall told me the story about what happened to her during that storm. She was going to school at Sardis. She was the same age as I was. She had a sister named Pearl who had a stepson about fifteen years old that was going to school with her. She said they had to go home facing that north wind. The teacher went along with them for a little piece, and then she turned off to go to her boarding place and they went on alone.

They had to pass an old abandoned schoolhouse. So they thought they'd go in there and stay a few minutes and warm up. They got in there and the boy said, "We can't stay here. We'll freeze right here." So they got out and started home. They usually had to go around a cornfield, but they thought they would go catty-corner across the field and cut off some distance. They got out there and snow was blowing so bad they couldn't even see their way nor where to go. So they got lost. The boy got down and scratched in the snow. He knew which way the corn rows ran, so he was able to get his bearings.

Annabelle said all the time she was saying, "Let's lay down. I want to lay down. I'm sleepy." The boy just pushed her and kept on. She said she didn't have on her heaviest coat that morning. It was pretty nice when they went to school so she got her second coat. I think she had on some gloves. She said finally that boy got her to her sister Pearl's house. When they got there, they pulled off her gloves, and her fingers were frozen, and her heels were frozen. And today she's got brown on her heels. That's how come her to tell me that story.

CHAPTER THREE

ઝ

The Trustees Got
the Best Teachers They Could

TEACHERS AND INSTRUCTION

"The trustees got the best teachers they could" was not meant to be an apology but rather a commendation. Finding qualified teachers, and providing the money to pay them, was one of the major tasks that faced trustees. Afterward, they had the task of convincing their new teacher to stay on—even if he or she was unhappy boarding with Aunt Matilda and Uncle Andrew or having every detail of his or her actions reported around the community. It would appear, also, that some boys' sole purpose in attending school was to aggravate the teacher and thereby gain the respect and admiration of their classmates.

In spite of the difficulties inherent in staffing rural schools, teachers were found and school bells rung. Many teachers were remembered as being intelligent, industrious, enterprising, and conscientious. They were good role models who helped country children desire additional schooling, encouraging them to "go on as high as you can."

Instruction centered around the recitation bench, as it was here teachers heard lessons, while remaining pupils were supposedly studying at their desks. Older pupils were assigned to assist teachers in instruction of younger students. It was common for teachers to punish or shame pupils who could not recite their lessons, and prizes were frequently given at year's end to reward good performance. One can conclude that schools, then as now,

Typical of many two-teacher schools, a large number and wide range of ages were what teachers were expected to cope with. The young man with glasses (center) likely teaches the older children, while the young woman with glasses (left) is, in all likelihood, the younger pupils' teacher. Courtesy Fannie W. Albert and Abbie W. Martin

were sometimes excellent, sometimes poor, and often somewhere in between.

I Thought We Wouldn't Have a Teacher Ever As Good As Miss Annie

NARCISSA CLEGG

Miss Annie instituted what she called the Literary Society. On Friday afternoon, she would assign us speeches and dialogues and other things, and we would practice them. We would have programs at night, and she would have my papa play the fiddle between acts. Everybody enjoyed it very much. When school got ready to be out, we practiced for more weeks than usual and had a bigger program. Elmer Gray was, as best I remember, the biggest boy in school. And Miss Annie would have him stand outside the schoolhouse, several feet away from the building, maybe as much as ten or twelve, and everybody had to speak loud enough for Elmer to hear. And if he couldn't, he'd raise his hand. And then that meant we should speak louder. That was so that when the exhibition came on, everybody could hear.

Well, I can say this now. After school was out, and I knew Miss Annie wouldn't teach the next year, I took a big cry one night. I just thought we wouldn't have a teacher ever as good as Miss Annie. The

45

next year, in the fall we got Mr. Noah Hilburn, and I loved him just as well as I did her. He was a bachelor man. I remember about him. He came up to our cotton patch with Uncle Jeff. My papa and Uncle Jeff were trustees.

Uncle Jeff said, "This man wants more money."

Mr. Hilburn said, "All the teachers in my class, they're getting $75 a month." County Line was only paying $65. And he said, "I'd also like to have $75 a month."

I understood that Papa and Uncle Jeff said, "If we've got the money in the county bank, all right." So they gave him $75 a month. That's the first I knew about how much a teacher got. But he was a good one, and he was worth it.

He didn't have exhibitions and literaries exactly like Miss Annie did, but I remember he got up a box supper. He said "We're going to have a box [case] of maps." It was a great big box. I don't know where he got it, but anyway, he had the money made up with a box supper. He ordered those maps, the first we'd ever had. It was a wooden, I guess oak, box which hung on the wall, more than four feet wide, and the maps were on rollers. They had a metal pull. A map of the world, a map of Texas, a map of the United States, a map of all the continents, and whenever we were studying geography, he'd pull them down and there we saw them. And as long as I went to school, that map box was there, and I wish we had it even yet. Of course, he'd lock it up when we'd get through with it. It was above the blackboard, and whenever the geography classes came, then those maps came down.

"We Need a Big Ol' Ugly Man Like You"

WILLIAM I. POTEET

I remember when I finished school one year, Miss Annie was my teacher, and she was very intelligent. She come back the second time to teach after we had a rowdy bunch that run the teacher off. On my report card, I'll tell this to my own confidence, because I feel good about it, my grades were good enough and I was a good enough student that she wrote across it, "Go on as high as you can." That's encouragement. I'm glad to remember it. I must have been in the fifth grade. I made two grades in one year when she come back. I started to school and after a few days, she said, "This is too easy for you. You can take up with this next group." That was after we had a bad teacher and had about three and half months' schooling. I'd done enough of it and she said, "You can handle it. You can make the next grade." So I went in the fifth grade.

Later on, we had a teacher named Mr. Lusk. He was a big ol' man. I remember Papa was one of the trustees that hired him. Papa said, "We need a man that will make these kids obey. We need a big ol' ugly man like you." He was talking to him on our front porch. He hired him. He was ugly. We liked him though. He took it well.

"We Was Gathering up Cedar Wood for You"
MOLLIE HUDNALL

Once when I was going to school, the teacher was a young married man, hadn't been married too long. So just as soon as school let out, he'd go home every afternoon. He would leave before all the kids were gone so he could get back home to his wife. He had an old plow point he used instead of getting a bell. He'd get out there and beat it with an iron to call kids in from recess. Some of 'em would take his old plow point off and hide it. I guess he finally had to get a bell.

One afternoon after school the boys all got in a fight, and the teacher had to stay at school until ever'body left for home from then on. There was about seventeen boys up there and ever' one of 'em got a whipping.

Another year we had an old maid schoolteacher named Miss Florence. [This teacher was mentioned by several persons from the County Line School. Her name has been changed.] School was just a playhouse, I mean. One day, some of the boys got to playing and forgot to come in after recess. They looked around and nobody was outside, so they knew they was in trouble. So they said, "What are we going to do?" Well, the teacher had already put their names on the board, and she was going to whip them when they came in. So the boys knew she liked cedar wood to burn in the stove because it smelled so good. So they gathered up an armload of cedar wood and came back to the building.

She said, "Why didn't you all come when I rung the bell?"

They said, "We was gathering up cedar wood for you." So she didn't whip them. She thought that was just fine.

She just didn't have any discipline!

She Slammed the Broom over the Teacher's Head

NARCISSA CLEGG

Miss Florence came to teach in 1919. Because of the big crop they had, school didn't begin until right after Christmas, the first of January. Miss Florence was an old lady, a white-haired lady who wore a little dust cap to school like the old dames you see in pictures of the Dame School. Most of her pupils were boys. At first, I think there was only one girl in the school. Other girls came later.

She was just no match for those boys. She boarded in the home with the Adairs, Uncle Jim and Aunt Blanche. She and Aunt Blanche were just two of a kind. Aunt Blanche liked her just fine, but Margie, Aunt Blanche's stepdaughter, didn't like her for some reason, but I don't know exactly why. The boys in school didn't like her either. For instance, one day they were talking about a horse. They called that horse a mare. She told them not to say mare; it wasn't nice.

They said, "Well, what shall we say?"

She said, "You should say 'she horse.'" You can imagine how that would go over with a bunch of farm boys.

She was from Canada, I understood. Anyway, she didn't understand a lot of things about country folks, and she had so many eccentric ways that we didn't understand her. She came into town to take the teaching job in a snowstorm and took a room at the hotel. It was a big snowstorm with deep snow all over the ground. My father was a trustee. She called out there by telephone and told him, "Come into town here and get me! I'm here in the hotel, and they don't have a fire in my room." That was just like all hotels were at that time.

He said, "I can't come into town. The snow is too deep, and the roads are too bad." So she just had to tough it out. Finally she got out there.

One day George and Oscar, my brother and cousin (they didn't like her and they knew Margie didn't like her, either), told Margie, "If you'll run her off, we'll give you five dollars." Margie laughed. Of course, it was a joke. A few days later at the breakfast table, Margie got mad at her and just grabbed the broom and ran and slammed it over her head. And I don't know what all she said. But anyway, it like to have scared Miss Florence to death.

So she said, "I'm leaving! I'm not staying!" So she and Aunt Blanche came up to our house. She told Papa that she was leaving, she was resigning, that she was not staying. And she left! I don't know how long she taught there. It might have been a month or two. Margie laughed and told George and Oscar that they owed her five dollars. She had run Miss Florence off. Of course, she knew that they never had five dollars to their name. That was a joke that was told for a long time. I don't think they got anybody else to teach that year.

I Worked All That Year for a Nickel!
LIZZIE UNDERWOOD

The first teacher I went to was Mr. Laughlin. He could teach you a few things. He taught you how to read a little and to write and to spell. For the little kids he was all right, but for the older kids he would get stumped. Sometimes the older kids would teach the younger kids. After I got up in the fourth or fifth grade, if I got my lessons real good, I got to hear the lessons of the younger kids. There was so many of us that you could take 'em outside and let 'em spell or read so the other class could have their lessons. That way we could get done with the lessons by the time to go home.

I was a good student except for my history. My history was bad. If anybody asked me about anybody but Washington or Jefferson or Lincoln, I wouldn't know much about 'em. They didn't teach history much.

The teacher had a desk up on the rostrum, like a little stage. There was some bookcases on each side. The boys on one side and the girls on the other. We could put stuff in them bookcases and leave 'em there at night, what we didn't want to bring home. Mr. Laughlin had a way with kids, I guess, because he had several of his own. He said before we started in, "Well, now you kids learn to spell." We was learning to spell dog and cat and things little kids learn. And he said, "At the end of school whichever one learns their words ever'day and don't miss one is going to get a prize at the end of school." Well, coming home of a evening, I'd start from over there, and I'd be spelling a word. I spelled them words all the way home until it was time to get home. By then I nearly knew 'em. When I was going back the next morning, ever' little bit I'd stop and look at my book so I would know how the words was spelled.

Well, at the end of school, the old man called ever'body's name that had good records. He called me up on the rostrum and said I

49

especially had good spelling, and he wanted to give me a little prize. *He gave me a chalk box and a nickel!* [This was spoken with great disdain.] There was chalk boxes there by the dozen with chalk for kids learning to write. I could have carried a chalk box off a dozen times if I'd wanted it. *I'd worked all that year for a nickel!* My daddy said he was proud of me even if I didn't get nothing but a nickel.

I guess my favorite teacher was Martha Wilson. I was twelve or fourteen. She was just a good teacher. She was kind to you, and she'd call on you for things. If you was having class, and she asked a question and you didn't know what it was, you could ask another one. That would give you a chance, don't you see? She said that a-way each of us would learn faster than we would otherwise. We would learn from each other.

They Were Like a Breath of Fresh Air

VIRGINIA HAYES

When I was in the fifth grade we lived south of Lubbock, and I went to Southwest Ward. We had two teachers, a man and his wife, Mr. and Mrs. Russell Dennison. They were like a breath of fresh air. They were city folks, you see. She was very beautiful and sweet, very cultured. It was really different for us farm kids. Mr. Dennison had a beautiful blue car. I don't remember what kind it was, but he volunteered to come and pick the children up because the territory was quite large. It would have been difficult for us to get to school. I'm sure the state paid him.

I was in the fifth grade, and Mrs. Dennison taught grades one through four. He taught grades five, six, and seven. I remember he was rather harsh, because he was so eager that we learn. His methods were rather hard on little sensitive people like me. I remember if you ever made a grammatical error, it was almost like he was making fun of you. He'd make us feel like a fool. But she was the sweetest thing.

During the year they would have us to their home for dinner— one at a time. They would come and get us and bring us back. When I visited, I never will forget, they had a refrigerator. None of us had refrigerators. She made lemon ice cream. That was the best stuff I ever ate in my life!

I remember one learning experience I had. Mr. Dennison had us do a debate. I thought that was such fun. It seemed like I always had to take the worse side. This debate was radio versus the newspaper for the news. Of course, nobody wanted to take the side of the newspaper. Everybody wanted to take the radio because it was the new thing, you know. I recall that he praised me. That was so special. You know, if somebody is kind of harsh, then if you get their praise, that's really meaningful. He told us that he really thought our side won, even though everybody knew radio was better.

I Never Did Get Nobody to Help Me with My Class

LEO E. CLEGG

One time we had this old maid teacher from Denton. She didn't care too much for me so I decided that I'd give her some reason to not like me. One day we was studyin' physical geography. We had fourth and fifth and sixth grade, I think, three classes takin' physical geography. There was sixteen in all. It was right after the noon hour when we was havin' that class. So she called on ever'body in class, all sixteen of us, askin' us how to carry on fertilizin'. There wasn't anybody that knew how to carry on fertilizin'. I wondered what to say about it. And when she got to me, she turned red in the face, and she said, "Leo, tell us how to carry on fertilizin'."

I said, "Well, we always carry it on a wagon." The whole crowd tore loose a-laughin'. She didn't have nothin' else to say. But she was sure mad.

I really got her another time. I got up to the board in math class. She was goin' to help us if we had a problem we couldn't work. I had a problem, and I asked her to help me work it. But instead of helpin' us with our math problems, she got in a big way a-talkin' about how she wouldn't marry a preacher, and she wouldn't marry a lawyer, and she wouldn't marry a doctor, and all kinds of men she wouldn't marry. About that time, it was time for the bell to ring so I never did get nobody to help me with my class.

Finally, I said, "You'd do well to marry anybody." Boy, did I catch it then.

She said, "I'll have you to understand that I could have had several husbands."

I shot back, "Well, why don't you have one then?" I knew I was askin' for it when I said it, but I was mad at her because she wouldn't help me with my arithmetic problems.

I Had to Stay with the Teacher Because
I Was Too Little to Walk to School Alone

MARY BOYDSTUN

It was not uncommon for the teacher to board with a family in the community during the school term, and occasionally a child would also stay with a family who lived near school. The uniqueness of this story, however, is that both the teacher and little seven-year-old Mary boarded at the same place. It was three miles from Mary's home to school and, because she was the only pupil living in her area, she could not travel alone. Therefore, Miss Delilah had the added responsibility of caring for Mary after school hours. Teachers never questioned what they were asked to do, however, and sometimes job requirements went well beyond the usual job description.

I started to school when I was seven years old. The first year I stayed with the teacher, Miss Delilah, and went with her because I was too little to walk by myself. We stayed with a family that lived near the school. I went back and forth with Miss Delilah, and on weekends I'd go home. I was very homesick sometimes. There was two others in my class—twins named Clay and Clyde. When we had lessons, the older kids helped us some, but usually the teacher took us up, all three together.

There was a door on each end of the school. They opened to the east and west. There were windows on both the north and south sides. The state provided the school textbooks. Generally, about the time school started, the county superintendent would come out and bring out new books. If we didn't get new ones, we'd just check in the books at the end of the year and then the next grade would use them.

Miss Effie Mae's Prince Had Come to Take Her Away!

NARCISSA CLEGG

One year our school was taught by Miss Effie Mae and another teacher. They were staying with the Adairs down there in their house in the middle of the field. But Miss Effie Mae didn't teach but just a little bit that year. She had a man friend that must have been running after her for quite a while. One day he came up there to where she was boarding, and Mrs. Adair didn't like it, for she was old-fashioned and all.

52

Miss Effie May met the man out on the porch, and he grabbed her and gave her a hug and a kiss. Mrs. Adair was shocked! She thought he shouldn't have done that.

The man told Miss Effie Mae, "I've come after you. I'm going to take you away." He took her off and married her. She resigned her school and left right then. I guess you would have to say that was kind of romantic. Her prince had come to take her away, even if Mrs. Adair didn't like it.

Some Folks Believed the Teacher Was Pregnant at the Time
GRACE PHILLIPS

When I started to school I was six. I started a year earlier than Mother intended me to because I was the youngest and I cried when the other kids left for school that day, so she decided I could go with them. Back then, the teacher gave you your book the first day of school. I came home with my books so happy and Mother burst into tears and had to go off into the kitchen and stand near the wood box and cry a while. My teacher was Miss Delilah. I recall when we read we always put our finger on the letters and then on the words.

In second grade, I remember us learning to spell. I'll never forget the words because we had Miss Flora [name changed], and she kept me in first recess because I couldn't spell the words. It was "autumn" and "leaves" and "September." That's pretty good words for second grade, and I couldn't remember those words. She kept me in at noontime, and I still couldn't remember them. Like I never learned to milk a cow; I made up my mind, and I still can't. So at the afternoon recess, she kept me in and my older sister Ruby went to her and took her by the arm and said, "That's my sister and you're not keeping her in anymore." She got me by the hand and led me out. That poor soul never did try to lord it over me anymore.

Miss Flora died during the year, and that school year was over then. There was great turmoil in the community related to her death because it was kinda whispered underneath it all about what some thought had actually happened. When she died, one of the men in the community announced that he and Miss Flora had been secretly married. They had to keep their marriage a secret because she would have been dismissed if it were known she was married. People said that she died from acute appendicitis, but some folks believed she was pregnant at the time, and that was the cause of her illness and death.

There Wasn't a Thing Wrong with Him Except Love Sickness

BERTIE THOMSON

I started to school in 1911 because I didn't start until I was eight. We walked three miles each way. We crossed the river twice because of the bluffs along the bank—we crossed the river to the east where it made a bend, then went across the cedar breaks, and then crossed the river again to the south. When the river was down, we'd have to go around through the hills. We had one room and one teacher. Sometimes we'd have thirty pupils. Sometimes the little kids would say their lessons for the big kids.

The first year I went there my teacher was Mr. Jack Duckworth, and he boarded with the Bairds. The Bairds had three children going to school, and one of the girls was Lee. Sometimes Mr. Duckworth wouldn't get to school on time or wouldn't show up at all. The trustees met, and they asked him to move from the Bairds. So from then on, Mr. Duckworth stayed with the Ackers. He had a buggy and a team of his own, so he could go back and forth. Lee was older, so when all this happened, she quit school.

One day Lee went down to get her mail at the Adair place where the post office was. Lee come back by the schoolhouse just before dinner and stayed, and after dinner Mr. Duckworth didn't take up books. He and Lee stayed at the dictionary talking. We had a great big dictionary that was bolted to the wall. It was on one of those metal things. The teacher and Lee got to talking, and he forgot to ring the bell at one o'clock. So all the kids simply ran off. We all run off, except my brother Lewis and Jim Gray and one of the Trout boys. Jim Gray was sick that day so Lewis stayed with him. There was three grown boys, Alf and Frank Gray and Willie Helms, going to school then. The girls wouldn't run off unless Alf Gray went with 'em. So we all run off. When we got down a little ways from the schoolhouse, we told Alf and Willie to go down there to the Adairs' and phone Mr. Acker to come get Mr. Duckworth—that he had spinal meningitis. There wasn't a thing wrong with him except love sickness. When they got down there and tried to call Mr. Acker, of course he wasn't at home.

When the teacher finally rung the bell about two o'clock, we all come back except Alf and Willie. We were just over the hill a little ways where he couldn't see us. Mr. Duckworth was going to give Alf and Willie a whipping because they didn't come in. So Alf and Willie quit school. These boys was grown, seventeen or eighteen years old or bigger. It was the last year they went to school. Of course, they was in the eighth grade; that was as far as they went.

She Made a Beautiful Wreath
of Paper Flowers to Go on the Grave
NARCISSA CLEGG

I'll never forget the Richardsons who were teachers at County Line when my sister Gladys died. She was twelve and was hit by a car, one of the only cars in our community. She died several hours later. The morning that she died, they called the teacher, Mr. Richardson, and told him that Gladys was gone. He said, "All right, we'll call off school right now for the day." He and his wife came to the funeral. She didn't know there would be any flowers because then we didn't have the undertaker. We all took care of our own. Mrs. Richardson made a beautiful wreath of paper flowers to go on the grave. Somebody else, I think Mrs. Settle in town, ordered flowers and brought them out there, which was very unusual for that time. And old Aunt Sissy McCombs, when she heard about Gladys, she had roses all in bloom. And she let them just strip her roses and make flowers and bring them over there. Roses to go on that grave. Mrs. Richardson was standing back there holding those paper flowers. She didn't know whether to put them on or not. We said, "Put them on!" Her paper flowers went on right among the others. It was an unusual way, but we did it. I just loved Mrs. Richardson for wanting to do that.

I Knew More Than the Teacher
ROBERT MARTINEZ

I went twenty-seven months to school up to 1929. So the last year I was in school, I was promoted to the sixth grade. We didn't go but

55

three or four months. All the farmers did that. They kept kids out to pick cotton, and then we'd have to get out early in the spring to hoe it.

So here comes a teacher—a man. Where did he ever get a degree teaching, I don't know! There were two little girls, the Prince girls, in my class. They, too, were promoted to the sixth grade. Well, he put the two little girls to the blackboard making fractions. In those days you took fractions in the sixth grade. That was difficult for me. When it came to arithmetic, I didn't have an easy time. So he had those little girls crying because they had been taught one way, and here he was teaching them another way—the wrong way—it wouldn't come out at all.

They were crying, so finally I told him, "We were taught different and you're changing it for them, and that's why they don't know what they are doing." I felt so sorry for them. They were younger than me. I was old. I was seventeen years old. Those days a seventeen-year-old was a man.

He said, "How did y'all do it?" I got to the blackboard and showed him. The little girls followed me exactly with no trouble. And he says, "Well, you go ahead and work these problems with them and help them." So we worked several. I kept on and kept on and finally I thought, "Why should I be here? I know more than this man." That's not an exaggeration or anything. I knew more than the teacher. So I just didn't go back to school anymore, but now I wish I'd have stayed.

When I Got to School, I Had to Memorize Poems
EUNICE HUCKABY

I started to school at age six to Mrs. Yantis and I loved her. You know, you always love your first-grade teacher. First-graders always love their teachers. I loved her very much. Her husband was also a teacher. I didn't have him because he taught the upper-level students, and she taught the younger ones.

I remember on my first day of school I had been assigned a seat, and I remember the teacher coming down and sitting down beside me and opening a little book, a primer, I guess you'd call it, and her saying, "Now, can you read this?"

I had seen the book, probably from my older sister Ruby or some

of the older kids who brought it home, and I said, "To market, to market, to buy a fat pig."

She said, "No, no, that's not the one." I was going pretty much by the picture, I guess. I just assumed that's what it said. And she said, "No, no, that's not it." Then she started teaching me. I don't remember how she taught me, but I know I couldn't read at that time.

I didn't learn to read from my older brothers and sisters. I guess, for one reason, we didn't have books like kids have these days. We didn't have that many, though Mother was good to read to us, and we took a newspaper that came twice a week. I remember that we took the *Pathfinder* and later the *Reader's Digest* and *Capper's Weekly*. But as far as children's books like children have now, we did not have those. My mother read a lot from the Bible. That was one thing she taught us a lot. She read from the Bible and read to us articles that she thought we ought to hear. At night we were all seated around and she would read from something.

When I got to school, I had to memorize poems. In fact, it seems to me every Friday afternoon we had what I think they called a Literary Society. We'd have a different type of program, but one of the things the teachers would do was to assign us certain poems to memorize. And we had to do a lot of that by memory. I remember one was the "Psalm of Life" by Longfellow. That didn't have any meaning at all then, but in later years it did. You know, I'm glad I learned that. I wonder if kids have to do that today. Many of them didn't mean anything at the time, but now I'm so grateful I had to memorize them.

My last teacher was Mrs. Wright, and we only had one teacher by then. I was in the eighth grade. I helped some of the younger kids. I would listen to their reading and stuff like that, but I guess my favorite teachers were Lois and Louise, the Smith twins. Lois taught the smaller kids, and I was in Louise's class. They were wonderful, wonderful ladies. What I liked about them when I think back now, they tried to motivate us to go on beyond our schooling. You know, a lot of kids, once they finished there, the seventh or eighth grade, that was it. They didn't go on. If you did, you had to go into town and stay with someone to go to school. Lois and Louise did encourage us to go on to school. I can remember several of the kids were about ready to finish school there, and they especially tried to encourage them. They'd say, "You know, you can go into town and stay somewhere, and you can work and go on and get your education."

Sometimes You Might Sit Half a Day before Your Lessons
BESSIE CLEVELAND

We came to Pleasant Valley in 1924, and I was in the third grade. I walked to school, but that wasn't any distance. My daddy just finished the third grade, but he was determined that his children would learn to read and write and work arithmetic. Now, he didn't worry about the geography or anything like that, but they had to be able to read and write. I remember learning to read. It was more like memorization.

I was a poor speller. One of my teachers used a pond, she called it. She'd draw a circle on the board. Then when we'd miss one of those sounds, we were put in the pond, either as a splash or with our faces drawn in. To be in the pond was punishment. I hated to be in the pond, but I was there a long time because I couldn't hear the sounds. Reading wasn't any trouble for me, but just the sounds.

A typical day at school would be to begin the day with some exercises that they don't want us to do anymore, like singing and Bible reading. But we always did that. Then the upper grades, the highest grade in the room, would have the first lesson. It was usually reading. Then the teacher would assign them a lesson for the next day. They could either do that or work on their math, which would be their next subject. Then she'd go to the next grade. The lower grades usually went to a table when we read. There would be about six or seven in my group. The teacher would start with the higher grades, then the middle grades, and finally to the lower grades. It might be an hour or so before she would get to all grades. Sometimes you might sit half a day before your lesson. But to people that didn't experience it, it's hard to realize.

The teacher read to us usually. The teacher read us Bible stories and other things. She read us *The Shepherd of the Hills* and I think *The Little Shepherd of Kingdom Come*. She was probably the one that influenced me to do more independent reading. I'd spend all the extra minutes I had reading, and even now I do.

I Wasn't Too Good at Spelling
WALTER CLEVELAND

The teacher would assign us work. Take so many pages ever' day. We'd have to read and do the work. In arithmetic we had to work up them problems. In readin' we had to read and get up and read in front of the children. We had to study a lot. One bunch would be up there giving their lessons, and the other bunch would be in the same room studying. The teacher never did miss a lesson. I had 'em all.

59

We had reading and math and geography and physiology. That was about it. Physiology was health. We'd study the parts of your body and what was good food and cleanliness and all that kind of stuff. Just the basics. Geography and history and spelling. I guess that was just about it. I wasn't too good at spelling. We had to buy our books. Bought 'em down here at the drugstore. I don't remember the names of the books, but I know we had Will and Mae in 'em.

We Did a Lot of Singing and Marching

NAOMI VINYARD

I started to school when I was seven. That would be in 1918. Miss Florence was my teacher, and I was the only one in the first grade. She got tired of me running up and asking her what every word was, 'cause I didn't know very many. She put me on an apple box on the stage right by her desk. I didn't learn to read, not at all, by the time she left. The big boys ran her off. I had gone most of the year to Miss Florence and she hadn't taught me a thing!

When I was in the first grade, Miss Florence never heard my lessons. I did have lessons from the older boys and girls some. She didn't hardly ever hear mine. A big boy named Jim was usually assigned to hear my lessons. She'd pick one of the best readers from the top grade, the seventh grade, and have them to listen. That's the way teachers did later on, too. They just didn't have time to do it all.

The next year Miss Howard was the teacher that taught me to read. She used flash cards. She started out with the alphabet, and when I learned all the letters, she started putting in words, and then I was reading before I knew it. I remember one time she gave us some little readers to take home to read. I kept reading mine over and over. So one day my older sister Mollie said, "Mama, I wish you'd make Naomi stop that reading. It's the same ol' thing, and I'm so tired of it. It's the same ol' thing everyday; it's the same ol' thing."

And Mama said, "Let her read if she wants to read. She likes to read. She'll be a good reader. You let her alone." She made Mollie leave me alone.

It depended so much on who the teacher was as to what we did.

When the Yantises were there, we did a lot of singing and marching and all kinds of things. Mrs. Yantis was real good. We didn't have instruments, but she would clap and say, "Tra le la, La le la, Tra la la la la le," and we'd march around and keep time. We did the figure eight and we did everything. We'd go around and around inside the school building. That was good exercise, keeping time to the music.

I Went to What Was Called the Colored School

A. B. LAMPKIN

I went to school in Anson to what was called then the Colored School—two rooms. One side was the high school and the other side was the elementary. The elementary went from the first to the eighth grade, and in the next room was the high school. We were a little bit different because the black school didn't start up until about Christmastime because it stayed closed until cotton pulling was over. I don't know how we got anything accomplished.

We had quite a few kids in school then. There would be probably close to a hundred and fifty kids with the two teachers. There was about fifteen or twenty of us the same age, but then there was some more that were older and some that were younger. Ours was a big room, and one teacher took care of all those kids in grades one through eight. That would be about eighty or so kids. We took turns with our lessons. While a group—say the third grade—was having their lessons then we'd study.

Any books we got was handed down from the town school, which was the school for the white kids. That didn't bother me because we didn't know any better. Not being exposed to anything better, we were grateful for what we had. I was too young to play basketball, but our basketball uniforms came from Anson High. Whatever they didn't want, when they got new uniforms, they would pass them on down to us. We had to share books, I remember that. We didn't have enough books, especially in the lower grades. We had to share the books. I don't ever remember ever doing any homework, because we didn't take any books home. When the other class was having their participation, we would do our studying and whatever work we had to do. We would do it right there. We had to do chores when we got home, so we didn't have time to do any homework.

61

I Memorized Poems and Practiced Handwriting

ABBIE WILLINGHAM MARTIN

The first year I went to school, there was a big old boy named John and he was a giant of a man. He wasn't all there, either. Quiet, but he sat on the very back seat in the back row. It was from John on down to the first-graders—all in the same room. But we learned. The room was full and we all did our lessons. The teacher heard us recite.

I listened to the children above my grade, and I couldn't wait to get to the next grade. I memorized poems and practiced handwriting. I remember a school play that was put on one time. Mama made angel wings for me. The little girls who were in the play had these white wings on their hands. It was very dramatic and very serious with us. We practiced and practiced.

Friday afternoon we had spelling bees. I was good in spelling. My mom made us good. As long as I was in school she'd say, "Don't let anybody beat you in your grades."

Close to the Front of the Book, There Was a Page Missing Where Spot Was

JUNA REYNOLDS

When I first started to school in the fall, it was so beautiful—the weather was so beautiful. We had the front door open. The seats were so that the little seats were in front. There were two rows, and they gradually got bigger as they went back. There were about fourteen desks in there. They were double desks. Ours was the smallest. Elene and I sat side by side, because we were in the first grade. We shared the same book. I remember right close to the front of the book, there was a page missing where Spot was.

We were by the door, and in the fall that was wonderful. The door was left open for ventilation. We would look out in that beautiful weather. You can imagine how much learning took place. But in the winter, our seats were a terrible place to be. The stove was in the back of the room, and we were up front by the door. Elene and I almost froze. I remember it was just murderously cold. We were the smallest in the room, but we were the farthest from the stove.

There was a little table that the teacher would have us come up to for recitation. Sometimes Elene and I wouldn't be in the same place in our reader. I would then come up and stand by the teacher

62

and she would hear my lessons. I might be on page twenty-three and Elene would be on some other page. If there were two or more in a reading group, she would have them come up to the table and set on the little bench, and she would hear their lessons.

I Taught an Eighteen-Year-Old Boy to Read When I Was in First Grade

EVA WALL SINGLETON

I went to Shady Grove until the third grade. They wanted to improve the school system and they realized that one room for eight grades was a difficult situation for any teacher. So the parents got together. I don't know whether they voted a bond or whether they just made a contribution, but they built a new school, and it had *two rooms*. Oh, we were so pleased when our school system had two teachers and two rooms. They kept the old school building for the church. We had the primary in one room and intermediate children in another.

We would go to the recitation bench and take turns. One child would read the first page, another the second page, another the third page, and so on until everybody had read. Then we'd start all over again—'round and around and around. The reader I remember was "This is Will. This is Mae. This is Fly. Fly is Will's dog." That was the *Playmate Primer*. Some kids had trouble reading. They came from poor, poor home situations, and they had really no background for anything. I had been so blessed because I was an only child, and my parents gave me all their attention. There were children there who had five or six in a family, and their parents didn't have time to help them.

I taught an eighteen-year-old boy to read when I was in first grade—on my way home. I was riding my pony home from school, and I would always stop at the last house before I got to our house. That was the Rhoades family. Mrs. Rhoades always had something good, and I loved to stop there. She always had a cookie for me. Her boy had been deprived of school because the father had no interest in educating his children. She did, the mother did, but the father made them work in the fields. So John, now, was eighteen years old, and he couldn't read or write. He was embarrassed to tell anybody.

I was like a little sister to him, so in the afternoon I sat on the

63

front porch and read. I'd tie my pony's bridle to the banister, and John and I would sit on the front porch, and he'd say, "Now, what did you learn today?" Then I would show him what my teacher had taught me. Then he would read it after me. And he said, "Now, how did you learn to write?" I'd say, "Here's my copy book." I had a tablet, but I wouldn't let him write in my copy book because I knew my teacher didn't want us to. He'd put the paper down and he'd learn to write. Then World War I came. He was called into service and had to go to France. He had learned enough from my first-grade teaching to write back.

I Started Crying Because the Teacher Didn't Call on Me
CORDELIA PATTERSON

I went to Dry Ridge School. The teacher had eight grades; she made my assignments, and I went home and did them. My daddy told the teacher one night—Sunday night, we were all together somewhere—"Cordelia doesn't have her assignment for tomorrow." But my daddy didn't get to go to bed that night until I got my assignment. When I got to school the next day, the teacher tactfully went around me and called on everybody else, and I started crying because she didn't call on me. My mother taught me to read, she taught me to write, she taught me to spell, and my daddy taught me all my math. I could add and divide and multiply. I started to school when I was seven.

We had an old organ in our school. At that time, some of the older girls in the eighth grade played the organ. The teacher didn't use it for music. She didn't have time. If the girls wanted to play it, we were allowed to. She made our assignment and quite often an eighth-grade girl would check it to see if I had done it correctly. Frankly, I don't remember her teaching me anything. She just made the assignments and saw to it that I had them, and I didn't know any better.

"Why Do Things Seem Sweeter, When We Can Possess Them Not?"
GRACE PHILLIPS

I had to memorize poems when I was a kid, and I can still say some of them. "The wild white rose, it was peeping through the brambles.

64

The Empty Schoolhouse

That wild white rose, it was dangling just beyond my reach." It ends, "Why do things seem sweeter, when we can possess them not?" The whole poem is about trying to get that white rose and never quite realizing that dream. Things we can't attain seem sweeter to us because we can't attain them.

I recall that my two brothers, Bill and Henry, were away at college one particular school year when I was having to memorize so much poetry. They even complained; they thought that was too strict. I think there were only three of us in that grade. We had to stand up every day and recite poems in front of the class. Of course, we were all in the same room anyway. I can remember hymns, too. When I go to church, somebody'll offer me a songbook, and I'll say, "No, I don't need that. I know all seventeen verses." I remember "When We All Get to Heaven" was on page 73 in the old *Waves of Glory* songbook, and it was in five flats. It was played all on the black keys.

They Would Tease Us and Tell Us We Were the Teacher's Babies

MAUD ARNOLD BAILEY

When I was a child, I also went to a one-room school. The teachers were not as well trained when I first started to school as they were after I began teaching. I don't think they had a prepared schedule like we had. There was one little boy with me in the first grade. We started in what was called the *Primer*. After we finished that, we were ready for the *First Reader*. About the only way we could tell what grade we were in was by the readers we had. I finished the *Primer*, *First Reader*, and part of the *Second Reader* the first year. My father and mother had taught me to read and to spell. I can remember the first word the teacher gave out. It was "marbles" and I spelled it. The teacher was a man and he was nineteen. This little boy my age and me, he'd call us up to the front—that's where the classes all recited. He'd take the little boy on one knee and me on the other. The older pupils called us Katus's babies. His name was Katus Pierce. They would tease us and tell us we were his babies.

I Read All of the Books and Some of Them Twice

WILLIAM I. POTEET

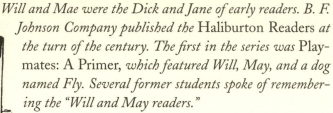

Will and Mae were the Dick and Jane of early readers. B. F. Johnson Company published the Haliburton Readers *at the turn of the century. The first in the series was* Playmates: A Primer, *which featured Will, May, and a dog named Fly. Several former students spoke of remembering the "Will and May readers."*

One of the first things I remember was, before I started to school, I went to visit one day. I was sitting between my big brother George and my cousin Jim, and I forgot where I was. I had learned to whistle like everything around home. And the first thing you know, I went *wheeeee, wheeeee,* real loud. Of course, the schoolhouse just turned to turmoil with everybody laughing. I was scared half to death. So at noontime, we was playing out in the yard and here come the teacher. She put her arm around me and wanted to know if George and Jim had put me up to whistling.

I said, "No, they didn't."

"Well, watch yourself and try not to whistle," she said. I naturally wouldn't have done it at all if they had tried to get me to.

When I learned to read, I remember: "This is Will. How do you do, Will? This is May. How do you do, May?" I'll remember that always. That was one of our first lessons. I don't think I knew how to read when I started to school. I learned at school. It wasn't very hard. I just sat down and read it. I could recognize the words. I think I did all right. In a few years, we got a little library. It was very little—small books like *Buffalo Bill* and books like that. I read all of them and some of them twice. I just loved to read. I loved it.

Our Teacher Would Require You to Say a Little Scripture Verse

CLYDE HODGES

I learned to read at home and at school. The teacher would read to you and point out words. She'd read to you, then my mother would help me at home. We had them ol' blue-back spellers. Geography and English books and arithmetic books.

Our teacher, not every morning, but I think every Monday

66

morning, would require you to say a little scripture verse out of the Bible. Everybody would have one. I still remember some of the scripture verses that I had to memorize. I remember one especially. The boys put me up to it—some of my cousins that were older than me—and that was the first year I was in school.

I said, "Jesus wept, Moses crept, and Peter come a crawling." [Another person remembered a version of this as "Jesus wept, Peter slept, and Johnny went a-fishing."] They put me up to say that, you know. And course, I said it. I was little, so I don't guess the teacher got on to me much.

I think the state furnished the books. Just had a seven-month school, and half of them kids had to stay out the first three months picking cotton. Made a living then picking cotton, you see. I never did have to stay out any to pick cotton. My daddy just wanted us to go to school. I never did have to stay out for anything. Daddy would get the cotton picked. Of course, we would pick on Saturday and pick some after we got in from school.

The Teacher Would Call Us up to Hear Our Lessons

FANNIE WILLINGHAM ALBERT

The first school I ever went to was north of Old Hobbs, up on the hill. I was about seven that year. Most kids started to school when they were seven, but my sister went earlier than that. The school-teacher was boarding with us, and my sister went walking with her to school. I think it was more than a mile from our house.

We had one teacher for all those children. There were about sixty. The teacher was Miss Middleton. She was nineteen years old when she was teaching here. We had just one big room, and the boys sat on one side of the room and the girls sat on the other. We had desks that way. She taught all sixty of those in the same room.

When we had our lessons, the rest of the pupils were busy, or were supposed to have been. We'd march to the front of the room to have our lessons. Had a little bench called the recitation bench, and the teacher would call us up to hear our lessons—to read or spell or work on the blackboard. We had a blackboard for our arithmetic.

Later on we had two rooms in the school. We called them the Big Room and the Little Room—Big Room for the big kids and Little Room for the little ones. There was a wall that separated them.

67

I Learned to Read from the Newspapers on the Wall

JIM POTEET

Most houses in rural areas were constructed as "box" houses. They were built with one-by-twelve boards placed vertically around the four walls to form both the frame of the house and the walls. The cracks outside between the planks were covered or "weather-stripped" with one-by-fours. The inside of the rooms was left with the open face of the raw boards. Families often covered these walls with pieces of paper—old newspapers, catalogs, and other materials available to add both warmth and "beauty."

I learned to read at home. Of course, I was eight years old when I started to school. We papered our little side room with newspapers and I learned to read from the newspapers on the wall. I could read from those newspapers before I ever went to school. I always heard my older brother's lessons. I was so near John's age. Mama would sit down in a straight chair, and John was right here on one side and I was on the other, and I got the lesson just like he did.

The first day I went to school, the teacher put us up to the board. They had blackboards all around. The teacher was Mr. Hilburn and he wrote from one to ten up there on the board. He put us first-graders up to the board to see if we could write to ten. I commenced to write and I just went right on. I got to thinking he might not like that. He had a pointed stick. But he threw up his hands and said, "Looky here what he can do!" Why, he had third-graders that couldn't do what I had done. I knew everything John knew, plus I got to listen to all the lessons of the older kids every day. I didn't really have to study; I would just hear the other kids' lessons. When you'd get up there to a higher grade you already had all the knowledge, if you listened. So I say schools like that are the best schools because you can learn from all the older kids.

CHAPTER FOUR

❧

The Teacher Could Whup
As Many Licks As He Wanted To

DISCIPLINE AND PUNISHMENT

The ability to establish firm discipline was the most important concern registered by trustees when employing a teacher. It was the measure used to evaluate a teacher's effectiveness, and failure to maintain order was reason for firing. If teachers were to be asked back the following term, they must quickly convince pupils they were in charge. As Henry Poteet stated, "The kids knew when they had teachers who knew what they were doing, and they knew when they had ones who didn't." When giving these interviews years later, the scorn and disdain pupils felt for ineffective teachers remained evident.

There were diverse methods of punishment described by the interviewees: hair-pulling, knuckle-cracking, head-thumping, and putting one in the corner, in the cloakroom, under the desk, and at the board with one's nose in a chalk ring. However, these measures were far exceeded by the use of corporal punishment as a means of discipline. Teachers were expected to spank for misdeeds as well as for failure to do assigned work. According to these stories, there were no regulations governing the severity of whippings. "The only rules and regulations was that they'd just catch 'em and whup 'em!"

Not all teachers relied on "willow-sapling discipline," of course. Many maintained effective discipline without being overly severe or abusive. What is clear from this research is that trustees wanted teachers who knew how to deal with the pranks and shenanigans of mischievous children.

They were willing to give teachers freedom to do whatever was necessary to ensure an orderly school.

She Went into the Classroom and Laid a Pistol on Her Desk

ABBIE WILLINGHAM MARTIN

Mama was just a fanatic about school. She had taught school over in Scurry County before she married. When she applied for the job, the trustees told her she couldn't handle the boys. There were some mean boys, and they ran off every teacher they had.

She said, "Oh, let me try it."

She went to school in a buggy, and I believe her family was living in Snyder. She went into the classroom and laid a pistol on her desk with her lunch bucket and a school bell. They never gave her any trouble.

If Kids Wouldn't Study As They Should, the Teacher Used the Hickory Stick

BESSIE CLEVELAND

If kids didn't do as they were told, wouldn't study as they should, the teacher used the hickory stick. Most of the parents had told their kiddos, "If you get punished at school, you'll get the same kind of punishment, but it'll be from your daddy, when you get home." That seemed to work pretty well. Of course, they got around that a lot. I'm the oldest, and I know when my younger brothers wouldn't get their lessons, the teacher would give them so many licks. It happened so often we formed a pact. We wouldn't tell Daddy because we wouldn't want the boys to get two whippings. Daddy didn't realize that until we were grown. We didn't tell him.

It was common for a teacher to punish with a spanking if you didn't get your lessons. You got a spanking for misbehaving, and then you got one if you didn't get your lessons. If you was just a little mischievous, she'd put you in the corner to stand. The teacher would sometimes put the older kids in the cloakroom. That's where we kept our coats and lunches. She'd set a kid in there and close the door for a while.

70

When I got in the older group, we had a man teacher, and we knew how to get around him. We pulled lots of stunts. We all liked him, but we soon realized we could do whatever we wanted to do. Like if we wanted to get out a few minutes early, if we'd band together and get the president of the school board's sons—he had two sons—if we could get them involved, then there wouldn't be anything done about it.

Some of the Boys Was Bigger Than the Teacher, and Tougher, Too

WALTER CLEVELAND

The only school I went to was Pleasant Valley. They named it Pleasant Valley because it was in a little low area. Ain't nothing left there now but a cistern full of rattlesnakes. My first teacher was Miss Patterson. I never got a whipping, but lots of boys would, all the time. We had mostly women teachers. Boys would get whippings for fighting and running off. They'd hide in the toilet, you know,

and them women would have to go down there and get 'em. That was the funny part of it. The teacher would send some boys after 'em 'cause they couldn't go get 'em.

I remember one time a boy lived up on a hill there, and he went outside and got hisself a rock. The teacher had us in a-hangin' pictures after school was out. This boy throwed a rock through the door and hit the teacher. He throwed it as hard as he could. And I mean he just lit out across that field as fast as he could. I never will forget how fast he run home. She knew who it was.

Sometimes parents would get mad at the teacher. Men teachers especially whipped too hard. Usually parents would get mad at the teacher for whipping their kids too hard. They'd have trouble over it. Some of the boys was bigger than the teacher and tougher too. They'd go to school until they was twenty years old. They didn't get a chance to go very long at a time.

She Lined Us All up, about a Half Dozen of Us, to Whip Us
WILLIAM I. POTEET

We had a teacher one year from Canada. She wasn't used to a one-teacher school. She didn't know how to handle boys. She was used to a dean, I think, or something, and it scared her half to death. She whipped us young boys twice when she wouldn't whip the big ones once. She didn't know how to handle them. She cut down on the lunchtime from an hour to thirty minutes. The older boys wouldn't go along with it so they tied up the two doors and then rocked the schoolhouse. Generally, we were in on it, and helped rock the schoolhouse. She lined us all up, about a half dozen of us, to whip us. She started on me and my brother Jim. By the time she got us whipped and one or two of the others, why, her switches were all broke up. She lined us up and did it again and we got another whipping. The older boys got just one whipping. They was the ones that really instigated it. We just went along with it, you know. We wanted an hour for lunch so we stayed out an hour.

As Soon As School Let out, the Kids All Went Wild
NAOMI VINYARD

Miss Florence wasn't too good of a teacher, and as soon as school let out, the kids all went wild. She wore a little "dame's hat." She was

72

about forty-five, I guess, but we thought she was old—*real old.* The boys finally ran her off. I know one day when it was real bad, real cold, and the wind was blowing, she told the boys, "We just won't have recess today. We'll just turn out early and all go home early."

One of the big boys said, "We're going to have recess, boys." And out the door he went, and the rest of the boys all followed. They didn't mind her at all. So she said to the rest of us, "If they are going to have recess, you all might as well, too." Of course, we little ones was just sitting there wondering what in the world to do. They didn't pay any attention to her at all.

One time later the boys got under the schoolhouse. It was way off the ground, and they was playing dogs and wolves, as they called it. These "dogs" would just bark and howl and bark, and the "wolves" would howl. It was a terrible noise under there. It was during recess, but she wanted 'em to go in. She'd ring the bell and ring the bell, but nobody would go in. They'd just keep barking and howling. So finally she told them, "Now I won't whip you if you'll come out from under there."

They said, "You sure you won't kill us?" Well, she had her a switch and when they started out, she'd let 'em have it.

George Stayed Outside, and He'd Dance and Whistle

HENRY T. POTEET

Miss Florence was very eccentric. Very proper. These folks out in the country thought that was dumb. They weren't ready for that. She always called everything by its proper name, and if there was any shade of it that didn't sound good, she would correct it and use a proper word for it. She heard the boys talking about a bull once, and she said, "No, that's not nice. It's a surly."

My older brother George went to that school, and he was as big as a man, and there were several other boys just as big going to school there, too. One day Miss Florence decided for some reason—I think it was because of the way the boys had been doing—she wouldn't give us but thirty minutes of our noon recess. We had fifteen minutes of recess in the morning and fifteen minutes in the afternoon, but an hour at noon. So after thirty minutes, she rang the bell to call us all in.

George had a watch and said, "We're not going in now." The

schoolhouse was off the ground—built up on rocks—and George and I and a couple of other big boys got under the house. We'd kick the floor so they couldn't hear anything. So Miss Florence sent one of the little girls up to the nearest trustee's house to have him come to expel George. By that time, George and the two big boys were over the hill. After the trustee came and gave the verdict, George came back down to the schoolhouse. He stayed outside, and he'd dance and whistle, just outside where they could all see him and hear him through the window. He was good at whistling. He'd dance and whistle. Of course, Papa, my dad, was also a trustee, and when he heard about this, he brought George home and put him to plowing after that.

Besides the fact that those kids needed a strong disciplinarian, they usually admired their teacher. And those teachers who disciplined, they were admired greatly. The kids knew when they had teachers who knew what they were doing, and they knew when they had ones who didn't. The big boys knew what they could get by with. When it got to be that we had two teachers and not such big classes, we learned more. There was something about the personality of the teacher that came through. The trustees wanted a good school and believed in education, and they got the best teachers they could, even if sometimes it was a pretty poor teacher.

The Teacher Put Me under Her Desk to Keep Me from Talking

CECIL A. SINGLETON

I went to a two-room school named Eureka. When I first started to school, I'd get in trouble for talking. I'd do a lot of talking. The teacher would put me under her desk, and she'd sit there with her feet—you know, legs—under her desk. She wore those long, high-topped shoes, laced all the way up, and I'd sit under there and run my finger up and down those laces. She never did kick me. I don't know why she put me under her desk except that got me out of the way. The kids couldn't see me because the front of the desk came down so you couldn't see around it. I guess I kept talking as long as she let me stay in the room, but when she put me under the desk, I had to shut up. I had to stand in the corner, and I had to stand at the board with my nose in a ring for talking too much. Sometimes the teacher would draw the ring on the board higher than your nose could reach without tiptoeing. That was torture!

The Teacher Meant Business and We Knew It

A. B. LAMPKIN

Discipline was no problem. The teacher meant business and we knew it, because when you got home—well! Discipline then was altogether different. You were not to talk back, you were not to be disobedient, and you just knew that. The principal would help the teacher with discipline. He'd spank kids right there in that room in front of the whole class. He had a razor strap, and sometimes he'd use a mule line or whatever he had. It was always a piece of leather, and he used it. In our school discipline was really no problem.

Miz Perkins Come up There and Jumped on the Teacher

DELIA HARDIN

There was a Perkins family that went to school with us for a while. Well, Charles was as mean as he could be, and Miss Wright gave him a whippin'. So Miz Perkins come up there and jumped on the teacher for giving him a whippin'. Miss Wright told her that he'd done so and so, and if he done it again she'd spank him again.

So ever' day Miz Perkins would sneak up there and slip under the window and get on the front porch and listen and see what Miss Wright was a-doin'. One day during class—Miss Wright knew she was a-doin' it—so one day during class, Miss Wright just walked over and opened the door and said, "Miz Perkins, it'd be more comfortable if you'd come in and sit in the desk." Miz Perkins didn't come back and sit on the steps anymore.

She Whipped Me with Her Hand

JUNA REYNOLDS

I got one spanking from the teacher. It was my birthday. I thought I should be able to do anything I wanted to since it was my birthday. I did something, and she told me not to, so I sassed her. I told her, "It's my birthday!"

She said, "I don't care if it is your birthday, you can't act any way you please." She whipped me with her hand. It didn't hurt, except it hurt my feelings.

The Teacher Would Pull His Hair

MARY BOYDSTUN

I remember a little boy that lived between our house and school. The teacher was always getting after him about something, and she'd pull his hair. He'd be talking to somebody in front or behind him, or aggravating somebody, so she'd pull his hair. One morning he come to school, and his hair was about that long. It was cut so close he just didn't have any.

He said, "I'd like to see you pull it now."

The teacher said, "Well, you've still got ears!"

The Teacher Whipped Me Forty-Five Licks

LEO E. CLEGG

Once me and this other boy got to fightin'. While he was lookin' for a willer [willow] pole, I got to lookin' for a club. He found a willer pole about four feet long and about the size of your wrist, with the edges cut off. He whopped me over the head and cut my head open. So we got in a fight and I got him down. He was finally willin' to quit after I gave him a good beatin'. He whipped me, too, but anyhow, he wasn't no bigger 'n I was. But he was an eighteen year old.

The teacher whipped us the next day with a willer switch that was four foot long. He'd change hands ever four or five licks. He whipped me forty-five licks. It was a switch four foot long. I guess my older brother, if he knew anything about it at the time—he wasn't goin' to school at the time—he might have jumped on him.

My back had bloody spots all over it. My shirt was stuck to my back from the blood when I got home. I showed my mother, but she didn't want to fuss. That was about two or three weeks before she died. She was the kind of person who didn't want to have any fuss or nothin'.

The teacher thought I was one of the tough nuts of the school, and I guess accordin' to the fight, it looked like it. He had heard that our school was one of the roughest in the state, and he was goin' to show us he was boss. They should have called the sheriff out there and let him know that he could whip us, but not with any four-foot

76

switches. Even in the Bible they just gave 'em thirty-nine licks. I mean it really did hurt.

One time another teacher made me stand in the corner. It was on Friday evenin', and I was just doin' somethin' to pass time. I was at the board and had a piece of chalk about one inch long, and I was writin' sideways. I thought it would be funny to write sideways. I didn't see anythin' wrong with that. The teacher put me in the corner for that. The corner was full of nails where we'd hang up all our coats and things. I bent all the nails down. Then I noticed the broom standin' near the corner so I chewed the end of the broom handle off. I couldn't think of anythin' else to do. I don't think the teacher noticed what I had done. I'd chew some off and spit it on the floor. I shouldn't have ever bent them nails down because ever'body had to hang their coats there.

That Was Unusual for an Older Girl to Get a Whipping
NAOMI A. MAYFIELD

The year that my sister Grace went to school, she got into trouble with the teacher. She and a boy had a fight. He pulled her hair, and she scratched him. The teacher was going to give both of them a whipping. He sent my older brother out to cut a switch off of a tree. He cut the switch and came in and asked if he could take the whipping for his sister. The teacher wouldn't let him, but he did let Grace leave her coat on. It didn't hurt her. Hurt her feelings more than anything else. That was unusual for an older girl to get a whipping. That was quite humiliating. He almost got in trouble over that.

There was a boy named Jim who loved to tease me. Once he was pretending to write me a note. He wrote this little note—or pretended to—and handed it to me. I was a little goody-goody, so I just took it up and handed it to the teacher. The teacher opened it, and it was a blank piece of paper. Jim laughed about that, and every time I see him, he still laughs about it.

"Have You Been Smoking, Prentice Merrill?"
BUDDY BURNETT

They were drilling for oil on the Guinn place. With a cable tool it took forty forevers to drill a well. They built little tar-paper shacks around the drilling rig to weatherize it. Mr. Casey was one of the teachers at our school, and one of the hands was boarding with the Caseys. Morris was the Caseys' son and he was about my age. He snitched a package of Old Gold cigarettes—ready rolls, we called them—from this guy who was rooming with them. He brought the package to school, and at recess he passed the word around. We were in the second grade, mind you. And at recess we all went out to the three-holer toilet, and boy, we had us a ball. *We had us some ready rolls.*

When the bell rang, we had to line up outside before we came in and come in one at a time. Just inside, there was a cloakroom where there was a monitor who took up coats and caps and placed them on pegs. I was the monitor for the boys. After I got the coats put up, I passed by Miss Harrell's desk. She was just like an old 'coon hound. She gave a sniff and said, "Prentice Merrill!"

I said, "Yes, Ma'am."

"Have you been smoking, Prentice Merrill?" I couldn't deny it. I had to admit I had been.

She reported us to Mr. Casey, who taught the older kids and served as the principal. He said, "You go home and tell your parents." You know how that is, confessing up. I was waiting as long as I could to tell.

The next morning on the way to school, my sister said, "Buddy, have you told Papa?" Papa was taking us that day in the car since it was rainylike.

Papa said, "What?"

And I told him. He sat out beside the school half the morning. Mr. Casey went out there and met him. It was a frame-up I know. At recess, Mr. Casey came into our room, and he told the boys to just keep our seats. He asked the boys if they told their parents.

I said, "Yes." Well, I had told him after my sister brought it up.

So he said, "All right, Buddy. Come up here." He took off his belt and gave me a whipping before all the kids in those four grades. This wouldn't be done nowadays. I can't tell you to this day whether that hurt or not. I was so scared. Most of the time, teachers whipped kids after school was out rather than before the entire class.

He Had the Teacher Whip Ever' Boy in School

LEWIS H. CLEGG

Did anybody ever tell you about the time when they had all the guys whupped at the school? Didn't? Well, I'll tell you how that happened. My brother Leo and Pat Helms kinda got into it. I got into it, too, I reckon. I was always into ever'thing. Uncle Jeff—he wasn't really my uncle or any kin to me, for that matter, but ever'body called him Uncle Jeff—well, he thought I was to blame for the whole thing, and he was on the school board.

He came down to school and said, "I'm going to have Lewis whupped if I have to whup the whole school." And he did. He had the teacher whup ever' boy in school. Uncle Jeff was on the board, so he could require that. Ever' boy in school got a whupping. They didn't spank boys in that day. They got whupped! They used cedar limbs. Why, I've seen them come out of there with bloody whelps on their back and legs. The teacher could whup as many licks as he wanted to—until he give out, I guess. There were no rules about it. The only rules and regulations was that they'd just catch 'em and whup 'em.

The Teacher Gave Me Sixty-Nine Licks from Here to There

WILLIAM I. POTEET

All of us boys got a few whippings from the teacher whether it was a woman or a man. The worst whipping I ever got was from Mr. Cantrell [name changed]. Pat and I were friends. But he got me in several messes. I got the awfulest whipping I ever got in my life because of Pat. Pat was crazy about this girl named Grace. One day when Mr. Cantrell was teaching, Pat must have seen Grace had a letter written. Another boy was crazy about her, too, and she was crazy about him for some reason. He was rough and tough.

Anyway, at lunchtime Pat and I went in the schoolhouse. I followed him in. Pat went to Grace's desk and pulled out her geography book and there's this big ol' stuffed letter. We looked at it a little bit. He folded it up and handed it to me to put it back. When I was putting it back, the teacher poked his head in.

The next day I put on extra clothes. I knew I was going to catch it. He kept me in and like to beat me to death. The teacher was Mr.

Cantrell. Harvey Cantrell. He was a big strong man. He put me on that platform and gave me sixty-nine licks from here to there—from my neck down to my ankles. *Sixty-nine licks!* A mesquite switch that long, about five feet long. Why he gave me so many licks I don't know. That's a beating. They'd have thrown him in jail now. Usually about fifteen or twenty licks is a whipping. Sometimes five or six licks. He really poured it on me. *Sixty-nine licks!* The boys outside told me later that they counted. He gave me sixty-nine licks! He thought I was guilty, see.

A few years later Mr. Cantrell got a job teaching in high school in town, and he came over to see me. I told him about that time he whipped me so hard. I guess he didn't pay much attention to me. He was a rough guy. Later he had a fight with a student in high school and they fired him.

She Come Down on Those Boys, Just Like Whippin' a Mule
CLYDE HODGES

Some of the teachers had trouble with the kids. Lots of them were trouble. I don't reckon I ever got a spankin' in school. I would have, this one day, but I didn't. The teacher just went crazy. She had a whole bunch of kids there, and before she got around to all of us, she just lost her head. She missed me, but I sure thought I was gonna get it.

There was a branch or creek down there, not far from school, a running branch, growed a lot of willers [willows] on it. This teacher had willer limbs that stood up at the corner of the room, and touched the ceiling—it was at least eight foot. She'd use them for whippings. She had three wrapped together, twisted together. She come down on those boys, just like whippin' a mule. Like to a cut one of the pupil's ear off. Well, they fired her. They had a board meeting and fired her. Oh, she had a temper!

The Teacher Threw Him down and Held Him on the Floor
MAUD ARNOLD BAILEY

There was a troublemaker, a boy about ten years old. His brother was one of the older boys. I guess he was about seventeen or eighteen. Well, this troublemaker—the teacher would have him come up and sit right beside him so he could keep an eye on him. The boy would come in and sit down on the back seat, and the teacher would tell him to come on up. Well, that enraged his older brother, and he jumped up and hit the teacher and almost knocked him down. But the teacher got the best of him and threw him down and held him on the floor and that frightened all us children. We ran out of the house, you know, crying. They sent one of the older boys for the trustee that lived nearby. The trustee came and settled the dispute.

I know one time we had a teacher who wasn't good about getting to school on time. Sometimes he didn't even come at all. One day he was late. One of the older boys asked him what was the geography lesson that they had the day before. The boy had missed school, you know, and he said, "Mr. Hatton, what is the geography lesson?"

Mr. Hatton said, "I don't know. I wasn't here yesterday."

The boy said, "Well, I thought you came for a little while yesterday afternoon."

"Aren't You'enses Ashamed? Well, You'enses Oughter Be!"

EUNICE HUCKABY

I didn't get any punishment from Mrs. Yantis, and I don't recall her ever having to punish us. I'm sure she had to correct us, but I don't recall her having to spank a child. I didn't see boys spanked at that age. But I did when I was older. I remember one boy named Ellis, I can't remember what he did now, but the teacher whipped him. It was a switch, I guess from a limb of a tree, and the minute she hit him he yelled, "errrrrrrr," real loud. We were all standing around watching this. I can remember his brother, who was a half brother— whatever it was they were spanking him for—he was trying to defend him, and he would say, "Ellis is a good boy, I know he's a good boy. He's honest."

One time we got in trouble when some kids from Mexico were in our school. J. D. Shipp was staying at Uncle Jeff's and Aunt Lindy's, going to school. We'd come down the road to their house and he'd join us, and we'd walk to school together. These little Mexican kids would walk to school with us each day. One time coming home, we harassed those kids, and it was wrong. J. D. would say, *"Ándale, ándale, ándale!"* That's the only Spanish word he knew. I think that means hurry. I didn't know what it meant then. But we'd say, *"Ándale, ándale!"*

These kids thought we were going to beat them up, I guess. And they'd run, and I believe J. D. would kinda hit at them. I'm sure he didn't hurt them really—he was just teasing them. Naturally, they didn't know but what we were going to beat them up. It was wrong.

The kids went home and reported it, as they should have. They were crying by that time, and their father came and talked to Uncle Jeff, and Uncle Jeff came up and talked to Papa and they called us in. Well, that was a court session.

I remember Uncle Jeff saying, "Now, did you'enses do this?" and J. D. said, "Yes, sir!"

"Well, aren't you'enses ashamed?" You know he'd say "you'ens" when he was talking about one person, but "you'enses" for more than one. "Aren't you'enses ashamed?"

J. D. said, "No, Sir!"

And Uncle Jeff said, "Well, you'enses oughter be!"

Papa talked to us and said that's not right. I can't remember exactly, but more or less, the essence of it was "Those kids are just like you are, and they have feelings and they need to be treated right." And it's true, it wasn't right. It starts right there in human nature and it was wrong.

If We Got a Whipping at School, We Would Get Another One When We Got Home

GRACE PHILLIPS

We had a big red-headed teacher who was quite strict. If you didn't listen like you should, she would come and take your chin, she'd put one hand on your chin and the other hand on top of your head and give a quick twist like a chiropractor. I'll tell you, you paid attention after that!

Usually boys were punished with a switch. Salt cedar. There's a lot of it that grew around there, and that really did sting. That was the best way to punish a child. Also, they'd take a yardstick and hit right near your hand. You know, if you're sitting at your desk, giggling and talking to somebody, and *Whop!*, a big yardstick comes down right near your hand, you start listening! In those days, the teacher could do almost anything and the parent wouldn't object. Mother, and I think Papa backed her up, always told us when we went to school that, if we got a whipping at school, we could plan on

82

getting another one when we got home. Teachers did have the backing of the parents.

The Teacher Came Back and Thumped Us on the Head
BESSIE DAVIDSON

We had a young man in the community who got his certificate, and he taught me one year. There was this big ol' stove and we'd all sit around this big stove quite a lot. There was three or four of us little beginners, and we were doing a lot of giggling and the teacher came back and thumped us on the head. I guess I was always easily excited, so I hit at him. I had long hair and braids, and he got hold of one of those braids and pulled my hair. He and I laughed about that years later.

I Got Eight Whippings All in One Year
JIM POTEET

I remember once some older boys got in a big scrap and two boys named Lewis and Jim were fighting. Everybody saw it—we was all watching. The teacher was Mr. Smith and he was going to whip every boy in school for either fighting or watching the fight. I remember Lewis and another kid named Guy wasn't going to take

their whipping. They was great big boys— as big as the teacher. Instead, they was going to fight the teacher. We had double desks and they was both sitting together. When it came their turn, they wasn't going to take a whipping. When Mr. Smith came to them, Lewis said, "Hit him, Guy."

And Guy said, "You hit him, Lewis."

They just sat there saying, "You hit him." "You hit him." "You hit him." And instead of them hitting the teacher, Mr. Smith just wore them out.

We had another teacher named Miss Annie. She was a good teacher, but she followed a poor teacher, and they didn't have a good teacher up at Cottonwood

School. So they put the two schools together. She already had all she could handle. Cottonwood had some big boys, and you put them with all the other big ones from our school, and that was too much for her to handle. That's when I got eight whippings. All in one year. She said to me, "If I have to whip you any more, I'm going to send you home." So about two weeks before school was out, I done something, I don't know what it was. She called me up and said, "You know what I told you?"

I said, "Yeah."

She said, "Well, I'm not going to send you home, and I'm not going to whip you." School was about out. She said, "You have never told me a lie. You've been honest about everything, so I'm going to let you stay."

That year one of the things that happened was with a girl named Grace. There was a pretty nasty note wrote on her tablet. I was the first one to school that day. Miss Annie came in, but she didn't find it, but I saw it when I came in. It was there on the big tablet and her seat was close to where I sat. You couldn't miss it. When Grace come in, she saw it and told the teacher. Of course, I was the first one in school. I said, "I didn't do it. I saw it when I come in, but I didn't do it." The only fight I ever had at school was over that. Grace's brother thought I did it, and we had a fight over that. They finally found out who did it. It was an outsider. The schoolhouse was never locked, and he just came in after school and wrote on her tablet.

One of my later teachers was Miss Effie. She was a little ol' timid girl. She didn't whip so many kids, but every time she'd whip one, she'd cry. I sat by a window there, and I'd slip out the window and play mumbly-peg anytime I wanted to. She never did catch me or say anything about me coming in. She didn't have no order, but she was a good girl. She had these big ol' boys, and she didn't know what to do with them. They wasn't mean; they was just ornery.

Now when Mr. Carter come out there, things was different. The first day he got this long switch and put it on his desk and said he'd come to teach school. I don't know how much school he taught, but he sure kept that switch hot. One of my other teachers was named Miss Hall, and she told me she didn't know why I was so mean. She said she didn't expect that from me, because my folks was Methodists.

84

She Whopped Me over the Head with a Pencil
ADDIE BOSTICK GREEN

Younger brothers and sisters were regular visitors in the school before they were old enough to attend. The visit might be for a special occasion, but it might be the child was sent to school to get him or her out of the mother's way. Teachers had plenty to do "keeping books" for all seven or eight grades without the addition of a squirming five-year-old, but they seldom complained.

I never went to any school but Riverdale, and I went there when I was six. That would be in 1906. The main thing that I remember about going to school was that I went to school to visit. I went to school with my older sisters and brothers, and I talked and I talked. Miss Maggie was the teacher and she whopped me over the head with a pencil to stop me from talking and I stopped. My first year in school—I don't no more remember anything about my first year in school than nothing in the world. Kids used to start in the primer, but I think I started in the first grade when I started. I was too little to remember much.

The Teacher Was Goin' to Whup Me Because I Fought
MARTHA PIKE

I went to the Cottonwood Flat School and lived on the old Hudnall farm. We walked to school, but in later years we rode horses. I'm one of the youngest of the family. Buddy is the only one younger than I am. I had twin sisters named Ninety and Nine. Some people would think I was making this up, but I'm not. They was named after the ninety and nine sheep in the Bible. People always was making a joke and saying there was a hundred and eight in our family. They said there was Ninety and Nine, and then there's nine more children in the family, which equals to a hundred and eight.

One of our teachers was Miss Ruthie, and she didn't allow no fightin'. There was a boy there named Cloyce. I never could stand that kid, so on his birthday—now, she didn't allow no fightin'—and on his birthday they was ridin' him on a pole. I was sittin' over on the woodpile because I didn't like him, and I wasn't goin' to have no hand in it. I don't know what, but somebody done somethin' to him, and he jumped off that pole and run over there and slapped me. Of course, I was older and bigger and, boy, that's when I tied into him and give him the whuppin' of his life.

The teacher was goin' to whup me because I fought. I said I wouldn't have nothin' to do with him 'cause I didn't like him. He just run over there and slapped me. So the other kids told her, "Now, Martha didn't have nothin' to do with it." That's the nearest to a whuppin' I ever got at school. I'd hated for her to whup me, anyway.

"Let My Boys Alone, or I'll Stomp Your Liver Out!"
LEO E. CLEGG

One afternoon after school was out, I was in the hack ready to go home. My brother Jack made a deal that he was going to whip a boy there named Raymond. But when it come down to it, Jack wouldn't fight, and Raymond wouldn't fight either. All the boys run over the hill to where they was gathering to see the fight, and they wouldn't fight. Well, they said, "We've got to have a fight. Somebody fight. Leo and Pat are about the same age and same size, let's make them fight."

I didn't want to fight. I really didn't want to go over there. They said, "Come on over. You won't have to fight." Well, I went along with 'em. I should have stayed over at the hack, but I didn't.

The teacher had done gone on home. He was just newly married so he went on home. Anyhow, they'd pushed Pat into me and me into Pat. Pat thought I had hit him. I tried to catch myself, but I bumped him without intending to. First thing you know, we was fightin' like ever'thing. We was bloody all over our fists and all over our noses. We was really hittin' each other. I got Pat down in some prickly pears. They had to drag me off to get him out of the prickly pears. We finally quit. I think this was on Friday, and when the teacher found out about it on Monday, he whipped all of us.

I went to school in town for one year. We stayed with my grandma. The boys found out we didn't have no grown men around, and they took advantage of us. One day I started home for lunch, and a kid named Joe Bailey had a big ol' limb, a mesquite brush it was, and he whopped me over the back with that. The rest of the boys pushed me around. I didn't know what I was gonna do. I couldn't hardly get away, and finally I broke and run and got away from 'em.

I went out north of town toward some hills. They went over to a hill and lay down on the ground where I couldn't see 'em. They was gonna catch me again. I went on around another way and got back way ahead of them. Then I hollered at 'em. They tried to catch me, but I was too far ahead.

They tried to take advantage of us. One day beside the house next door south of us, they had a big number three washtub piled full of rocks. We was goin' down the road, and there was some boys there, two was twins about my age. I was eight then. My cousin Wesley was twelve, and he had the strongest arms of anybody I ever saw for a kid no bigger than he was. His mother died when he was three or four years old, and he had to fight his way on ever'thing.

These boys was throwin' rocks at us like ever'thing. There was a fence about knee-high, and Wesley jerked out his pocketknife and started over the fence after them. There was four of 'em, and one of 'em was fourteen years old and one was thirteen. The biggest one broke to run in the house where his mother was. He told her, "There's a boy out there with a pocketknife that's gonna cut us all to pieces."

Here she come out there just a-ravin'. She said, "Let my boys alone, or I'll stomp your liver out!"

Wesley said, "If they don't stop throwin' rocks at us, I'm a-cuttin' theirs out."

She realized what the story was and said, "Now, you boys are going to behave yourselves out here and quit throwing rocks at everybody. You ain't goin' to do that." She put a stop to that. Wesley sure made a believer out of 'em.

"I'll Whip That Country Kid for You"
DONO DARDEN

One year we went to school in town. We was from the country, you know. We went on the first day in a horse and buggy. Got there a little bit early and, you know little boys, they always go to the out-door toilet—used to—and get aquatinted. Well, my brother Jack had three fights that morning before school started. One little boy sort of made fun of Jack's clothes and immediately he had a fight. And he whipped him; his name was Alley.

So a kid we called Snake told Alley, he says, "I'll whip that country kid for you." And Jack heard him say it. Well, he popped him, and he give him a whipping. So, the little boys run to tell another boy named Ross. Now these boys was all taller than Jack.

And Ross says, "Well, I'll clean that bumpkin's plow." And the little boys was all hovering around him, and a couple of 'em run to tell Jack he was going to get his plow cleaned. So Jack went to meet him, and he didn't say anything; he just hauled off and knocked Ross cold. Now that was unusual, you know, to get knocked completely out.

When Ross got up and dusted his clothes off and staggered around a little bit, he says, "Well, I didn't even know the little devil's name."

And Jack invited 'em, he says, "Any of the rest of you want some, I got it ready for you." He was really stirred up. He didn't get in trouble. The teachers never knew anything about it.

The Principal Once Used a Buggy Whip to Punish Kids
IRA HESTER

Back then boys or girls would go to school until maybe they looked like grown people. Bigger than the teacher. Maybe they'd be nearly twenty years old, or something like that. We had a principal once who used a buggy whip to punish kids. It was really one of those old-timey buggy whips about six feet long, and boy, when he got ready to use it, he didn't hold back. Usually back then, our parents always told us, "If you get a whippin' at school, you'll get one at home." Well, you don't get that today. They don't want their little sweetie to be touched even. To my knowledge, I never did get a whipping at school.

"I Just Come to Drive the Buggy"
NARCISSA CLEGG

Sometimes children didn't do too well in school. There was a boy in our school, I'll call him Jacob, and he didn't understand anything. I guess he was mentally retarded. The kids all called him an idiot. He was a great big tall boy. The teachers had just passed him along with his younger brother in the same class. Well, he couldn't get his spelling. So the teacher was going to punish him one day—that's what

88

teachers did then when you didn't do well in your studies. And the teacher made Jacob stand up and chin the wire that was across the platform that was put up for a curtain. And he had to just chin it real hard. Well, some of the bigger boys didn't think what the teacher was doing was right. They felt sorry for Jacob. Sam was the biggest boy in school—actually he was a man, seventeen or eighteen—and he started up to the front of the room toward the teacher—he wasn't going to let the teacher do that. When the teacher saw what was happening, he let Jacob stop. Sam turned and went back to his seat and nothing else happened. But there would have been trouble if the teacher hadn't let Jacob stop, and the teacher knew it. Sam was as big or bigger than the teacher was.

The year before that, there was another incident with Jacob, but that teacher handled it different. Jacob was up at the board—the teacher always assigned him a problem along with the others. Well, I was a little kid, but I happened to see this. Jacob's brother came over and helped Jacob with his problem. I guess it was a simple problem. Anyway, the teacher said, "Jacob, did you get your problem?"

And he said, "Yes, teacher, I did."

The teacher said, "Explain it for me, will you?"

I don't know if he explained it right or not, but he explained it. The teacher said, "Well, Jacob, you did get a problem, didn't you?" And Jacob's face just broke into a smile, just like a little kid's. He was so proud to be bragged on. And then the teacher said, "Jacob, why do you come to school, anyway?"

Jacob—you know, he was a big ol' boy nearly as big as the teacher—looked at the teacher, still proud of himself, and said in all seriousness, "I just come to drive the buggy." They came to school in a buggy, and he was the oldest. That was true. We all knew it. He just came to school to drive!

Boys Would Throw Paper Wads and Would Get a Whippin'
BUDDY HUDNALL

We lived about three miles from the schoolhouse. It took us about forty-five minutes, maybe an hour, to walk. It depended on how much we played on the way. Miss Loleet was my teacher for about five years. There was about thirty or thirty-five kids in all. Boys would throw paper wads and would get a whippin'. Once we threw some paper wads and the teacher asked us if we did. She asked me if I threw paper wads and I had to say, "Yeah, I did." So she gave me a whippin'. If my parents found out that I got a whippin', they might not whip me at home, but they would sure give me a good tongue lashing. If you done some talking or something you shouldn't have, the teacher would make you stand in the corner or come sit down beside her and sit there.

CHAPTER FIVE

❧

If You Prowled Somebody's Lunch Basket, You Could Expect to Get Your Ears Beat Down

RECESS, RECREATION, AND LUNCH

"A wonderful time of day was lunch," exclaimed Eva Wall Singleton. It was an oft-repeated sentiment, as recess and lunch were universally remembered as the favorite times of the school day. Such games as hopscotch, jacks, marbles, and hide-and-seek have survived to entertain today's child, but in early decades of the century, kids were also playing lesser known games: mumbly-peg, little-white-house-over-the-hill, sheep-board-down, and red line. Also played were innovative games, such as wolves and dogs and stink base, for which players made up rules to suit themselves.

In these rural schools, play was often gender oriented, with girls playing jacks and hopscotch, building playhouses, and imitating the actions of their mothers. They joined with boys in less rowdy games, such as little-white-house-over-the-hill and hide-and-seek, but it was the boys who had the wild chases called for in wolves and dogs. From these interviews, apparently one of the favorite activities of the boys was aggravating or teasing the girls. Storytellers rarely remembered specific rules for games but remembered "We had fun!"

Lunches were plain and reflected the daily fare of farm people. Biscuits, pork, and sorghum were occasionally supplemented with fried pies, gingerbread, or tea cakes. Trading food items was a common practice that relieved some of the monotony of a limited diet. In spite of the plainness and tedium of the contents of their lunch buckets, respondents remembered them with nostalgia. "Man, that was good eating!" and "Mama was one of the most finest cooks" testify to the satisfaction these children felt—at least in hindsight!

I'd Play Mumbly-Peg All Day Long

JIM POTEET

Mumbly-peg was a version of mumblety-peg, a game in which a jack-knife is tossed in various ways to make it land with the blade in the ground. The loser must draw a peg from the ground with his teeth. The name is derived from the word "mumble" meaning "to bite." The original name was "mumble-the-peg."

I remember one of our teachers would play games with us. He'd get right down and play with us. He was a sport, I'll tell you. He was a really good sport. We often played mumbly-peg. The girls along with the boys. The girls usually didn't have their own knives, but all the boys did, and we'd share. I don't remember all the rules, but I know there were strict rules that you always followed. You'd take a pocketknife and flip it to make it stick up in the ground. You could keep flipping until you missed. The first time you missed, you'd have to let the next person have a turn. You'd start off flipping the knife off your knee, and you'd flip it off your arm and flip it off your elbow and off your chest and shoulders, and off your head and then you had to flip it behind you. To win you had to do all those difficult things, if you didn't miss before you got to the last thing.

Every throw had a name. When you would stick the blade through your fingers and throw it, I think that was called Picking the Crow. One type of throw was called Shearing Old Pete, and the last one was Finding the Guinea's Nest. That's when you'd throw it over your shoulder to make it stick up back behind you. There was names like Breaking the Chicken's Neck and things like that. I don't remember them all. But you had to count the eggs when you found the Guinea's Nest. As soon as you missed you have to let the next person have a turn.

If you was good and got the first go, you could go out on the first time, and nobody else would get a turn. I went out lots of times. If you beat the other fellow, he had to Root the Peg. On the last throw, you would leave your knife in the dirt. Then you'd take a stick with your eyes shut. You could hit the knife three times to drive it in the ground as deep as you could. Sometimes you'd drive it plumb out of sight. Then the other fellow would have to root the knife out with his nose or pull it out with his mouth. I'd play mumbly-peg all day long. That's the reason I got so good.

One Game We Played Was Little-White-House-over-the-Hill

EVA WALL SINGLETON

The ground around the school was so nice. There was a road that ran in front of the school, a dirt road, and the land across that on the other side of the fence was virgin land. The boys went over there to play ball. They had a big open area. They didn't have any basketball or tennis, but they had baseball, and sometimes they played marbles. The girls jumped rope and played jacks and lots of circle games.

We had lots of competitive games, like relay games where you'd pass a ball over the top of your head or between your legs. We played wolf-over-the-river and games like that. The one game that the teacher had trouble with was pop-the-whip. Sometimes the child on the end would get hurt. The teacher discouraged playing pop-the-whip. But they played it sometimes without her knowing it.

One game we played was little-white-house-over-the-hill. You had to make up what you were doing, you had to pretend you were engaging in a certain activity, and the other side had to guess what you were doing. If they guessed, they would run after the players on your side, and whoever they tagged, had to come on the other side. It went something like this: We'd say, "Here we come!" They'd say, "Where are you from?" and we'd answer, "New York." They'd ask, "What's your trade?" We'd say, "Lemonade." Then they'd tell us, "Get to work and show your signs, if you're not afraid."

Then we would give them the initials of what we were doing and would act it out. Like if our team decided to be "Grandpa chopping wood in a red coat," the initials would be "G C W I R C," and we'd pretend we were chopping wood, and the other side would have to guess who we were and what we were doing. You might be churning butter or knitting a sweater and things like that.

But the Girls Didn't Play Marbles

NAOMI A. MAYFIELD

We played in the hills and canyons until we finally made up money and bought a basketball, which we just pitched around. We played wolf-over-the-river. You'd play that by having two lines or bases for a safe area. There would be somebody who was "it" out in the middle, and he was supposed to catch you when you ran from one base to the other. You'd run from one side and try to reach the other side. The "wolf," or the person who was it, would be in the middle. As you ran from one base to the other, the wolf would try to catch you by touching you. If you were caught, you had to join with the wolf to help him catch other players. This proceeded until all were caught. A boy named Wallace was my age and we were quite competitive. Sometimes I could outrun him, and sometimes he could outrun me. We played hide-and-seek and kick-the-can and mumbly-peg. We all played that, too. Even the girls. But the girls didn't play marbles.

We had what you call an old sinkhole there. I was fascinated by that thing. I wouldn't go in it, but other kids would. I was afraid of it. I just remember it was a big hole, and there was a little trail where you could get down in there. Then you had to drop the last part of the way, and it kinda went back under a bank. Some of the boys would run and jump into it.

Once I ran up to it like I was going to jump but wasn't. I had no intention of jumping. And some boy pushed me in and I sprained my ankle. I landed on my ankle and it sprained. I remember sitting up all night crying. Mother would put hot water or cold water. She tried everything. I didn't sleep a wink that night.

We'd Bring Old Dishes and Make Out Like We Were at Home

FANNIE WILLINGHAM ALBERT

We had an hour for lunch and then recess in between, morning and afternoon. Recess seemed about fifteen minutes, but I guess it was

thirty. At recess we played wolf-over-the-river. At that school, the
little girls that I played with would have a playhouse out under a
tree. We'd bring old dishes and make out like we were at home. We
marked out an area with rocks for our house, and the small girls
would play in the playhouse. We didn't actually bring dolls to school.
We'd just pretend, play like.

The boys all wore hats, and the girls wore bonnets because that's
all we knew to wear then. Hair ribbons were popular then, too. All
the big girls wore the ribbons. We had two dresses—wore one dress
one week and the other one the next week.

We Made Our Playhouses out of Rocks

JUANITA VINSON

At school, we played wolf-over-the-river and flying Dutchman. We
also had homemade toys to play with. Daddy made us slingshots out
of rubber inner tubes. We also had stilts and Tom-walkers. Tom-
walkers were like stilts except they were made out of tin cans with a
wire through the top of the can that was long enough to reach up to
the hand, so you could walk and hold them on at the same time.
When we made our playhouses out of rocks, we'd sweep the ground
clean with broom weeds that we used to make our brooms.

I Was Not Going to Stand for Him Cheating
ROBERT MARTINEZ

When I started school at Harmony, I couldn't speak English. Nothing, nada, nothing at all. There was a boy named Fred who was a little bully. He was domineering, even to his sister Mable, who was older than he. So, he'd do whatever he wanted to with us. He was big. Oh, he was big. I was not going to stand for him cheating when we played baseball. It was just the five of us Martinez kids and Mable and Fred and two of the Wallace kids. So, there was not enough to play much, but if the Martinezes didn't play, then there was just two of them on a team. They wanted us to play with them. My sister was quite a bit older than I and better in English. I'd tell Fred, "Si you play good, I play good. Si you play fair, I play fair." I was using the "si" in Spanish for "if. . . ." My sister made fun of me. She said, "Si you play good, I play good?" She was making fun of my English. "That's bad," she said.

The Rest of Us Would Be Dogs
LEWIS H. CLEGG

Wolves and dogs was one of the best games we had. Two boys would be the wolves, and we'd give 'em a certain length of time to get gone. Usually they'd go straight west into Rough Creek toward the canyons. The rest of us would be dogs and we'd go find the wolves. One time we couldn't find 'em at all. I tell you what, sometimes we'd get to playing and we'd forget to take up books. The wolves wouldn't be where we could find 'em.

"Tell the Teacher, Deelie's Dead!"
DELIA HARDIN

One time during recess, I got caved in on down below the schoolhouse. We was digging in a canyonlike area down north of the schoolhouse. There was a big pour off and we dug out under there. We had us some toys and built us some benches, kinda like a little playhouse. It might not have caved in but two of the boys ran across the top of it, and when they did, it caved in. I was in there and Geraldine Seaboalt was, too, but they didn't know she was in there.

One of the girls was just jumping up and down screaming, "Tell the teacher Deelie's dead!" My sister Dot and Clyde Garrison was digging, and they finally found Geraldine and dug her out. I guess it would have really killed me, but we had an old apple crate for a table in there, and I was right beside of that. It was kinda holding the dirt up off of me. Years later I was going to go through Carlsbad Caverns and I said, "I just can't do it." I could feel that thing caving in on me all over again.

She Was Buried and She Could Have Died

DOROTHY HEAD

We'd dig in the sand down in the canyon a little ways from the school-house. One time Deelie got buried down there. She and Geraldine Seaboalt. We had dug back under the bank, and somebody ran up on the bank, and it caved off. Clyde Garrison and us dug her out. They were buried, I mean completely, under that much dirt. Geraldine was out at the edge, and we found her first. We didn't know Deelie was in there because she was so far in there we couldn't hear her crying.

Somebody looked around and screamed, "Deelie's in there, too." When we got Geraldine out, she was screaming loud. We got Deelie uncovered. She was buried so she could have died. There must have been just enough air around her body. She was back in there digging, and Geraldine was not so far in. I didn't know what happened. I mean, dirt fell around my feet, and I turned and looked and there was all that dirt. Lucille Seaboalt was jumping up and down yelling, "Deelie's dead! Deelie's dead!" She didn't even know her sister Geraldine was under there, too!

"Somebody Just Squzzed My Hand"

GRACE PHILLIPS

The main thing I remember about school was our recreation time. We played wolf-over-the-river and sheep-board-down, which was similar to hide-and-seek. The sheep was the one that got caught. The wolf got him. We played baseball, and a good part of the time we didn't have baseballs. We'd use a rock. It was hard to hit a home run when you were batting with a crooked stick, hitting a rock. We'd sometimes have a twine string ball, which was homemade. We never had store-bought balls.

Great fun was running off at recess and just forgetting to go back to school. The teacher had a bell she rung. There were two restroom areas. The boys would go over the hill to the west and the girls would go east. There was a play area in between. It was all right to play anywhere as long as you didn't venture into the restroom areas.

We loved to go to the ol' sinkhole. I think about it now and just have nightmares. I can't believe the things we did. We went in this big ol' sinkhole. It had a cave—it would be called a natural bridge, I guess, but it was a cave through there. The boys, if they wanted to be real mean, they'd get the girls in the cave and they'd build a fire at each end where you couldn't get out. The smoke would be just terrible. It was dangerous. One time we got in there and there was a snake near the other opening, and they had a fire built back on the other side. I think about that now, and it's just the worst thing I can imagine.

There was one boy in school who wasn't too bright, and his nickname was Squzz [rhymes with fuzz]. We had a game we played where you stood in a circle with everyone holding hands. A person was in the center of the ring, and he had to try to catch whoever was squeezing the other one's hand. Well, this poor ol' boy didn't know that was the purpose of the game, and someone squeezed his hand. He said, "Somebody just *squzzed* my hand." So he was Squzz from then on.

Then we nicknamed another boy Clabber. His family lived in a little cotton picker's house, and they didn't have cows, of course. Our cows were being very fruitful at that time, so we would give them milk. The mother got sick and needed some clabber. Clabber is what happens when you let milk set for several days without re-frigeration. It turns sour and then turns to clabber—a little like cottage cheese. Well, we had lots of clabber, and they sent the boy down to get this big two-gallon bucket of clabber. So he was heading out home with his bucket full of clabber and he stubbed his toe. The clabber went all over the ground, and he fell right on top of it. He was covered from head to foot with this white clabber. So from then on we called him Clabber.

We Fought for an Hour, I Guess

LEWIS H. CLEGG

I was only eight years old and this kid named Guy Murphree beat me up one day at school. We fought for an hour, I guess. I couldn't go to school the next day. My wrists was both swollen. Mama doctored me up. So Guy kinda ruled the roost around there for the rest of the year. But then Papa sent me to town and, boy, I fought ever' day down there. I nearly had to.

I had a boy by the name of Jones that was my buddy, and we'd start home together and fight before we got home. It was just as much fun as a ball game to me. I came back and finished up the last month of school in County Line. Ol' Guy jumped me again. And I was tough enough that I just beat the tar out of him. I wasn't afraid of him, I didn't mind fightin' him; I didn't care, I'd just as soon be fightin' as anything else.

Just about the time we started back to school after the schoolhouse burned, the boys chose up sides, and we put one group on one side of the hill and the other on the other side, and we had a rock fight. When school took up, we went in, but when recess come, we'd take our places and start back where we was. That lasted about three days until one of the boys got a rock right in the mouth. Knocked a tooth or two out. So that broke that game up. I remember one time we all chose up partners and wrestled. And that turned into a fight. So we stopped that one pretty quick.

The One That Knocked out the Most Tops Was the Winner

BESSIE CLEVELAND

When we played on the playground, we all had to play together. There wasn't enough boys to make a baseball team; they couldn't have two sides. And when we played basketball we played boys' rules because there wasn't enough girls to play alone. When we wasn't playing ball, we'd play red rover and wolf-over-the-river and hopscotch and marbles. The boys tended to play marbles more than girls, but I played a lot, too. We'd play tops, too. Boys and girls both played. You had to have two tops. You'd draw a circle and each player would put one top in it. It could be a top without a spindle. Each player would try to knock out as many tops as they could, and they'd get to keep the tops they knocked out until the game was over. The one that knocked out the most tops was the winner.

When we played marbles, we didn't play for keeps. Of course, the boys did play for keeps on the way home from school, especially those that lived quite a long ways away. They'd fix them a ring and shoot at the marbles, and if you got it out you could keep it. A really good player would have a whole pocketful. Some kids would have what was called a steelie, a steel ball. But most of us would rule those out because we didn't want our marbles broken. The steelies would break them. When they played with steelies, I usually got my marbles and went home.

Girls usually played jump rope and played hopscotch and jacks. We'd all play drop-the-handkerchief, pop-the-whip, and tug rope. We had a rope to see which side would be the strongest. The boys usually all wanted on the same side because they felt like they were stronger. Usually in Pleasant Valley the girls outnumbered the boys. So it wasn't such a struggle with us most of the time to win. There were more of us. The boys would say, "Now, we're going to beat you girls today." But they usually didn't.

Often Times We Played Red Line

HENRY T. POTEET

Often times we played red line. That's where you'd draw a line from yonder to there, and you'd choose up sides. Two ways you could get people on your side. Usually two strong people, one from each side, would say, "Here, let's pull." If you could pull the other fellow across the line—others could grab him and hold him and pull him back— you either went across, or they'd be pulled across or you could turn loose. It was a little like tug-of-war. Another way, if a person is standing there while two are pulling, you could run around him, but you'd have to run around him all the way and come back to your side. If anybody from the other team touched you while you were doing it, you'd have to be on their side.

The Empty Schoolhouse

We'd Wind Socks up to Make a Big Ball
and Sew It up with Thread

LIZZIE UNDERWOOD

One time Daddy went to Coleman County and brought me back a little rubber ball. We took some old gray socks and wound 'em 'round and 'round that ball until we made a pretty big ball, and then we sewed it with thread. We'd play ante-over at the schoolhouse. Then we'd play stealing sticks. You'd choose up half of the kids on one side of a line and the other kids on the other side. We had a pile of sticks. Each side had so many sticks. You would try to steal from their pile and they would try to steal from your pile. If you got caught trying to steal their sticks by getting tagged when you were across their side of the line, then they got to keep the stick, and you had to be on their side and help 'em. If we had an old rag ball, we'd play ball. It wasn't played like they play now.

On Easter, we had lots of cack-berries—they're what some people call cactus berries. We had a teacher named Jack Duckworth. He boarded down at Mr. Adair's and come up to school in a buggy. One morning on the first day of April, we made it up to all run off and leave him there by hisself. We was going to go cack-berry hunting and stay until time for school to turn out. Well, we all stayed until dinner [lunch]. All of us but four took off over the hill and hunted cack-berries until we got tired. We came back to where they could see us and set down and played games. Mr. Duckworth told us we would have to stay in ever' day for a week at dinner except for ten minutes. He kept us all in but them four, and they got to go outside. We never minded staying in. We'd go in and get our lessons. Someone would say, "I'll bet they're having a good time out there by themselves."

There was a big long tank [earthen pond] with a big tank dam down in a draw close to the school. The teacher told us to stay away from that tank. She told us to stay off the tank dam. Everybody would get busy doing something, and we'd slip off down there. It was just a little ways down there. If you went off the tank dam and start sliding, you'd go way down there nearly plumb to the end of the tank. The teacher told us to be careful not to go down there by ourself. When it was cold, the water would freeze over. One day some of the kids threw a big rock out in the tank, and it froze in there.

Well, we started running back from there, and one of the boys run into that rock. He fell flat on his back, and it knocked him out. So we all had to get a hold of him and drag him off the ice and get him up and take him up to the school.

I guess the teacher suspected something so she asked what happened to him. One of the kids said he fell and hit his head. She said, "What'd he hit his head on?"

I said, "Well, you just as well know it now as later on. We was all down there doing something we oughten to have done, and he fell on the ice and hurt his head." So she didn't punish us. She just talked to us. She told us it was always better to tell the truth.

On April Fool's Day, We'd All Go off Together

LEO E. CLEGG

One April Fool's Day, the teacher said for us all to bring a picnic and we'd all go off together. We went over to a big rock on a fishing hole on the river. We brought our lunch. The Abner boys [name changed] —they come. I don't know what they brought or whether they brought anything or not, but they hadn't had a bite of meat or anything like that in I don't know when.

The teacher had brought some wieners, so we all had meat, but the Abner boys dropped theirs in the sand. They was going to knock off the sand and eat 'em. They couldn't get all the sand off the meat.

The teacher said, "Don't do that. We've got more meat." She gave them more meat, and they couldn't hardly believe they got meat for lunch.

After lunch the older boys and girls paired off, and they was goin' over across the river to another hole of water where the bend of the river was. So the teacher and one of the other kids was holdin' the fence up high as they could, so we could all get through it. One of the girls about the same age as I was—she was kinda timid, like me—I was hangin' around behind. I wasn't goin' with nobody, and the rest of 'em was walking along together.

So they said, "Hurry up, Leo! Hurry up, Leo! Hurry up, Leo! We're gonna let the fence down."

This girl was just barely through the fence and she just stood there. I was in a hurry to get through the fence, and I didn't realize she was there. I bent over to go under the fence, and when I did, I run my head up under her dress. I backed out right quick, and they'd done let the bob wire back down, and it jabbed me in the back end, which made me jump forward right into her again. Talk about an embarrassed guy. *I was!*

She said, "What'er you tryin' to do?"

I couldn't explain myself. I was too embarrassed; I didn't know what to say.

Playing Hooky on April Fool's Day Was Usually Forgiven

BESSIE CLEVELAND

I remember one year on April Fool's Day. We had a woman teacher that year. All of the kids decided they just wasn't coming to school. Well, they come to school that day, but then we were just going to disappear. And we did. We all left the school building, a few at a time. I didn't live very far, but I didn't go home. I hid in the shinnery lane. Took our lunch and had a picnic. None of us had watches, but when we thought it was about time to go home from school, well, we went back to the school building.

Some of the kids had been spotted by their parents before the day was over, and they took them home, and then brought them back to school. Of course, the teacher reported to the parents. My daddy thought it was all right. Just a joke. Playing hooky on April Fool's Day was usually forgiven.

The teacher asked us the next morning, "Now, what kind of punishment should I give you?" She knew where some of us were all the time. She said, "Well, I'm going to let those that didn't run off go to the cistern." That's where we went to draw water. "You all go out there and play a while. I'm going to switch the rest of them." She didn't. But she gave us all some candy. That's the way she punished us. She scared us to death. We all thought we were going to get a paddling, but we didn't.

They Caught a Pig and Brought It in the Schoolhouse

MARTHA PIKE

On April Fool's Day when Miss Minnie was teaching, we run off, but we only thought we was runnin' off. We looked back, and she was goin' with us. So we all had a picnic down on the creek or wherever we went. On April Fool's Day, you was supposed to run off. I remember one time we all had lunch buckets. After we'd eat our lunch, we'd leave our buckets outside on a kind of a humplike thing. Anyway, some of the neighbor's pigs got out and come up there and was trying to get into our buckets. The teacher told Jim and Jay to run out there and bring our things in the schoolhouse. They run out there and caught a pig and brought it in the house. That's how ornery them two was.

We Had the Maypole on the First of May

FRED BROWN

We had the Maypole on the first of May, I guess. We had a big pole with those streamers coming out. The boy would take one and then a girl, you know. You'd go round and round the pole, singing and everything until you wound it up. This old lady said, "They shouldn't do that. All they want is to do that so boys and girls will be right up together." She didn't like it, but she was probably right.

Talking about long dresses. My mother was telling me about in 1926, Nehi soda pop came out. It was in those tall bottles, and they depicted the Nehi as "knee high." They showed it as a girl's leg past her knee. One of our dear old ladies said, "That is ridiculous. They're just carrying it a little bit too far."

A Wonderful Time of Day Was Lunch

EVA WALL SINGLETON

A wonderful time of day was lunch. I think we had about forty-five minutes for lunch, or maybe it was an hour. But anyhow, we all brought our lunches; we had no other choice. We would trade things to eat with each other that we liked. My mother made wonderful cinnamon rolls and goodies and individual chocolate pies and things like that. So I had lots of friends around noon, and they wanted to trade with me.

I carried my lunch in a little bucket—kind of a little water bucket. Later Mother bought a lunch pail. It was a g-r-e-a-t day when we had a piece of fruit. Once in a while, if Daddy went to town, he'd bring back oranges or bananas or apples. Oh, everybody wanted a bite of the fruit. There was one family that had very little, and Mother would put in extra things, and she would tell me I could share with them. Of course, I was an only child and many of my schoolmates were from large families. That was really the first thing in my life that helped me to see compassion for others.

Later there was a girl named Hattie who was deprived. Mother had taught me enough about sharing that I noticed Hattie wouldn't eat with the other girls when we had lunch out on the grounds under the trees. Hattie always went off by herself. When I saw what Hattie was doing, I told Mother about her. Mother told me I should eat with her, and I said, "No, I want to eat with my friends."

Mother said, "Hattie needs a friend." So Mother made little individual things, like pies and sweet rolls and things. I began to eat with Hattie and share some of the things Mother put in my lunch with her. Soon, the other girls began to notice that I was eating with Hattie, and it wasn't long before they joined us. Hattie was shy and needed someone to be her friend first.

"I Ate My Lunch, But I Didn't Have Near Enough"

WILLIAM I. POTEET

I started to school in 1915. I was close to eight years of age. Of course, schools then were only five to six months a year and didn't start before November or December. We walked to school. It was about a mile. Everybody walked except for a few families that drove a hack. We never even thought about nothing, only walking.

For lunch we usually took a syrup or lard can—the syrup can was a gallon can and the lard bucket was a little larger. Mother made our bread, which was biscuits, and put in a slice of ham and a boiled egg. I don't remember much about dessert, but Mother was good about making cookies or what we'd call now cupcakes. We usually had some of that nearly every meal.

At lunch we'd go out under a tree beside the schoolhouse. Of course, if it was cold, we'd stay inside and eat at someone's desk. Mother put us five boys' lunches together, and my sisters' lunches would be separate. So we boys ate together and we each got our part to eat. Once my little brother Henry came in the schoolhouse after we'd gulped our lunch down—he was a little fellow—and the teacher was still eating at his desk. The teacher asked, "Henry, have you had your lunch?"

Henry said, "Yes, I ate my lunch, but I didn't have near enough." That was probably true with most of the kids. You know kids are always hungry.

That Was a Christmas Treat, to Have Fruit
GRACE PHILLIPS

I don't remember much about school, but I do remember the lunches. We had plenty of food at home, but school lunches were different from our usual fare. We never had to go hungry. Baked potatoes were a big item. When you'd bake them, you'd take the stuffing out, and you'd put butter and onions and such stuff in it. And you'd put it back in the shell. You'd take it and eat it, skin and all. Mama would sometimes make a potato salad out of them and stuff it back in the same shell. They were mighty good at lunchtime. We didn't take corn bread in our lunch. It was for crumbling in sweet milk. Biscuits would be easier to keep. And we'd put bacon or ham between the biscuit—whatever part of the hog we were eating on at the time. We had boiled eggs, if the hens were laying at that time, and sometimes fried chicken.

We'd always kill a beef. We'd kill it in the wintertime and we'd hang it up and we'd eat it before it ruined. Sometimes we had cookies and cakes. Tea cakes especially. The real delicacy in later years was when we got peanut butter and crackers. That was big stuff.

We seldom ever had fruit. That was a Christmas treat, to have fruit. If we had fruit trees on the farm, it didn't ripen during the school year. Of course, we started late and got out early. School was after cotton picking—first things first. We got out in early May, in time to hoe cotton. During the snows—when we had snows and such, we wouldn't have school.

My favorite teacher was Lois Smith. She was one of the twins, Lois and Louise Smith, who both taught there. She was a very loving teacher, and she was interested in each of us as individuals. I could go talk with her, and she asked me questions about what I wanted to learn. She would get the type books I wanted to read and to look at. Also Lois and Louise had more class than most of our teachers because their brother owned a grocery store in town. They brought great lunches to school. When they were through with lunch, they threw their lunch sacks in the little canyon not far from the schoolhouse. So we would head home in the afternoon and hide behind a bush until they were out of sight. Then we'd go back and raid the lunch sacks. We'd get apples, and oranges, and sometimes Oreo cookies. That was the first Fig Newtons I ever had. We were bag ladies, let me tell you. The original. And *that was the best stuff!* We'd be a little late getting home from school but nobody cared. We felt good. You know, I've often wondered if they threw those things away on purpose, knowing how much they would mean to little country kids. We were probably too proud to accept food directly.

We had cotton pickers come to our school. I remember we had a girl called Ray-who-he-a. I have no idea what her name actually was. Ray-who-he-a was what we called her. It was a Spanish name, no doubt with a Texas accent. I'm sure it wasn't anything like what her name was. She came to our school for a little while during cotton picking time. She spoke a little bit of English. We walked to school together, and I recall she had one piece of chocolate candy that used to be made thick, like big drops. And, oh my, I thought that sure looked good. She plopped it all in her mouth, but she decided she liked me. So she took it out of her mouth and bit off half of it and gave it to me. And I ate it! Good stuff!

Some kids brought fried pies all [the] time. Two kids in our school—Wallace and his little brother Willard—brought fried pies to school. One day they bit into them, and they weren't any good. They were just awful. When they got home, Wallace asked his sister Mollie, "What in the world did you put in those fried pies? They had bones in them!"

What happened was that someone had fixed up a big plate of scraps for the dogs, and Mollie was fixing the pies for frying, so she picked up the wrong bowl. She thought the bowl of dog scraps was pie filling. She made up this bowl of scraps into fried pies, and the kids took them to school! They were just awful. [Such a mistake is easy to understand when one remembers what early morning was like. It was late autumn, winter, or early spring when the children were in school, so it would have been dark outside. The only lighting in the kitchen was a small kerosene lamp, so two bowls side by side could appear very similar.]

They Was a Poor Family, I Mean Dirt Poor

LEO E. CLEGG

There was something kind of funny, and yet it was serious, too. We was all sittin' out on the north side of the schoolhouse in the shade eatin' our lunch one day. You know how kids are. If they had a piece of biscuit they didn't want, they would throw it away. Well, the Abner family lived just over the hill from the schoolhouse across the creek. They was a poor family, I mean dirt poor. They ate mostly boiled maize and boiled corn, Papa said.

One day one of us boys at lunch threw a piece of biscuit away. We seen one of the Abner boys go over there to see what it was. He picked up that piece of biscuit. He didn't get biscuits at home. He grabbed that and ate it. When we saw what he was doin,' someone else would throw a piece of bread away, and the boy would pick it up, whirl around so we couldn't see him and eat it, dirt and all. The other kids got to winkin' at one another, and somebody would throw another piece of bread here or yon, and he'd run from one place to another grabbin' a piece of bread. He thought he was in high heaven gettin' that bread. Lookin' back on it, it was pitiful, just pitiful.

Another time one of the Abner boys come to school, and his mouth was all green. The teacher asked him why his mouth was so green, and he said he'd been a-grazin'. *He'd been eatin' grass!*

I don't know how they kept from starvin' to death. They had an old dirt farm that wasn't worth a thing. I wouldn't have had it if you'd give it to me. My dad said he'd come by their house, and they would always beg him to stop and eat with them. He wanted to be sociable and all, but all they ever had would be boiled maize and boiled corn. Used to people would take maize and shell it and grind it and make it into flour, and you'd never know the difference.

I was at their place in 1914, I guess, and they had a dugout with a brush arbor built in front of it. It didn't have any doors or nothin'. The dugout was built on the side of a hill. The dust was about three inches deep. Soupy dust. I don't see how they kept from chokin' to death on all that dust. That was about the poorest family I ever seen. I don't believe there was any worse anywhere. They was a poor family, I mean poor!

It Was Good, Man, Was It Good

WALTER CLEVELAND

For lunch we carried biscuits and bread and sausage. All the kids brought something. It was usually cold biscuits and meat, and biscuits with syrup poured in them. We'd stick our finger in the biscuit and pour syrup in it. Stick your finger in it, fill it full of syrup, and close it up. It was good, man, *was it good.* We didn't have paper napkins or wax paper, so we'd usually take a cloth to wrap things up in. We all carried our lunches together. All of us kids would share the same big dinner pail. We'd usually eat outside. The teacher wouldn't let us eat in the building unless it was raining or cold.

Those Fried Pies Were Still Hot at Lunchtime

NAOMI VINYARD

For lunch we usually took sandwiches made out of biscuits and ham and boiled eggs. And sometimes fried pies. We'd put in a few cans of pork and beans. One time we forgot our lunch. We went horseback that day. So one of the boys asked if they could run back home—it was about three miles there and three miles back, so they did. Mama decided that since we had forgotten our lunch somebody'd be back for it, and she'd just made a lot of fried pies. She made some apricot fried pies, and they were still hot when they got there.

When my brother got back to school with our lunch, the teacher had just let us out to eat. It was a hot day and he was riding this horse. We had to get a spoon and spoon those pies up. We'd usually eat outside. We usually took a hack. It was a two seater. Different from a buggy that usually had one seat. We'd usually leave our lunch in the hack until lunchtime, and that's where we ate. There were so many of us, and we always brought those buckets. We were still using a common dipper to drink out of. We'd draw a fresh bucket of water and all drink from it, and then pour what was left over back in the cistern. Couldn't waste water, you know.

A Lot of Times We'd Exchange Food

IRA HESTER

You take back when I went to school, we had no planned athletic activities. You just did whatever came natural. I had a cousin; he and

I would fight all the time when we were out at recess at noon. And of course, as a lot of people, different ones have told you, most of us took our lunches to school in syrup buckets, half-gallon buckets, or a gallon bucket, whatever you had. It was usually a biscuit with sausage. One biscuit with sausage, and maybe some kind of sweet. My mother would make sugar pies. She'd usually try to have it planned where she would have some kind of sweet. I'm the fourth child of ten, but we didn't meet together at lunch. We took our own lunch. And a lot of times I would have something that maybe another student didn't have or didn't get to eat at home, and he'd have something that I wasn't accustomed to too much, and a lot of times we'd exchange food.

Everybody Had Homemade Sorghum Syrup
CLYDE HODGES

I tell you what, we had a cold lunch every day. We carried lunch to school. Most of 'em carried a gallon syrup bucket with a lid on it. We had plenty to eat, though. We had sweet baked taters, and a lot of people, as long as it lasted, had sausages and pork ribs, stuff like that, you know. And everybody had homemade sorghum syrup. Every community had a syrup mill. You grind the cane, and the juice comes out, and they had a big cooker—build a fire under it. And they cooked it down. It would take all day. A lot of people cook it too fast, but the best syrup was made when you cooked it slow. We had a little snuff glass about so high and that big around, and we'd fill it about half full of sorghum syrup. Then put a biscuit in the top for a lid. Some days, I wouldn't want nothing but baked sweet taters. Oh they was good, I thought.

And we had boiled eggs. I went to school with an old boy whose name was Willy. Some of the boys told him, "Willy, you can't bust that guinea egg on your forehead with the sharp end." And he just kept beatin' and a-beatin', and the blood went to spewin' and he stopped. I guess he decided he couldn't. He died with a scar on his forehead. He went to his grave with a scar on his forehead from the sharp end of a guinea egg. Them guinea eggs are sure hard.

Sometimes Mother Would Put in a Little Glass of Jelly or Preserves

MAUD ARNOLD BAILEY

Mother was a good hand to fry pies, and we had a large orchard and she dried a lot of fruit. She would cook this dried fruit until it was real tender and she'd make pies, fried pies. That was one thing we'd take for lunch. And always sausage and biscuit. Mother made biscuits. We didn't hardly know what it was to eat light bread. We didn't take sorghum to school. We had it at home, but I guess it would pour out on the way to school or something. She never did put that in our lunches. Sometimes mother would put in a little glass of jelly or preserves. We had eleven children in our family. Ten grew up. I was number seven of the children. I had a lot of bosses. We were talking a while back about leadership. I told them that I don't have any leadership qualities because I was always told what to do.

He Loved That Fried Chocolate Pie

INA DINGUS COWAN

When I was a child in school we took our lunches. They'd let us go outside and eat on the woodpile. We always liked to roll our lunch up in a newspaper. But mainly people took little syrup cans with a lid on it. My sister Merle was extra good at making butter rolls. We had butter rolls for school nearly every morning. She'd take the biscuit dough and roll it out and put butter and sugar and roll it up and bake it while we were having our breakfast. So everybody would have a butter roll. Merle did that. She made wonderful ones.

I was about eight when I first ate peanut butter. It was about 1914 or '15 or somewhere about there. Then after that they came out with pork and beans. I thought that was the best thing I ever put in my mouth. They were in a small can, and I remember how much I loved pork and beans, but now I won't touch pork and beans at all.

We lived out in the country and the Watkins man—he was a peddler—came by our house and gave us chewing gum and candy. That's why we liked to see him come. The Watkins man would trade for chickens or eggs or milk. When I was teaching we milked four or five cows in the morning, and we lived on the cream that we'd sell

III

and the eggs. We had five hundred leghorn chickens. That was our living. We always ate well. That was one thing. We grew our own food. It was a matter of working hard. You could keep a cow. My father kept a cow right here in town as long as he was able to take care of a cow. I guess he was one of the last ones that kept a cow here in town. He raised his own pigs here, too. Life wasn't nearly as easy in those days. We drew the water out of the cistern and washed on a rub board, but it was quite a satisfactory life. I'm glad I grew up and had this kind of experience.

After I married, my husband's brother was a young boy that was still in school. He took a fried chocolate pie every morning to school. His mother would mix up cocoa and sugar and some heavy cream. . . . And they'd dip in there and get enough to stir that up and put that in a pie shell, raw pie dough, and then fix it where it wouldn't run out and fry it. She fried that. I've never seen that anywhere else. This was my bother-in-law who was fourteen. My husband's mother would do that. As long as that kid went to school he had to have his chocolate pie. That was just a joke in the family. *He loved that fried chocolate pie!*

If You Prowled Somebody's Lunch Basket, You Could Expect to Get Your Ears Beat Down

DONO DARDEN

We carried our lunch in a lard bucket. We usually had bacon and bread. Now, it was a pretty light lunch. Left over from breakfast. Ordinarily you had scrambled eggs and bacon. Hardly ever had beef—it was pork. Fights at lunch didn't happen very much because food was too valuable. Wasn't no argument, if you prowled somebody's lunch basket, you could expect to get your ears beat down. Now, by George, it would just call for a fight.

The Empty Schoolhouse

CHAPTER SIX

⁊

Life Was Hard Then,
But We Done the Best We Could

SOCIAL AND FAMILY LIFE

Social life in rural communities was wedded to the school. It was here Friday night "literaries" took place, as well as box suppers, pie suppers, singings, parties, revivals, and patriotic gatherings. Holidays were often celebrated in conjunction with the school. April Fool's Day was for pranks and playing hooky. "You were supposed to run off from school" on that day. Sometimes there were Easter egg hunts and Fourth of July celebrations, and always there was Christmas. Many parents gave each child his or her Christmas present at the school Christmas party.

It is difficult to overestimate the influence of the school on social activity in the community. If there was a funeral, school was dismissed. Churches used the buildings for Sunday school, sermons, and revival services before congregations grew large enough to build their own structures. Any event that brought the community together—whether singing school or traveling magic show—was usually held at the school.

Freedom from school, the delightful days of summer, was remembered with enthusiasm by many interviewees. Although summer often meant hard work in the fields and in the home, it also brought long days drenched with sun, a chance to be outside away from the restriction of school. One could go swimming, eat roastin' ears and black-eyed peas, walk barefoot in the fields, and lie on a pallet at night and watch for shooting stars.

Life was difficult for many families as they struggled to ensure that food, shelter, and clothing were adequate and that enough money remained to pay taxes and the occasional doctor bill. Narrators told poignant tales of seeing children who were hungry, of wearing hand-me-down clothes and feed-sack dresses, of doing without all but the basic necessities. A common thread, however, was that families did the best they could: "We made do!"

One of the Happy Times Was on Friday Night
EVA WALL SINGLETON

One of the happy times in the school was on Friday night when the parents would come to school with their children. Some of the children would sing. I always got to tell a story; I liked to tell stories. Then they would have some that would play the piano. They would have piano solos and other little instruments played by children, and the parents would come, and every child would perform whatever he could. If there was a child that wasn't really capable of doing something by himself, he would be in a group number. I remember those were such happy times. We put on our best dresses and the boys their nicest clothes, a little tie and nice pants, and they got up and performed.

At Christmastime we always had a Christmas tree. You could put a gift on the tree for one other person, so you would get a gift, and the teacher would always give you something—maybe a stick of candy, maybe a little ball, maybe a hair ribbon, or maybe a pencil. They always gave you something. They didn't let any child get more than two things. You would draw names or you would bring a gift for a girl and a boy would bring a gift for a boy. I remember the teacher was so sweet and loving. She always had a few little things hidden back in case somebody didn't bring one. She never let them feel embarrassed or ashamed. She had an extra one. I always thought that was so sweet.

"Heavy, Heavy Hangs over Your Head"
ADDIE BOSTICK GREEN

We went to play parties, and we went to dances. We'd ring up in the middle of the floor, sittin' in chairs, and there'd be one that would get something, and he'd go and hold it over your head, and he'd say, "Heavy, heavy hangs over your head." And the person whose head it was over had to guess what it was. And another game they'd play was spin the bottle. Ever'body would be sittin' in chairs in a circle, and they'd set a bottle in the middle of the floor, and somebody would spin it. Whenever the neck of the bottle pointed at a certain person, then he'd have to get up and spin the bottle. Another way to play was whoever would spin the bottle would get to kiss the girl it was pointin' to. That was a popular game, especially with the boys.

Later on I think some of the kids played winkems. All the girls would sit in chairs arranged in a circle. Their partners would be standin' behind them with a handkerchief held in both hands. A boy who was "it" would sit in the middle of the ring and wink at one of the girls. The girl that was winked at, she would try to get up and run to the boy in the middle. Her partner would try to grab her by putting the handkerchief over her head to keep her from leaving him. If he was fast enough, she'd have to stay. If the girl was faster, she got to go to the boy that winked at her, and then her partner had to sit in the middle and try to get a new partner.

I Didn't Believe in Hypnotism until Then
CLYDE HODGES

When I was a kid, lots of Saturday nights they would have what we called box suppers. They'd sell chocolate pies and this and that, you know, to raise a little money. Oh, you gave a dollar then for a chocolate pie, that was pretty high. But we'd buy them. They would raise money that a-way. They'd auction 'em off. You wasn't supposed to know who brought which pie until somebody bought it. But my girl would always tell me which pie to buy. She never made me guess. She'd have a way of letting me know it was hers.

I remember one time over there at the schoolhouse, they had a little show come in there. Hypnotism deal. I never did believe in hypnotism 'til then. I believe in it now. They hypnotized a cousin of mine. He was grown—put his feet in one chair and his head in another. He was stiff as a board. You could walk up there and sit on him. He wouldn't bend. I seen that with my own eyes. You could sit on him, and he wouldn't bend. I didn't believe in hypnotism until then.

She Come Riding a Horse with a Low-Neck Dress On
NARCISSA CLEGG

At the end of Mr. Hilburn's first school—it was out in June—my cousin Alfred Gray was teaching over across the river at a school called Riverdale, and their school was out the same day. They arranged to have a big all-day picnic in the valley between the two schools, Riverdale and County Line, in a big grove of cottonwood trees. So everybody from both communities, and even some from Cottonwood School up on the divide, came and spent all day. Somebody got a big freezer from town and put up a stand and sold ice cream. Then everybody had their dinner.

Of everybody that went, there wasn't but two or three people that was dressed for the hot sun. The Barrons came out from Rotan, Mrs. Barron and some people with her. They were the only ones with long sleeves on. We all had on our best. I had on a dress with a

These boys at Riverdale School, Kent County, are engaged in one of the rites of spring, the much-anticipated Easter egg hunt. Courtesy Luther Bryan Clegg

∞ *The Empty Schoolhouse*

low neck and short sleeves, and we all came up with sunburn. *Oh my! How we had to doctor ourselves!* Miss Jessie was teaching at Cottonwood. She come riding a horse with a low-neck dress on, and she was like everybody else. Oh, how she got sunburned! All the young people at least got burned.

After dinner, I know we had speeches, because I had one. I had to say a reading. I said the "Psalm of Life," one of Longfellow's poems. I can still tell you every line. They didn't play games. They just talked and visited. Everybody had a good time. At the end, one of the trustees said, "I want the two teachers, Alfred and Mr. Hilburn, to stand up here, and I want everybody to come around and shake their hands." It wasn't exactly good-bye, but it was an appreciation or something. And I know we all went around, and when I got to Mr. Hilburn to shake hands with him, he said, "Keep up the good work you're doing." I don't know if I was doing good work, but I was making Es for excellent and all, so I guess I was. That was a real encouragement to me. He said, "Keep up the good work!"

Papa Put on One of Aunt Lindy's Dresses and No One Knew Who He Was

WILLIAM I. POTEET

I remember my dad—we'd gone over across the river to church at the Riverdale School with John Dillingham. Mr. Dillingham was an ex-barber and went back to barbering later. He was living on the farm then. Anyway, he shaved my dad. Papa wouldn't shave. He'd just clip his whiskers off with scissors. Well, Mr. Dillingham shaved him. We had a big BYPU, which was a Baptist youth group. They had a big program at the end of that gathering. So the teacher thought it would be funny to get a dress from my Aunt Lindy and put it on Papa and parade him up and down on the stage, and they'd try to guess who he was. Well, they couldn't figure out who he was. There was a group of people there from over at Spring Creek beyond Hobbs—and Papa finally said as he paraded back and forth, "I'm from Spring Creek." They'd cut up a lot, and they almost had to throw them out, they got so noisy. "I'm from Spring Creek," he said and walked out the back. Nobody knew who he was. They never did figure out who he was since they'd never seen him before with his beard shaved.

I Had a Hat with Great Big Roses on It

OPAL WATSON NANNY

The first time I ever remember going into church, it was in the schoolhouse. Lots of times they didn't have a church building and they had church in the schools—and political meetings and even funerals. I was a little girl, real little girl. I don't know how little I was, but my mother and daddy had taken me to get me a hat. In the store, they had a cute little one that had little tiny blue flowers on it, and they wanted to buy it. But I saw one with great big roses on it, and I wanted that. And I squalled and I kicked and I took on, you know, until Daddy said, "Well, it's not going to keep the sun off of her, but neither one of them will, nor the rain, so let her have it."

So I got it and they took me to church next Sunday, and I would wear the hat. I got in there and there was this boy and his girlfriend there in church, you know. They were adults, of course. And she had on a hat just like mine. I never forgot it. I decided, even at that early age, old people did know a little something. I must have been less than five years old.

I Cried Because My Dress Caught on Fire

NAOMI A. MAYFIELD

Real candles were often placed on evergreen trees indoors during Christmas celebrations. They represented the ultimate fire hazard. Without running water or any real means of fire control, it is astonishing more homes and schools were not destroyed by fire from candles.

We used to have a community Christmas tree at school. Everybody took their Christmas gifts to the schoolhouse and they passed them out. Each family would have something there for each member of the family, or at least for the children. They had real candles on the tree. I had this dress that my folks had bought me. It was bright orange with pockets—a pretty dress. I got too close to the candles and it caught fire and burned a hole in it. I cried because my dress caught on fire. Mother had a piece of green material—the dress had some green trimming on the pockets—so she had to make me a whole yoke out of that green material. But she fixed it. We had two school dresses each. In May we could all go barefooted, but not 'til May. Of course, we couldn't walk to school barefooted. We'd take our shoes off when we got there. It was too rough in that country to go barefooted.

My brother Marvin went to school, but my sister Grace didn't go to school there much. She was younger than Marvin but she had a lot of trouble with her eyes. Dad was blind after we went out there and Grace had the same thing. They called it granulated lids, then. It was inherited and she was treated with silver nitrate. It's a wonder she has sight today. She still has a lot of pain with her eyes. She didn't lose her sight, but she missed a lot of school on account of it.

My grandfather came every summer and held a revival. One summer he came for a revival and brought a Mrs. Snyder with him. She was a wealthy woman and did things for people. She took a real interest in Grace, and saw she was just going to become blind if something wasn't done. She asked if she could take her home with her to Oklahoma City. So Grace went, and they sent her to school there and gave her treatment for her eyes. So Grace left us. She never attended much school here.

I Was Grown Before I Ever Knew You Was Supposed to Have a Christmas Tree

BILL CLEVELAND

At school we'd have a Christmas tree. We didn't have much on it. The teachers would usually buy you something—a handkerchief or something like that was as much as you ever got. Usually the school would have apples and oranges for ever'body. We decorated the tree with popcorn and paper links, paper chains. Some of the men would cut the tree out of the cedar breaks. We didn't have a tree at home. I was grown before I ever knew you was supposed to have a Christmas tree. Us kids would take a branch off of the tree at school and take it home. And that was as near as I ever knew of having a Christmas tree. We lived out toward Sardis, and there wasn't any cedars out there.

People Had Christmas Then, and It Didn't Cost No Big Bucks

CLYDE HODGES

We usually got out of school some for holidays. For Christmas they'd dismiss 'bout three or four days. We didn't even know there was any Thanksgiving going on, and we didn't know then what Halloween was.

Sometimes people'd pull tricks on each other at Christmas. I remember when Christmastime come, they would pull tricks on their neighbors. Dad had a surrey. Me and the kids thought more of that surrey than we did the first automobile we ever got. We got up one morning, and it was sitting up on top of the roof of the house. Someone had come in the night and put it on [the] roof of the house. Yeah, seven or eight big stout men, you know, they set that surrey up on the roof of the house. They come back and helped get it down later. Same ones that put it up. That was at Christmastime, just for fun.

Oh, I tell you what. People had Christmas then, and it didn't cost no big bucks. You could take Christmas night then, and you could look all over the country, and the sky would be full of skyrockets 'til midnight. Some of them all night long. You could buy a whole bunch of Christmas fireworks. Didn't cost much.

For Christmas we'd get a pair of socks, an apple, or an orange. Ever' kid then hung up a sock on the fireplace. It'd be filled full of fruit, candy, and apples, and maybe the sock wouldn't hold it all, so there'd be some sitting down on each side of the fireplace. I tell you what, kids then got a lot of Christmas presents that they thought a lot of. Each of the cousins back then would buy or make a Christmas present for the other cousins, you know. And you could get a pair of good socks then for twenty-five cents.

My Dress Was Made over out of Mother's Wedding Dress
CONNIE HAYTER TUTT

I wore the same dress to school all week. As soon as I got home, I'd take that school dress off and put on an ever'day dress. I don't know about the boys since there weren't any in our family, but they probably did the same thing. Washing was such a problem. The mothers usually washed all day Monday and they ironed all day Tuesday. I guess I had two school dresses. This dress . . . was made over out of Mother's wedding dress. My sister also had one just like it. It was made the same way except larger, and it was from my mother's wedding dress also. After these dresses wore out, my mother used the material to make quilts out of the good parts of them.

The only time in my life that I remember thinking we really were poor was one Christmas when we just didn't get anything for Christmas, except that my mother sat up all night and made new doll dresses for our dolls. That was our Christmas present, new doll dresses for our dolls. Our dolls had china heads and hands with cloth bodies. They were store bought some years before. Rotan wasn't established until 1907, and I was born in 1901, so I guess we must have shopped at Snyder or Sweetwater, or maybe Roby. We ordered things out of the Sears, Roebuck catalog or Montgomery Ward.

Sometimes we'd have a Christmas tree at school, but I think the Christmas trees would be mostly at church. Our parents provided whatever gifts we got. I'm sure a lot of kids didn't get anything at all except a sack of treats and a little candy provided by the church. Now, that was a treat. We didn't have oranges except at Christmas. We would have oranges and nuts and apples, I guess, and some type of hard candy; stick candy is what it usually was. The only social things we had was at church.

He Just Stuck a Firecracker in the Wrong Guy's Face

LEWIS H. CLEGG

One time this big ol' overgrown boy—he was about sixteen, I guess —was throwing firecrackers around at the school Christmas program. He was nearly drunk; that's what was the matter with him. Somebody should have taken him home, but they didn't. He stuck a firecracker in Papa's face. He just stuck it in the wrong guy's face. Papa hit him before he knew what he was doing. I was in the schoolhouse when it happened.

What happened after that—Papa went down to town and just paid his fine. Told them what happened. Then, of course, the sheriff sent for the kid to come pay his. Never was any more said about it. It was the custom that, if you got in a public fight, you was fined. That happened a lot. Down in town once there was this ol' boy named Dry and he was just a-whooping it up. There was another man named Moore. He just came up and he knocked ol' Dry completely out. Just with one lick. And ol' Dry had to pay a fine for getting knocked down. That just made Dry so mad he nearly died.

I Knew I Was Gonna Get My Tail Beat

DONO DARDEN

One summer my cousin and I—we were about six years old at the time—thought we'd smoke us some tobacco. His dad, my uncle, dipped snuff, and my dad smoked RJR tobacco. Dad carried his tobacco in his pocket all the time, so you couldn't slip that. But Uncle Oscar got this little brown jar of snuff, and he'd dip some out in a little tin can to carry in his pocket. Well, that would give you a chance to swipe some of his snuff.

We thought, Tom and I, how fine it would be to smoke tobacco and not have cedar bark flaring up and scorching our eyebrows and giving us away, you know. Well, we slipped some snuff out, and we tried rolling cigarettes. We went down to the cow lot and got some corn shucks and used horse manure to practice on, but we didn't have no luck. We couldn't make those corn shucks stick together—couldn't crimp 'em around. So, we swiped some pages out of the back of the Sears, Roebuck catalog. Then when we'd try to roll up our cigarettes, why, the paper'd tear. We wanted to smoke and talk with a cigarette in our mouths like the cowboys did.

We didn't know exactly what we was saying, but we wanted to cuss and sound pretty ugly. We practiced cussing some, and we got this snuff, and went off down in the pasture close to the tank. Goin' to smoke—goin' to strike a match on the seat of our pants like the cowboys did. Well, we didn't have no luck doin' that, so we had to strike a match on a rock.

We rolled our snuff cigarettes and lighted them both off one match—we saw some of these cowboys where both of 'em would light two cigarettes off one match—and when we sucked, both of us sucked that snuff right down our throats. It made us sick at our stomach. I never was so sick—I knew I was goin' to die, and I knew I was gonna get my tail beat. But I wanted to die around Mama, you know, so we went to the house and Mama stuck her finger down our throats—made us both vomit—washed our faces with a wet rag and then put it on our throats.

I knew I was goin' to get a whippin', and Dad whipped with a razor strap—a two-layer razor strap—and he'd hit you hard. Hot dog, he tore you up!

Mama told him, "You set a bad example for 'em—you ought not to whip 'em so hard."

122

And he said, "Do as I say, not as I do." And he made it stick. Now you can believe that. Well, that cured me. I never did learn to smoke.

Lo and Behold, I Went Head over Heels into the Well
LEO E. CLEGG

It was one summer and my brother Jack and I was havin' to fill the water trough for the horses. We didn't have a pulley or nothin'. We had to pull that water up by hand. My big brother Lewis was a-plowin' down in the field before dinner. So Jack and me got to playin' and squirtin' water at each other and into each other's eyes. You know how kids will do.

The rim of the well was only about four or five inches above the trough. I thought I'd get up there and sit on the edge of the trough and lean back against the well. I leaned back, and lo and behold, I went head over heels into the well. Fourteen foot into the well. I could see daylight plumb to the bottom of the well. That water was in there, and I landed on my head and shoulders, so it didn't hurt me a bit. I knocked water halfway to the top of that well. I went to hollerin', "Draw me out! Draw me out! Draw me out, quick!" Jack couldn't draw me out. About that time Lewis come in from the field, and they both drawed me out. Later my brother Wallace died in a well, so I guess I was lucky.

My Mother Ran a Little Store in Our Home
BUDDY HUDNALL

My mother ran a little store in our home, must have started it in about 1908. She'd bring groceries and things from town, buy 'em at a wholesale company. Later, we had a gas station and a post office called Hud. She kept school supplies and groceries—staples like flour, salt, and canned goods. It was tempting as a boy to sneak in the store and get candy and things. We'd have a lot of rules, but I'd break all those rules. When you have candy all the time, you get to where you don't care too much for it. Mama would get candy in barrels—stick candy, lemon sticks, peppermint sticks.

She'd get a barrel and get the candy mixed—different kinds. She'd keep dried fruit in ten-pound boxes, prunes and peaches and apricots. She'd either sell 'em by the pound, or you could buy the whole box. We kept the store until 1931. We ran the post office and people came up to our house to pick up their mail.

My Mother Was a Great Cook

A. B. LAMPKIN

When I was growing up, we didn't know what light bread was. We ate a lot of red beans, and we had a lot of stew. My dad always told us that a lot of fried foods wasn't good for you, and you should avoid it. We ate boiled meat or baked meat. We had stew meat and we'd carry that to the field in a pot. It would be hot during the summer so you didn't have to heat it up or anything like that. We had fried chicken on Sunday. That was a delicacy.

We used to kill our own hogs. Me and my sisters and my mother, we would handle the chitlins. They are the intestines. We used part of them to stuff sausages, and the other part, we'd clean them and just boil them. We made cracklins out of the skin. I haven't had any good crackin' bread in a long time. After they would kill the hog, they'd scrape it, and it was our job to take care of that skin and the inside, like the liver and the hog maws. Part of that was cooked with the chitlins. The maw is sort of like the stomach, it kind of grinds the food up for the pig. We ate the brains. Eggs and brains are good. I tell people about eggs and brains, and they are repulsed. But that is one of the best parts of the hog.

We never did kill a beef, but we raised our own chickens and garden. About everything we had to eat, we raised it. Of course, we bought our flour and meal because we didn't have a grinder for corn. We had a big can of lard. We didn't worry about sunflower oil and all that kind of stuff. My mother was a great cook. Everything I liked had to have gravy with it. Gravy was, I guess, my favorite of whatever I was eating, whether it was smothered chicken or whatever else. They used to tease me a lot because for a while they said I wouldn't even eat the meat, I'd just eat the gravy. My mother would make gravy by putting a little grease in a skillet and sprinkle flour in it and let it brown. She'd stir it to keep it from burning and season it and cook it until it got to the color she wanted. Then she'd put water in it and let it boil down. Sometimes she'd make milk gravy the same way except she'd use milk instead of water. We had only one cow and we kept her for milking.

My Mother Was One of the Most Finest Cooks You Ever Saw

LIZZIE UNDERWOOD

We never did have no trouble having enough to eat because my mother was one of the most finest cooks you ever saw. She'd go in the kitchen and take nothing, and when you set down at dinner, you don't know what you're going to get.

One year Mr. Limming, over there across the river, had lots of peaches and we canned a lot that summer. We had an old hack and one day we started down to the orchard and we saw ten or twelve trees with the prettiest yellow peaches on 'em. I told Mama, "Aren't those pretty. Let me jump out and get one or two." I got out and looked, and I said, "Mama, the ground's covered with 'em." There we was, giving a dollar a bushel for peaches. That was a whole lot then. We'd taken two or three peaches up to Mr. Limming's house.

Mama said, "Mr. Limming, what's the matter with those little peaches?"

He said, "Not a thing in the world." It'd been two years since he had farmed that part of the orchard. He had two crops of Alberta peaches. Early he had the big Albertas and something had happened to 'em and they got rid of 'em early. And it come a rain and the trees bloomed again.

Mama said, "Why don't you dry 'em?" He'd eaten dried peaches but he didn't know how to do it. So she said, "Do you care if we pick up a bucket off the ground and take 'em home and dry 'em and see what they're like?"

He said, "No, but don't get you a bucket. Get you a bushel basket, and I'll help you get 'em."

So we brought 'em home and Daddy had made a shed for sheep

that was not very high and it had new tin on it. Mama had some old sheets about wore out. And we put them sheets up on that shed and poured the peaches over easy on that hot tin, and in two or three days they was the prettiest things you ever saw. So when Mama got some fixed—we always had lots of hogs, butter and milk and eggs and things like that—she said she believed we'd go back and get some more peaches. She decided she'd take some of them peaches to Mr. Limming. She took him nearly a gallon bucket full of peaches after she'd dried 'em. He said they was the best peaches he believed he ever ate. I don't know how many trips we made, but we dried nearly two hundred pounds on the halves.

When we went to school, Mama would cook a great big pot of them peaches and make fried pies. Instead of frying 'em she'd put grease over 'em and put 'em in a big ol' pan and bake 'em. The kids got to where they tried to trade us out of our fried pies.

A Big Rattlesnake Was Coiled Up in the Fruit Ready to Strike

JIM POTEET

We used to buy dried fruit in a big box. Raisins, or apricots, peaches, or something like that. We'd break the top loose, and you could reach in there and bring out a handful of fruit. So Mama had the box in the kitchen and went in there to get some raisins. She started to raise that little lid there. She said she didn't know why, but she raised it a little and looked in. Usually she would just reach in with her hand and pull out a handful of fruit. But that morning she looked in first, and there was a rattlesnake there coiled up ready to strike. Can you imagine—a big rattlesnake coiled up in your fruit ready to strike!

Snakes were usually pretty bad during the years when we had lots of rats and mice. One year the rats just took that country over. They'd just gnaw a hole in the floor and come in the house or barn or wherever they wanted to. That's when the county agent came out there and made up a bunch of rat poison. We killed rats until you couldn't hardly live around there because of the smell.

We'd go in the kitchen after supper. We had a board sitting there just right, and we'd wait until after the supper dishes were done and wait about fifteen minutes. Then we'd go get that board and slap it over that hole so the rats couldn't get out of the kitchen, and then we'd kill those rats. That was our after dinner entertainment. They were rats, not mice. I went down there behind the barn one time with a shotgun in the daytime. They was just lined up there, and I killed five in one shot.

Sure Enough, Both Cats Fell in the Cistern and Drown

LEO E. CLEGG

I remember one time at home, we had a cistern full of water. Papa tried to keep a lid on it all the time, but we didn't always do it. Two big ol' tomcats got in a fight one mornin' just before we got up. All at once, I didn't hear 'em anymore, and I thought they went in the cistern. Sure enough, they both fell in the cistern and drown. But we didn't know both fell in, for we found only one.

Two or three days later the water got bad, and we knew what had happened. If we had brought them right out of the cistern when they fell in, the water wouldn't have been bad, but we didn't know there was two cats. We had to draw that whole cistern full of water out. It took us a day or so to draw out the water. No tellin' how much water was in that big ol' cistern.

One time we was livin' with my grandma in Rotan. She was takin' care of me and my sisters and our cousins. There was six of us kids. She took care of us while we went to school. She didn't want us to get sick on her with all that bunch of kids. So she took a quart jar of honey and mixed red pepper in it and made it real strong with red pepper. And ever' one of us had to take a teaspoonful of that honey with red pepper in it ever' night. It was supposed to keep us from takin' a cold. There wasn't any of us got sick that year, so I guess it worked.

"You're Going to Be Called Abigail!"

ABBIE WILLINGHAM MARTIN

When we first moved to Fisher County in about 1884, we found a grave on the place. It was a grave made in 1875. We knew whose grave it was, but we didn't know why it was there. The name was Levi Thomas, and it was carved on a broken wagon wheel. The date was Christmas, 1875. Later my daddy and granny and Uncle Jackson put a stone there. But they never found out who he was or why he was there or what he died of. They surmised he was a buffalo hunter. Papa tried as long as he lived to find out more about him. He advertised about him, but we never knew any more.

I'm so proud of my heritage. I was named for a Negro slave. She lived with us for many years after the Civil War. I have a picture of me with her when I was a small child. I'm sitting on her lap. They said that when they took us to the photographer, she said, "Mr. Picture Taker, would you put her little hand on top of my old hand." And that's what he did. You can see the picture today. Just like that. I've always cherished that. We called her Aunt Abbie.

They just named me Abbie, but when I went to Britain Training School, I had a Latin teacher that roomed next to me, and I loved her better than any teacher I ever had. She said, "I'm not going to have you called Abbie." She said, "I'm going to be an old maid all my life, and I never would have wanted to marry except I might have a daughter and name her Abigail. Don't let people call you by the short version. You're not going to be called Abbie anymore. You're going to be called Abigail." Right then I became Abigail. Any class I had, I was called Abigail.

I think I learned to read at home. My mama was very interested in our learning. Papa was too, and Papa kept up his study all his life. He studied more things. He studied medicine and the Bible and geology. He was always studying things. We sat around a dining table with a lamp in the middle, and while we got our lessons, Papa was studying right at the table with us. My father hired a number of Mexicans. He spoke Spanish and wrote it both.

Mama, of course, was patching blue jeans, overalls they called them then. I imagine that's what she was doing.

This Asafetidy Bag Smelled Awful

IRA HESTER

Asafetida—country folk said asafetidy—was the gum resin obtained from various Asiatic plants of the parsley family and was often used in folk medicine to repel disease. The foul smelling asafetida bag was believed to ward off colds, the flu, and certain other common ailments. It could be purchased at the drugstore and was placed on a string and tied around a child's neck. Other folk cures were also employed: a big dose of castor oil was given for constipation and a spoonful of kerosene mixed with honey or sugar was used to relieve croup.

Did you ever wear an asafetidy bag? Well, all I remember is this string tied around the neck and down here was this asafetidy bag. It smelled awful! You bought it. I just wonder if they were recommended by the doctor. It was used to keep off diseases and germs, you know. My mother always saw that we stayed in pretty good condition. So she was giving us a one-a-day pill, and my brother that was younger than me said he couldn't take it, and I said, "Well, give it to me, and I'll take it." I had already taken mine. So I took two, and I stayed in the peach orchard all that afternoon using the bathroom.

In the Wintertime, We Had to Wear Knit Underwear

BILL CLEVELAND

I remember when my oldest brother got his first pair of long pants. We laughed at him and Mama like to have whipped us. He wasn't going to wear 'em. And he was seventeen years old. In the wintertime, we had to wear knit underwear—union suits—they were called. In the summer, our mother just made our underwear out of whatever material she had—flour sacks or anything she could get. Everybody wore union suits as far back as I can remember—those old long things with buttons in the back with a flap or a slit.

"Poor Little Thing—Maybe Someday She'll Have Something Nice"

ABBIE WILLINGHAM MARTIN

Mama would say that, whenever the kids would play, that I never wanted to play anything but house and preaching. She said she'd look out her kitchen window and I'd be sitting on the cellar with pans and rags, and I'd have the lamps and lanterns polishing them. And the brass rim around the cedar water bucket, I'd be polishing it, too. Mama said she'd say to herself, "Poor little thing—maybe someday she'll have something nice."

When we were playing church, I wanted to do the preaching. One time Papa was breaking a mule to the wagon. You'd break a mule to the wagon with another animal that was already broken. The partner would be an old dead head, one who wouldn't cause any trouble. So Papa was breaking the mule and was driving around over the place, and he stopped the team and tied them up in the yard. I didn't know it was a wild mule there, so I gathered my congregation together—my younger brothers and sister and all the other children around. I got up in the back end of that wagon and began to preach. I got all excited and began waving my hands like that, and the team, or rather the mule, got scared and broke loose and ran away and tore up the wagon. Threw me out, too. I didn't use the wagon for a pulpit anymore for a while.

Anything with a Little Sweetening Was Good
THELMA BURK

When I was growing up, when we was out playing, we'd look for things to eat. We would go cactus berry hunting, or we'd look for gum wax from mesquite trees or pick algerita berries. We didn't have much candy and I guess anything with a little sweetening was good. Algerita berries was on a little hollylike bush. When the berries was ripe, they would be orange and tiny, maybe like a BB from an air rifle. We would sometimes thrash the bush and get enough to make a pie. It tasted real good. We'd put a sheet or something under the tree and get a nice amount for our pie. Sometimes when we walked through the hills, we would stop at the shittim trees and get the white wax from them and chew it. It was like gum wax from mesquite trees, but it was white and would not dissolve. It was more like chewing gum. You could chew on it for a long time.

I Was Real Careful in Seeing after My Gardening
DONO DARDEN

One year the grasshoppers ate the crops up. The next year was drought, and my grandfather, Mother's father, gave us 160 acres. But we starved out. We moved from there to Clyde in Callahan County, and Dad got a job as a Watkins man, you know, a peddler, for a couple of years. And that's where I learned to sell. We'd sell peaches, overripe peaches that fell off the trees. You'd put three in a little brown sack, you know. Put the one with the biggest soft spot on the bottom and the one with the most red, the most color on top.

One time I got a job setting out sweet potato plants for a Mrs. Brown for twenty-five cents, sunup 'til sundown. I was very careful to be there promptly at sunup. Well, I put out sweet potato plants all day. And then decided I had made all of the money I wanted. Mrs. Brown told me I made a good hand and gave me four extra plants. I planted 'em like she said. Heaped 'em up and drew water to pour on 'em with these long buckets we used to have to draw water. And I scraped up fertilizer out of horse lots and heaped around 'em. I raised two bushels of sweet potatoes from those four plants. I've never been able to do that since. But I was real careful, you know, in seeing after my gardening.

That's What the Big Boys Done to Get Rid of Albert's Lice
LIZZIE UNDERWOOD

One time the Ashton kids [name changed] somehow or other had got lice in their family. You know how white those nits are and how they showed on red hair. Boy, you could just see 'em workin'. They'd scratch their head an awful lot. When they'd scratch, a lot of 'em would fall off.

Well, one of the boys named Albert had 'em and someone told the teacher. The other kids didn't want to sit by him because he had lice. He had 'em awful bad. His hair had been cut and left short where the lice sure did show. Two of the bigger boys chewed to-bacco. They got some creosote dip and weakened it down with to-bacco juice enough that it'd kill the lice and not hurt Albert's head.

Well, the way they got the oil on Albert's head was they got him and another kid to wrestling. The one that kept the other on the ground the most got a quarter. Well, during the time, one of the big boys poured this oil on Albert's head and while they had him down one of 'em gave his head a pretty good shampooing. And when he got up, Albert said that somebody poured something on him. Jake said, "No, you just got over there where me and Harvey goes to spit." They said, "We'll rub it in good and then we'll wipe it off with a handkerchief." And that's what they done, and they got rid of his lice.

I Lived in the Feed-Sack Era

GRACE PHILLIPS

I lived in the feed-sack era. The W. Leo Daniel era. W. Leo Daniel was the leader of a country and western group—only then we called it a hillbilly band. His sponsor was a feed mill that sold chicken feed in printed feed sacks—fifty and hundred pound sacks. We didn't always have to wear the same dress all week because we usually made our clothes out of feed sacks. We were more prosperous then. Made good dress material. It usually took three feed sacks to make a dress for a woman or young girl, so if you had two sacks alike, you'd see if your neighbor had one to match. You'd trade around the community until you had enough alike to make whatever garment you wanted. But still we would have to come home and change clothes after school—after you'd have eaten about four biscuits. You'd stick your finger in and pour the biscuit full of syrup because you'd be so hungry you'd eat anything when you got home. Old cold fried potatoes or anything.

The Lifestyle Then Wasn't What It Is Now

LORENE HENDERSON

When you move the school, you lose the community. The church stayed here when the school was moved to Hobbs, but now the church is gone. Completely gone. Of course, a lot of families are gone, too. On this farm across the road, there was four families lived on that half section. There's nobody living on it now. They all made a living, too. Of course, the lifestyle then wasn't what it is now. Then you could milk your cow, kill your hogs and chickens, and raise a garden. When you have that, there isn't too much you need. You could take your crops to town and buy whatever else you needed.

If I Had Another Life to Live, I'd Teach Again

RECOLLECTIONS OF TEACHERS

Part II contains the oral histories of teachers who taught in one- and two-room schools in rural West Texas in the first half of the twentieth century. Occasionally, as with Josie Baird, the narrator also has an account in part I, having been both a pupil and a teacher in rural schools. These recollections of what teaching was like in earlier days give valuable insight into the history of education. Here are the pioneers who "stood by the stuff" before custodians, book clerks, school nurses, cafeteria staff, and conference periods were considered basic. A tribute to their unflagging spirit was Picola Foreman's assertion, "If I were younger, I'd do it again."

Teachers in rural schools were little different from their urban counterparts in intent and purpose. Both had lessons to plan, pupils to teach, and "pranksters" to discipline. However, one can imagine the challenge of teaching all subjects in grades one through eight to a diverse room of pupils, some almost as old as the teacher, while keeping the fire going, the water bucket filled, and the floor swept. It would seem rural teachers could give a firm "Yes!" to the question Maud Arnold Bailey was asked at each pay period, "Miss Maud, do you swear you've earned the money?"

More fortunate were teachers in two-room schools where pupils were divided into primary and upper grades. Here one had a cohort with whom to share the professional load as well as an adult companion with whom to fellowship.

The interviews reveal teachers were aware of their limitations in dealing with such a variety of ages and levels, but they usually did not complain. As summarized by Ina Cowan, "In that school we had 108 children for two teachers, and I had 58 in my class. Looking at it now, you couldn't get around, but it never did dawn on me to do anything except to get busy and grab it." That was the philosophy that governed most of the teachers interviewed—"Get busy and grab it!"

CHAPTER SEVEN

✵

I Was the First Person
in My Family to Get a Degree

TRAINING AND EMPLOYMENT

What were the qualifications for becoming a teacher in the early rural schools of West Texas? The answer is given by several teachers in this chapter: you had to be eighteen, have completed seventh or eighth grade, and have passed a teacher's examination administered by the state of Texas. It was helpful when looking for a job to have completed college courses. School trustees often gave preference to those with more experience and education, but college credits were not required. The Gilmer–Aikin Bill, passed by the Texas Legislature in 1949, required that teachers have a four-year degree and certification. Prior to that time, some larger districts hired only teachers with degrees, as recounted by Bessie Cleveland.

    People who intended to make a career of teaching usually continued their college work by correspondence, on Saturdays, or during the summer until the degree was granted. Interviewees spoke of leaving home long before daybreak and driving great distances to the nearest college in order to attend classes.

    Employment entailed being interviewed by all trustees, and this sometimes meant going from house to house, or as Fila Campbell remembered, from field to field, to talk with the local trustees. However, when the job offer came, especially during the depression era of the 1930s when jobs were scarce, there was great celebration. Imagine Louise Standard's exhilaration when one of the trustees shouted to her after a board meeting, "Louise, you've looked long enough. You're going to teach school!"

"W-e-l-l, Miss Josie, You Was Elected"

JOSIE BAIRD

At that time teachers could take a board examination, and if you could pass the subject matter, you could teach, if you were eighteen years old or older. That summer I went to West Texas Normal School in Canyon. It was the review of all the subjects you ever heard of in grade school and high school, plus the extras, like child psychology—you can imagine being ready for child psychology—and how to teach reading, and maybe how to teach something else like penmanship. I think I took a test over thirty-odd subjects. It was given at Canyon at the end of the term, but it was graded down in Austin. If you were of age and you made the score, you got your certificate sometime soon after that.

I taught that year to help get my sister Delila out of high school. It was a hard year at home, so I helped out. Cotton crops didn't make anything much, and cattle didn't bring much. The next year we were both planning to go to school. Daddy had said he hoped we

County Line School, Fisher County, with teachers Josie and Delilah Baird, 1927. Miss Delilah, with her hands folded, is on the far left and her older sister, Miss Josie, is on the right. Seven of the interviewees are pictured here: Leo Clegg, Clifford Clegg, Henry Poteet, Mollie Hudnall, Josie Baird, Naomi Vinyard, and Eunice Huckaby. Courtesy Luther Bryan Clegg

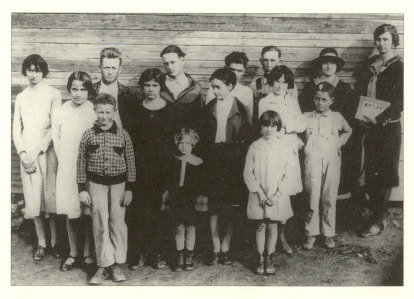

made enough that year. We made a good cotton crop, but it brought nothing practically. So we sent Delila to school, and I decided to teach a year. I hadn't intended to teach any more until I had some college work, but I had a certificate for another year so I came down to town. We didn't have a car, and I came down to town on the mail car. Anybody that lived out in the country, if they wanted to go to town, they just went with the mailman. I don't know if Daddy paid him something or not. He or Mother probably took me over to meet the mail car.

I came to town, and the people I stayed with during the last year of high school, I went up and spent the night with them. Daddy told me there was a man he knew that ran a service car. Daddy said, "You go down to Bob Smith and tell him I said to take you wherever you need to go." I was going to Roby to the courthouse to find out how many vacancies there were in the county, which is what you did then. They would give you a list of the schools that still needed teachers and what they needed them for. So Mrs. Vaughn—the lady I was staying with—she wouldn't let me get the service car. She took me to Roby.

They needed a teacher over at Palava, so the next day I was going to get Mr. Smith to take me over there. That's where the superintendent recommended that I go. But Mrs. Vaughn insisted that she would take me. She said that, if I didn't get the job over at Palava, she knew that they needed a teacher over at Capitola. So we went to Palava first. The county superintendent said that they were having the board meeting that day and that I should go right on over.

That was real strange going in before these men, not knowing a one of them, and they didn't know me from Adam. They asked me all kinds of questions about how much education I had and so forth. I didn't have any college work, except for one summer course, and I just had one year of teaching experience. The other girl that they were considering had two years of college. They took us one at a time, and I don't know what she told them.

When they were through with my interview, they told me to wait for a little while and they would make a decision. We waited out in the car, and one of the men came out and told us that they couldn't decide between us, but they would let us know in a few days. That was a way of not hurting either one of us, I guess. Mrs. Vaughn had a little more experience. She had taught school once when she was younger. So she said, "Well, we're going on over to Sweetwater to shop for a little while, so if you think you will have your mind made up by then, we'll stop by on our way back."

He said that would be all right. See, they were going to have a board meeting afterward. So we went ahead and went to Sweetwater—we hadn't intended to go to Sweetwater, or at least I hadn't.

We came back by and one of the men who was a trustee ran a filling station, and he was going to tell me the decision when we came back. He walked around the car, looking down at his toes, and I just knew he was going to tell me I didn't have the job. Mrs. Vaughn had already decided that the other girl had more college than I did so would probably get hired. So he just walked on around the car, and said real slowlike, "W-e-l-l, Miss Josie, you was elected." He was just seeing how I would react.

That year I lived in a teacherage. We built our own fires there. We got ninety dollars a month, except the principal, I think she got a hundred. We got ninety dollars a month, plus two and a half for building our own fires and carrying our ashes out. I just taught there one year, and then I went back to school.

She Knew the Bank Was Going to Go Broke

HENRY T. POTEET

Since we lived way out in the country, I had to go away to Hamlin to high school. I was to help with a man's daughters and his son and be their big brother to protect them. And I would go to school and would help with the chores. Then the next year I went to a consolidated school and stayed in a home where I milked cows morning and evening and went to school.

The last part of the year, I fixed it up to stay in the old college in Hamlin and go to the public school. Then, I had fourteen and a half credits. It took sixteen to graduate. Well, I stayed out and trapped the next spring. What should I do and where should I go? So I decided in the middle of the year, January, to sell my horse and my saddle and let my brother sell my spurs and I'd go to college. I headed off to Bethany in Oklahoma. I hitchhiked. I got to Seymour the first night, stayed in a hotel for a little bit of nothing, and I think on to Walters, Oklahoma, the next night. And on to Bethany. *Three days to go three hundred miles!*

I got up there to school and I went to the bank, and I said, "I want to write a check for my money to come into this bank."

Mrs. John Stockton said, "Do you have to do that? Can't you wait?"

I said, "No, I should do it now." She knew the bank was going to go broke. That was the year of the depression when so many did. So she persuaded me to write the check for just half of it. And Monday morning the bank closed. It was devastating, but I only lost half of my money, thanks to her.

I had been in Bethany for about six weeks, and Dr. Willis Dobson, who later became an English professor, was the registrar then. He called me in and said, "Mr. Poteet"—like he talked—he said, "Mr. Poteet, you didn't graduate from high school."

I said, "I know it, but I'm doing all right on these college subjects." He looked at me, and I looked at him. I said, "Can't you count some of this I'm doing back on that and let it finish it?"

He said, "I guess so." That's the last I heard. To this day I don't have a high school diploma even though I have two college degrees. Here's the one thing I was taught: If you will try and learn, you can make it, and I think I've been learning all my life.

I taught one year. I had to teach on an emergency certificate. They said you'll have to have a regular certificate before the year's out. They could pay me every month but they'd hold up the last check until I got my certificate. I took American and Texas government from Hardin-Simmons by correspondence so I could qualify in Texas. The county superintendent gave me the test, and he sent it in. Well, at the end of the year, I was going up to Oklahoma to get married. So I went down to the county superintendent and he said, "Yes, I've got your certificate." But he said, "Look here." In Austin, they'd dated it to end before it began. So I never had a valid certificate. He said, "It's all right anyway," and he gave me my check. I wish I'd have kept that certificate. I'd have it framed now.

There Were More Than Twenty-Five Applications That Year

LOUISE SMITH CALLAN

My twin sister Lois and I taught two years at County Line School. My brother Dewey had a grocery store in Rotan, and he knew a lot of people who lived out there so we placed our application, and he talked with them. At that time, you know, it was the beginning of the Great Depression. I think there were more than twenty-five applications that year, and many of them had degrees and teaching experience. So I guess we were just lucky because we only had two years of college. Later on we taught school for several years and did our work in the summer and took extension courses. We went to Boulder, Colorado, and to TCU in Fort Worth some. Finally we got the degree.

I don't think I would have taken the job out at County Line if Lois hadn't been hired too. We were very close, being twins. We looked so much alike that sometimes people couldn't tell us apart. One time my boyfriend came to see me and when we got ready to go, Lois walked on out with him. She said she got in the car, and she just died laughing. He didn't know which one was which. When we went to Hardin-Simmons College, we were Mike and Ike, look-alike. We dressed alike. We never wore anything unless the other one wore it. That was our fun. At County Line school, I was always Lois and she was always Louise. The kids called us Miss Lois and Miss Louise later, but I believe out there they just called us Lois and Louise. We were so near the ages of some of the big kids.

I Took the Examination for the Certificate

FILA CAMPBELL

I graduated from high school in 1917. I started teaching at Center about four miles west of Roby. I was just out of high school. My dad had promised to send me to college, but he decided he couldn't or didn't want to or something. He said, "If you'll go down in the cellar this summer and study, you can get away from all the children." And I did and took the examination for the certificate, and got a certificate for four years.

I got a job at Center and had to go out and talk to the trustees. I went from house to house, or rather from field to field. I wasn't afraid to teach. That first year I made forty dollars a month, and the school year was six or seven months. It was a coincidence, but I stayed with my husband's people. Of course, he wasn't my husband at the time. I didn't know him, for he was away in college. I walked about a mile to school each day.

I Was the First Person in My Family to Get a Degree
BESSIE CLEVELAND

When I graduated from high school, I went to college at Gainesville Junior College, but I had the misfortune of having typhoid fever, so I didn't go the rest of that year. They were good to me. I went for nine weeks, but they let me come back to finish that year. Then the next fall I was going to Wesleyan in Fort Worth. I went in to get my physical from the family doctor, and he said, "No, you can't go." He said, "What you've got to do is stay out in the sun as much as you can. That typhoid fever has done something, and you shouldn't try to go to school." I just didn't feel real good.

I took correspondence courses, three of them, and got my first teaching certificate. I didn't take any courses in reading. I didn't teach for a while because schools that depended on the state for money had to hire teachers with degrees. I went back and enrolled in school in 1942 and took three courses by going to McMurry in Abilene on Saturdays. But by then the war had started and teachers were scarce so I got the job at Pleasant Valley. I was twenty-seven then.

I only taught at Pleasant Valley two years. When I started, I got $97 a month. At that time we had nine months of school, so I got less than $900 for the year. I got the job there because I knew all the people and had lived there always. When they couldn't find a lower grade teacher, my cousin was a board member and knew I had a certificate. So he told the board, "I'll tell you something. I'm going to resign." Your kinfolks couldn't be on the board at that time if you were a teacher. He said, "Now, I'll resign and then tell you who you might get until you can find a teacher." He suggested that I might teach, and then he walked out the door. That happened on Friday evening, and the board met again on Saturday. They decided to hire me and called me.

The first two years I taught, the kids called me Bessie. Just Bessie. I had grown up in the community and taught them in Sunday school, so I was just Bessie. After two years, I thought I needed more money, so Roby needed a first-grade teacher, and the county superintendent, Mr. Dalton, told the superintendent at Roby about me. The superintendent came to interview me and gave me the job. I got $110 there.

Starting out like I did, it was a privilege to me. When I finally got my degree, I'd been out of school ten years. I went back in the summer and took courses by traveling to Abilene on Saturdays. I had just one aunt that was proud of me. All the rest just took me for granted. She couldn't hardly stand it because she said, "Nobody shows you any charity. We're proud of you." I was the first person in my family to get a degree.

She Turned to Her Husband and Said, "She'll Do, Daddy"

ALINE DARDEN NORTHRUP

How I came to be at County Line was that I was teaching at Dowell, and they weren't going to let teachers teach anymore if we didn't have a degree. Some of us met at Roby, and the county superintendent told us that he had in his hand a note from some of the trustees out at County Line, and they needed two teachers. So I went home and got the car, and my friend Bernice and I went out there and

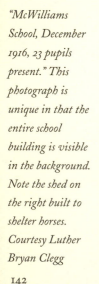

"McWilliams School, December 1916, 23 pupils present." This photograph is unique in that the entire school building is visible in the background. Note the shed on the right built to shelter horses. Courtesy Luther Bryan Clegg

142

applied. We went around to see all the trustees. Oh man, we felt like we had been on trial. They usually got around to asking how old we were, and if we were fixing to get married, and where we went to school, and things like that. I know when I went to see one of the trustees, his wife was standing over there listening, and finally she said, "Well, I'm going to ask a question." I told her all right. She wanted to know something about methods of teaching. And I told her what I planned to do for reading and arithmetic and things like that, and she was satisfied. So she just turned to her husband and said, "She'll do, Daddy." Bernice and I both got hired. I got paid sixty whole dollars a month for eight months.

So we were hired for that year. We were hired for the next year, too, but Bernice got a job in New Mexico. So they had to postpone the opening of school until they got someone else hired. There was somebody on the school board that had to resign, and somebody had to take his place before one of his relatives could have the job. You weren't supposed to hire your kinfolks if you were a trustee.

I Had Grown up in the Community, So When They Needed a Teacher I Was Hired

OVESTA McCLESKEY CLAY

I started teaching in Frankell, in the same school I attended as a pupil. I made the whole sum of sixty dollars at that time. When I first taught there we had four or five teachers and a superintendent. That was in the early 1930s. It was during an oil boom and Stephens County was full of people. I had grown up in the community, so when they needed a teacher I was hired. By that time I had finished three years of college. They tell stories on me that I paddled some of the children. I don't know whether I did or not because that's been a long time ago. I disciplined those children any way I saw fit.

There was a fellow that lived down in the canyon below where the school was. He came up to school one day. I had his little girl in my room, and he was not happy about her grades or something. They said I just lit into him. Of course, I knew all those people as well as you could know anybody. The superintendent was telling Daddy about it later. He said, "I thought I'd better go and see if she needed any help, but after listening to her outside the door, I decided I needed to go in there and help the man instead." I guess I was really giving it to him. Back in those days it was a different world.

I rode to school on the school bus, and sometimes I even drove it. In those days we didn't have paved roads, and when it rained, Mr. Johnson would get out and dig the mud off the wheels and I would drive while he was doing that.

I got married and quit teaching for a while, but during World War II, when my husband Comer was overseas, Frankell School had dwindled until it was just one room. There was about a dozen children going there then. They came to me and said would I please come; they needed a teacher. Well, I had a baby at that time about six months old so I hired a neighbor woman to come in and help me with the baby. I taught there for three months in that little school. It was a different place entirely from when I had taught there earlier. The area had dropped in population so that the school went from four or five teachers to only one. That's the way the whole community was. It had once been a thriving community and now it had dwindled to a handful.

I Said, "Well, If I Can't Teach It, It Won't Cost You Anything"

MAUD ARNOLD BAILEY

When I went to get a job, I went to see the trustees before school started. One of them said, "Well, we had a young man here last year. The older boys run him off." He said, "I'm satisfied you've forgot more than he ever knew. If you're willing to try it, we'd like for you to have this school."

I said, "Well, if I can't teach it, it won't cost you anything." I taught school throughout the year and had no trouble at all.

I got paid a voucher. We had to make reports at the end of the month and turn those reports into the county school superintendent, and he, in turn, gave us a voucher for our pay. It wasn't very much, seventy dollars, I think. Then we would take this voucher to the bank. I'd go to the banker at Rising Star and I knew him well. He was a notary. The voucher had to be notarized, and when I'd take it in, instead of him giving me the oath that they were supposed to, he'd say, "Miss Maud, do you swear that you've earned the money?"

I always got a voucher. I never had to accept script. That's where you don't get your full pay—you don't get the face value of the script, you know. That happened here at Cisco, and the superintendent and his wife had a new baby, and they named her Scrippy.

Miss Weaver Said, "We're Going to Be Professional!"

INA DINGUS COWAN

Really, I didn't intend to teach. It was back in the 1930s. I had a little two-year-old boy. The grandmothers took care of him while I was at school. But I was just going to teach until we got on our feet again and the crops were better. But Miss Weaver—she and I taught together for several years—would have nothing of that. We were going to be professional, she said. And professional teachers do this and professional teachers do that. We were going to be professional, she said, so I was going to school. You wouldn't believe it, but I never went to college a nine months' term in my life. I took all the extension courses I could get, all the correspondence I could get, and in summer drove from here to Abilene on unpaved roads. I would leave my house at four thirty in the morning to meet seven o'clock classes in Abilene. They would let us come Monday, Wednesday, and Friday. We had to make up some work for those other two days, but we attended those three days. They counted it. Summer school was twelve weeks in those times. And we did that for twelve long weeks. Of course, I got to loving it. I just loved the teaching and the children.

In 1935, when the subject of teacher retirement first came up I was opposed to it. I said, "No!" I wasn't going to give the teacher retirement three percent of my salary. I could spend those three dollars myself. I never had any idea of retiring, ever. Storing money so you could retire? Why, that was the most absurd idea I ever heard. I just wanted my whole check. Now Miss Weaver and I had this special kind of relationship after all those years teaching together. I admired her greatly. I would do exactly what she said if she would tell me. We each had respect for the other fellow. She permitted me to think what I wanted to think, and I permitted her to see it her way. We two sometimes didn't agree, but I never had a cross feeling toward her nor she toward me, that I knew of. So I said I wasn't going to join the retirement program. "Now, listen, Miss Cowan," she said, "This is the *professional* thing to do, and we are

145

professional teachers. We are going to join the retirement program."

I said, "Well, okay then." So we joined it early, in 1935. It wasn't until 1938 that they started making all teachers join the teacher retirement system. Every teacher who started teaching in 1938 or later had to join. When I did retire, they reached back and paid me for every year I had taught. That was one and one-half of our salary times how many years you had taught, and I had taught forty-two years. So now I say, "Thank you, Miss Weaver!" every time I get that check. That's what I live on. She was a woman ahead of her time.

Nobody Ever Came into the Job As Ignorant and Unprepared As I Was

BARGY FIELDS HARGROVE

I began teaching at seventeen years old, bluffing for eighteen. I graduated from high school in 1932. So I taught in 1933 and '34. I taught with Marjorie Smith from Rotan, and she quit in the middle of the year. I don't remember the little girl's name that took her place. However, she got off to a bad start because, when she sent in her application, she said that she could teach the children tap dancing. That just didn't go over well in that community. They didn't want any tap dancing.

When I went for the interview, they asked how old I was. I told them I'd be eighteen by the time school started. School had never started before October, but that year they sprung one on me. School started in September, and I had to tell them that I did not have a certificate and couldn't get it until I was eighteen, but if they would let me go ahead and start, I wouldn't ask to get my money until I got my certificate. When I got my certificate, they could pay me. They said it was okay, so I got to keep my job.

Nobody ever came into the job as ignorant and unprepared as I was. I had taken two courses in education, and I came out of there wondering why on earth was I there, and what was that about except I couldn't get a certificate without it. Nobody had even bothered to teach me about lesson plans. I think they brought up the subject once. But nobody showed me what it was all about. So I came in without a lesson plan. Nothing! The county superintendent had furnished me with a list and sent the books out—each book the kids were supposed to have. Then I had to figure out just what you were supposed to do with each one of those books!

I Had to Go out and Talk to the Trustees

FORRESTER PRICE

I taught at Bitter Creek, a little one-room schoolhouse over in Mulberry Canyon in Nolan County. Bitter Creek was the creek where the town of Sweetwater got their drinking water. It's over across the mountain southeast of Sweetwater. It was the fall of 1928. That was the last year they had a school at Bitter Creek. There were nine of us in my family. I was the youngest of the nine, and I had a sister who was the oldest of the nine, and she taught school the first year they had school at Bitter Creek, and I taught the last year.

We were farmers, and it was important to us that we should go to college. It was that or be a farmwife for the rest of my life. I always thought I'd like to be a nurse. It was one of my older brothers that encouraged me to go to college. He was a teacher and come to Roby as a coach, then worked himself up to principal, and finally superintendent. My older sister was a teacher and he was a teacher.

I finished high school at Trent in 1927 and went on to Abilene Christian College. I got my teaching certificate and I started teaching there at Bitter Creek. I taught one year there and came to Roby in the fall of 1929. After I came to Roby, I went to school every summer until I got my permanent certificate. I never did get my degree, but I taught enough years to get a permanent certificate. I don't remember how much money I made at Bitter Creek, but the first year I came to Roby I made seventy dollars a month. It went as far then, nearly, as big salaries do now.

I got my job at Bitter Creek because the county superintendent recommended me. Of course, I had to go out and talk to the trustees. You just had to go out and tell them how long you'd gone to school and such. I had to go to each trustee's house. It was an ordeal, especially when you were out in the country and had to go from place to place. I didn't have a car, but I guess someone took me around.

I Had No Idea of Making a Teacher,
But Decided I Would Try It

BESSIE DAVIDSON

After I finished high school and got my diploma, I taught two years at Kelley. My first certificate that I got, I just got information on what I was supposed to take tests on. I took a test and got a second grade temporary certificate. So the next two summers I went to Canyon—that was the nearest place that specialized in teaching—and got a first grade certificate.

When I finished high school, I had no idea of making a teacher. But that summer, I was staying over on the farm and one of the trustees came over and asked if I wanted to teach at Kelley. I said, "I'm not a teacher yet."

He said, "Well, you can get a certificate. I'd really like to have you to teach."

I didn't think I wanted to teach, but after the trustee left, my father said, "Why don't you do that? You might like to teach." Well, I thought it over, so I taught in the two-teacher school for two years. The first year I taught, I took the first four grades. One of the young men in the community was the principal. And so I found out I liked it. We just had a seven-month school because they never started school until cotton picking was over. They picked cotton out of the boles then rather than pulled the boles off the stalk.

The next year I taught, they built the principal a teacher's cottage, and they put up a windmill. I stayed at home just like I did when I was going to school all the time. I was close by. Anyway, I didn't much like the principal, and he didn't like me too well, either. I decided I wasn't going to teach the next year.

There was a little school called Kessler not too far from our farm. Homer Kessler had been the teacher, but by this time, he had a family of children. When the town of Dodson came in, a railroad was built to Wellington, and we were just half a mile from this railroad. And they couldn't find a teacher. They had built a schoolhouse just about a mile down from a switch they had at a little building by the railroad. So since Mr. Kessler didn't want to teach, he asked me to teach over there, so I decided I would try it. It was a one-teacher school.

It was quite different from the one-teacher school that I went to when I started. The building was new, the furniture was all new,

148

there were blackboards and everything. And instead of having a big stove out in the middle of the room, they had a big stove in the back with a jacket around it. Everything was new and nice in the building. I never did have but fifteen or sixteen pupils. And out of that group, I had four or five or more Kesslers. The older Kessler men were brothers and had children who were getting up to about the eighth grade and were getting ready to go to school in Wellington. They were quite interesting to teach.

I will tell this one event about my getting to the school. I always loved horses, and I had a horse, and that was one of our fads to ride horseback in those days. I went down to see the school and get ready for the school children to come. So I rode my horse, and I thought that was the way I would come to school because we only had one car in our family. When I got ready to come home, I started to get on this horse. I never did get on her; she would move around and around. Each time I would try to get on her, she would move to the side. I finally gave up, and I had to lead her home.

She Didn't Know Buttermilk from Salt

CARL HENDRIX

I graduated from Commerce High School in 1915. I was twenty-one years old in the fall after I graduated. My father's health broke down, and he thought a change would be good for him, so we went to West Texas. We had a section and a half of land. I applied to teach at Grady School but Ellen Kelley and a girl named Amanda, that I later married, already had the jobs, so I farmed for two years. I broke ninety acres of land. Ellen Kelley, the teacher I mentioned, was a lady who lost her leg—I think it was her left leg—to a rattlesnake bite. The doctor who had doctored her went off to a meeting somewhere, and he evidently forgot to tell some other doctor to see after her. He left the leg bound and circulation was cut off, so they had to take the leg off. She was living near Coleman and decided to come to West Texas in about 1916.

Grady School was located about eight miles west of Rotan and about a mile north on the main road that went from Hobbs to Rough Creek. It was a two-room building separated by doors. You could open it all up and slide those doors back and have it all in one big room. The building served as a church and Sunday school rooms as well as a public school. There was no denomination. They didn't have any regular pastor.

The way I got my first job as a teacher was through my wife. It was unusual for a husband and wife to teach in the same school. As I said, Grady was a two-teacher school and my wife Amanda had been teaching there for several years before we were married. Well, the year we married, she was principal. Ellen Kelley had taken a job somewhere else, and this year that I'm talking about, there was another girl in the community who taught with Amanda, but she didn't know buttermilk from salt. That year they had to cut their school short for some reason. The trustees told Amanda that they wanted her to be principal the next year. It was going to be the last year for the school because they were going to be consolidated with Hobbs. The trustees said, "We want you to be the principal and you select the person you want to teach with, but we hope it will be Carl."

She said, "Oh, I think it will be." And it was. She was my principal, and I was teaching the little kids, and they just loved me to death.

Before school started we had to go to Roby for the Teacher's Institute. It lasted several days, I don't remember, three days or maybe a week. We had lectures and that sort of thing. Everybody in there had something to do. I remember I was to tell them about magazines. I had gotten some together. I had to borrow some because I didn't have any. But they never did get to me. I was tickled I never did have to speak. That let me off the hook.

"Louise, You're Going to Teach School— You've Looked Long Enough"

LOUISE STANDARD

Mr. Bolter was the county superintendent, and he came to me to ask me to teach at the little one-room school at Mountain View. My daddy was a trustee. Mr. Bolter said, "Floyd, I'm going to ask you to resign tonight. I want the rest of these trustees to elect Louise as the teacher for Mountain View. You'll have to resign."

Dad said, "What if I refuse?"

Mr. Bolter said, "I don't think you will. I'm bigger than you are."

Later that night, Mr. Bolter came down our street and flashed his lights across our bedroom at about 11:30. He yelled, "Louise, Louise, you got it! You got it!"

I said to my husband, "Max, That's Mr. Bolter's voice. What on earth is he talking about?" I grabbed a housecoat.

My husband said, "Don't you open that door!"

I said, "You know it's Mr. Bolter." I got my housecoat on, and I said, "Mr. Bolter?"

He stepped out of the car, and the moon was shining real bright when he came on up on the porch. He said, "Louise, you're going to teach school next year at Mountain View. You've looked long enough." I'd been out of high school one year.

Two years earlier when I was in high school, we had music up in the music room. We girls liked to go up to the music room and dance at noon. I had this friend who was teaching me to dance. Mr. Bolter was the superintendent then and had asked us not to go up to the music room during lunch hour, but we'd sneak up there anyway sometimes and dance. He said one day, "The next person I catch in the music room during lunch hour is going to get a whipping." Well, he caught us. We heard his footsteps, and they stopped. He turned around and went on and got his bell. He gave us plenty of time to get down the steps and get out of sight. So we got out of sight and got in line and marched in. And there wasn't anything said about it.

Well, when I opened this little school at Mountain View, on opening day, Mr. Bolter came out and made a little speech for my students. I followed him to the door to tell him good-bye. He shook his finger at me and he said, "The first time you catch one of those kids in the music room dancing, you give them a whipping." He smiled and left. I realized then that I hadn't put anything over on him.

You'd Get Your Job by Going from Trustee to Trustee
MITTIE McKENZIE GEESLIN

I taught school in Mills County, ten miles north of the town of Goldthwaite, which was the county seat. I didn't teach school in town. I graduated from high school in 1917, and then I took a review, and I just got a second grade certificate, which meant I could teach through grade seven. I didn't have any ambitions to teach high school.

151

However, I did teach eighth grade if a student came and wanted to go to eighth grade. Why, I even taught Latin a little bit. You know, one student.

I started teaching in the fall of 1918. You'd get your job by going from trustee to trustee and talking to all of them. That was cotton country. It was the year of the drought, and the year of the war. School started that year the thirtieth of September, which was early for a country school to start. Of course, that was cotton country then, but it isn't now.

The day before school was to start, I started sneezing at noon. The next morning I got up, and oh, I felt so bad. I couldn't go to school. First day of school; I was heartbroken. I was taking the flu. It was the bad flu of 1918. So I went home, and I stayed two weeks before I came back to school. By that time, the family I stayed with had moved across the field, so I walked. Earlier, I was close to the school, and that's the reason I got that boarding place, because it was not too far. But now I walked across a muddy field. About a mile, or a mile and a half maybe. When I was sick, we just turned out school. I was the only teacher. One teacher. So then we came back and started over. There were about twenty or twenty-five students, I think.

The second year I taught in another little school and stayed with my brother. I got the whole sum of fifty-five dollars that time. It was a school called Cedar Knob. At the end of that year in December, they didn't know whether they would get state aid or not. So the county judge, who was the county superintendent ex officio, said, and the trustees did too, "If you can find another school, do it. We don't know whether we will get state aid, and we're out of money, and if you can find another school, do it." They were in need of teachers then, so I got a school out on the Colorado River at Hannah Valley, got eighty dollars a month. But they didn't have enough money to run but for four months. We didn't start 'til January the first, you see.

After I'd been teaching at Hannah Valley a few days, Cedar Knob called me back and said their state aid came, and would I come back and take my school. I was boarding at a trustee's home, and he said, "No." Cedar Knob told me they turned me loose. I felt complimented that they would offer it back to me. Well, I said, "No, I can't come back to Cedar Knob. The trustees and the county superintendent both told me to go on and find a school if I could, and so that's what I did."

I came up to Tarleton for summer school. I worked on my permanent primary certificate. I went one summer in Denton, and I went to Tarleton three summers. And I taught every winter.

I married in 1924. My husband was married to his first wife who died of the flu epidemic and left a two-month-old baby. The first time I saw the child, he was two years old. We started going together. He worked out at Star, and he boarded diagonally across the street from us, so we started courting. But we couldn't get married because of the depression. It wasn't really a depression; just hard times. Hard times—jobs were hard to get—so we waited three years. I wore this ruby ring three years. That was my diamond. And then we married in 1924, and that was the end of my teaching. Except the little boy was five years old by that time. I taught him first grade at home, because children didn't start then until they were seven. And his birthday came in October, and we didn't have the money to pay tuition on him. So I taught him first grade. He always made the honor roll in school.

Of All Who Took the Examination, I Was the Only One That Passed

VICTOR WOMACK

My folks came to McCauley in Fisher County in 1906 when I was eight years old. McCauley at that time was a pretty good town. We had a school with three or four teachers. My father was a doctor. He was one of three doctors there, and they had two drugstores all in McCauley. McCauley is nothing now. Nothing there. I graduated from high school in Royston, a few miles from McCauley. My father had a drugstore there where he practiced medicine. I graduated in 1914, and there were only two girls and I in the graduating class. They wanted to teach school, so they decided they'd take this examination for a teacher's certificate. They made some preparatory studies, of course, so I did the same thing they did, and I went to take the examination. I never intended to teach. Of the twenty-some-odd people who took the examination, I was the only one that passed. So I got a second grade certificate, when I was sixteen years old. That summer I went to Stamford College in Stamford, Texas, and got my first grade certificate.

My father was an asthmatic and he couldn't do much practice because of his health. We went out to Hobbs and he practiced out there. Hobbs was a two-teacher school then. There was a man from Fort Stockton visiting us out at Hobbs, and he knew I had a certificate. He said they needed a teacher out at a little school named Carmel in Pecos County and suggested I contact the trustees. I decided I would. I wrote to them and told them my qualifications and they employed me sight unseen. I went out there to teach and I think I had fifteen students. The school was out in a pasture about a mile from the ranch house where I boarded.

In Pecos County the teachers had to gather for about a week before school started for training. It was called a Teacher's Institute, and I went to Fort Stockton for that. I don't think I learned anything at the institute. The county superintendent was in charge.

"I Aim to Make Teachers out of My Kids. That A-way They Won't Have to Do No Work!"

STELLA GIPSON POLK

My oldest sister Jennie and her husband Lee taught in a little two-teacher school when he was called into the army. I was sixteen years old, so I took the examination to become a teacher. When Lee left for the army, I came to help Jennie teach. She moved into Lee's room with the bigger kids, and I taught the younger ones. Only Jennie couldn't teach algebra. The trustees decided that the three boys taking algebra should come to my room for algebra after my pupils were dismissed at three.

Most trustees were farmers or ranchers and seemed embarrassed to do business with a woman. Hiring a teacher was a necessary evil to them. If I asked what or how they thought I should teach, they'd say, "You just teach the school, we'll do the plowing." Before I could be paid, I had to have a voucher signed by two trustees. At the end of the month, I'd send my voucher for the trustees to sign home with their children. Only two signatures were required, but I always got the signatures of all three trustees. I didn't want to show favoritism.

I remember once that one of the trustees was very different from the others. He had a chip on his shoulder. At the county judge's office on the day he was to sign my contract, he never looked at me once. After he signed it, he walked by me and said, "I aim to make teachers out of my kids. That a-way they won't have to do no work!"

When my daddy was trustee at Mason, they made the rule that no married woman could teach, and I know my daddy just blew his top because he argued that a married woman made a good teacher. But they didn't allow them then. I can remember that well.

The Trustees Asked Her to Send a Picture of Herself

COMER CLAY

When I first started teaching, I taught at Wylie, a small school just south of Abilene. Years earlier my mother had taught school before I was born. She was born in Kentucky and was named Valley Maude Hill, but they just called her Valley. I think she started teaching before 1900. I know she taught one year in Evant and then in Hamilton. In 1902, she applied for a job teaching in Merkel, out west of Abilene. The trustees wrote her and asked for her to send a picture of herself. She didn't have one to send them so she wrote back and said, "I don't have a picture, but I'll vouch for my looks!" She was a pretty woman and maybe a little brash, but she got the job. She went out to Merkel to teach, and that's where she met my father. They were married and lived in Abilene where I was born.

CHAPTER EIGHT

❧

I Tell You,
It Pays to Teach Phonics

TEACHING AND METHODOLOGY

Whether a teacher had eight children or fifty-eight, there were certain things that had to be done. Providing the curriculum was a major concern. What to teach and how to have time for all pupils was continually on the minds of teachers. As Bessie Davidson lamented, "Here you're trying to teach a first-grader to read and an eighth-grader algebra, and every point in between." More often than not, teachers taught the way they were taught, for many of them had attended small rural schools. They followed the examples of their teachers, hoping "to make everything come out."

When problems arose beyond the teacher's ability to solve, there were sources available for help. The trustees, although often stern and unbending, wished to uphold community standards and were quick to assist teachers mired in difficulty. Fila Campbell related how trustees came to school and watched while she administered corporal punishment to two unruly boys. Also, the county superintendent was always willing to instruct and advise, sometimes more than teachers wanted. Parents usually wanted their children to do well in school and, as Picola Foreman observed, "were real congenial." She described their attitude as "If you have any trouble, just come to us. We'll settle it!"

I Taught Children the Way I Was Taught

JOSIE BAIRD

I had a two-year certificate and taught two years on that before I went back to school. I taught at Cottonwood Flat the first year in the fall of 1924. I was the only teacher. I had about twenty or so children including six little Mexican children who didn't speak English. I taught the children the way I was taught. I had gone to a rural school, and that's all I knew. I worked out the time schedule so I wouldn't give all the time to one group. I remember I learned to write fairly well when I was in grade school, but when I was in college, and high school too, I had to take so many notes, I got to where I'd just scribble. But I had to set copy for the children to write by and, I thought, this will never do for them to write like I do. So I got a writing course that you could get for a little of nothing and practiced writing so I could show them how.

I used the older children quite a bit to help the younger ones. Especially with those little Mexican children that didn't speak any English. I didn't have older Mexican children. I had one little Mexican girl who could speak English who was in a different family. We did encourage them to speak English, but Spanish was all they could speak. They tried. I had a boy named Jesse who liked to work with them and the little Mexican girl who could speak English—she was in the third grade—she helped them with their reading. She saw what I did with them, and she'd show them the pictures and get them to say the words, and show them the words and let them read. And they learned.

One little tot one day—I know he felt like that I'd overlooked him—one day he said, "Teacher, teach me." He'd learned that much. At another time, when I taught in a one-teacher school, I had fifteen Mexican children who didn't know a word of English and I hadn't studied Spanish. Later on I studied some Spanish, and I think that's the reason, because I felt if I was going to teach in the rural schools in this area, I needed to know some Spanish so I could understand the kids better.

At that time Cottonwood Flat school was north of the cemetery and a little bit east, and when they had cemetery working, we could join in. I stayed at the Dowden home, which was still farther north. There was a little canyon between the school and the house. If it was icy, we slid down the trail.

That year I made a hundred dollars a month for six months, and I paid twenty dollars a month board. I slept with the daughter; that was just expected. The children just called me Josie, not Miss Josie. Some were almost as old as I was. I know some people kind of look askance at that, but I grew up in the community, and some of the older ones had called me Josie all my life. We went to the same church, and it would have been rough to have changed it.

I Never Will Forget How We Did Units

MARJORIE SMITH WHITFIELD

When they started talking about team teaching in Fort Worth in the sixties and seventies, I said, "Mercy goodness! That's what I started with, you might say, team teaching." I never will forget how we did units. We'd use kids to help others. Sometimes the two of us teachers would put our classes together and have class. When I taught with Miss Wright, we did things like that. I said I didn't want to teach first grade, and she said she didn't want to teach seventh-grade algebra. So we decided to split where I would have some of the oldest ones and some of the youngest ones.

There was a ranching family in the community who didn't let their daughter go to school. They thought she was too little and it was too far for her to go. They didn't have any way to send her. When I went out there and boarded with them, they asked me if I would teach her to read and teach her numbers. So that first year that I was not teaching the first grade, I got materials—the finest little book that ever was—and I taught that child to read. Of course, she was apt. So I taught her to read and taught her mathematical processes.

The next year the little girl wanted to go to school so bad it was pathetic. So they let her go. She could do third-grade work. So I said if I can do that in one year with a child at home, maybe first grade isn't so bad. So after that I didn't mind teaching first grade.

Great Was the Explosion about Reading Time!

ALINE DARDEN NORTHRUP

Victrola was the brand name for a popular record player during the 1930s. Manufactured by the RCA Victor Company, Victrolas were sold across the country. Any record player or phonograph, regardless of the brand, was often called a Victrola. One can think of similar examples in today's vocabulary: Kleenex used for tissue, Xerox for copying machine, and Coke for soft drink.

Bernice Elliott and I taught together. She had the older children and I had the younger ones. Each room had a stove, but there was only one flue. They were back to back. I had only ten desks. Over toward the windows I had my reading table, which was a long table, and we had another small table that we kept the Victrola on. We had records and we sang. I believe it was Bernice's. Mr. Dalton, the county superintendent, come out one day and he was just flabbergasted. It was just before Easter, and we had taken white tissue paper and put it on string and made curtains for the windows. Then we cut out colored tulips.

He was just amazed. "And you sing?" he asked.

Oh, yes, we sang and we did exercises.

Bernice and I carried our lunch all the time, and one day, for some reason, I didn't put the can of beans just right like I always did. I usually put it at the edge of the ashes to keep it warm. I stuck the can down too far in the coals. And great was the explosion about reading time!

I guess one of the most difficult things I had to do was to keep the wood fire going in the wintertime. Some of the men would come around once in a while and cut wood. For the most part, the big boys had to do it. I had some twin boys who were real good to help.

At that time we didn't use as much phonics as we did later, but I used lots of flash cards, and I let the children write the words on the board, and we'd string the flash cards together to make sentences. I read lots to the children, and they caught on real quickly.

One of the girls in my class went to town on Saturday and had her ears pierced. Her parents sent all the paraphernalia to school on Monday for me to doctor her ears. So I said, "Oh, boy!" because one ear got infected and, oh, it was bad. In those days the teacher was the doctor too. There's been a many a bottle of cough syrup come to school, and you'd give it every two or three hours or whatever.

I remember one boy who went to County Line got one of the girls off and told her a dirty joke. She came running to Bernice, and we just couldn't tolerate that, so he wound up with a couple of spats. Well, his mother and dad were unhappy and said, "Oh, that girl lied." And to this day they won't accept his guilt. I can still see Bernice's face when she came out and handed me the paddle. She said, "You keep this in your room now."

I Had a Schedule for Each Class
MAUD ARNOLD BAILEY

I started teaching school in 1912. I was twenty. I am ninety-six years old. I taught in Mitchell School eight miles west of Cisco. I had sixty students. In 1911, I went to Hankins Normal College at Gorman [which operated from 1905 to 1912], where they prepared teachers for one-room schools. I had a schedule for each class. I tried to stay on schedule and combine courses, where I'd have a class on the floor in spelling while I'd also have a class sitting nearby in some other circle. If it was a reading subject, I always had them reading orally. I would give out the spelling lesson to these little ones while another class was reading a story. That way I managed to get out at four o'clock.

When I was teaching at Mitchell, the trustees had a rule that if two boys had a fight the teacher had to whip them both. I never did believe in spanking. One of the boys where I was staying got in trouble. I had to make a motion as if I was whipping him. That night at the supper table, he said, "It didn't hurt, it just made my new overalls fit tighter." If children missed a certain number of words in spelling, or didn't get their work, I'd have them stay after school and recite for me. If they talked—had a rule against talking—I'd have them to remain after all the others had marched out, and I'd talk to them about what they had done.

I taught phonics and spelling. I would tell the class, "Now, tomorrow we're going to have the story which will come next in the reader, and I want to see how many of you can tell me the story tomorrow morning. That will necessitate taking home your books tonight and reading it." The next day I'd say, "Now, how many of you can tell me the story?" Nearly all the hands would go up.

I Tell You, It Pays to Teach Phonics

JEWELL BRANCH

I had one family, the Watkins family, that had two sets of twins, and they had kids in my class from first grade to seventh grade, at least one child in every grade, all in one family. I wonder sometimes how in the world I ever taught those children. I taught phonics quite a bit. I'd start out with the short *a*, like in at, cat, rat. Then the broad *a*, like in father, and the long *a*, like in nature. Then we started on the other vowels. I tell you, it pays to teach phonics.

I had some good readers. We'd all work together. Sometimes I'd have different groups. Sometimes, at the end of the day, I'd remember that not all groups had read aloud. So maybe there would be ten minutes left in the day, and I'd call up somebody and say, "You haven't read to me today. Get up here." And I'd have that person read aloud. Sometimes you'd have kids that could pronounce words good, but they wouldn't know what they meant. I had one little girl once like that.

I Would Ring My Bell and They Would Hear It and Come In

BESSIE DAVIDSON

I never had any real bad discipline problems. Not anything serious. I never was the type to let kids tattle. I had a way about me that would let my students know I meant business. They were all neighborhood children, and I knew them. The first year that I taught, I had twelve little beginners.

You asked me about how I taught reading and what I did with so many beginners. Well, I don't think I taught them anything, actually. They were all neighborhood children, and the parents did more teaching than I did. The students would come and stand by me and read, and I would have them go to the blackboard and do interesting things. I must say that discipline never was a problem with me. I was especially interested in the fourth grade where they could really learn.

161

You know, I can't think of any real advantages of the small schools, mainly because of the diverseness of the group. I guess one of the greatest disadvantages is the very idea of having everybody. Here you're trying to teach a first-grader to read and an eighth-grader algebra, and every point in between.

My first experience, I just had the first four grades for two years. When I taught by myself, I taught all eight grades. I had such few pupils that these older children were not hard to handle at all. I just tried to find magazines and things for them.

I hired one of the boys to be my janitor, one of the Kessler boys. He would stay after school and carry ashes out of the stove or clean them out, help me sweep, or some little things like that. He lived closer to the school than I did, and he'd go early and have a fire built. We had coal rather than wood. At the other school, I remember I would have to stay after school and clean my room up.

Walking home wasn't easy, especially in the winter. My hands would nearly freeze. We were a mile and a half from the school, and we would have to cross the barbed-wire fence, and it was so hard to get through that fence.

Every teacher had her own personal bell. In a two-teacher school, why, maybe I would have a recess that the other teacher didn't have. But I didn't use my bell like the principal did. He was the one who would get out and ring the bell and line them up and march them in. And then when I taught in the one-teacher school, the children would scatter out on the playground, and I would stand out there and ring my bell and they would hear it and come in. I had this ding-ding-ding bell, and we would have drills by it. It was the only one I had, and I used it all the time in the country school.

The Subject I Enjoyed Teaching the Most Was History
VICTOR WOMACK

It was quite comical because I had two in the first grade that year, and I had kids on up to the eighth grade. It was difficult to work out a schedule where I could get everything in. With some of the beginners, I'd have some of the older ones let the little ones read to them or recite to them.

I guess the subject I enjoyed teaching the most was history. I'd kind of tell them the stories, I suppose, and I'd follow the text as much as I could. I'd supplement that with personal accounts and readings I had done. We had history books and geography books, and readers, of course.

For reading we'd set the kids on a bench—a row—and we'd have one read so far, and another one would pick up and read after that to where they would all read some every day. If they couldn't pronounce the words, well, I'd have to help them, of course. I don't think we used phonics. Our lesson was assigned, maybe so many pages a day. If it was a short story, I'd assign the whole thing, but if it was a long story, then I'd assign so much. They were all supposed to read the assignment and be ready to read at recitation time. If a child didn't do his assignment, I didn't punish him for it but would lower his grade. We had written assignments, too. Maybe a short story of some kind or an essay, you might call it, and we'd grade them on spelling, writing, punctuation, and everything.

The Year I Taught I Had One Boy That Had the Itch
CLARA HAYTER WOMACK

Several interviewees spoke of someone having "the itch." The itch was both uncomfortable and embarrassing, for it usually indicated a lack of hygiene and cleanliness. The itch was the common term used for scabies, a contagious skin disease caused by a parasitic mite. The mite burrows under the skin to deposit eggs, causing intense itching, hence the term, "the itch." Children who had it were usually restricted from school until their symptoms disappeared.

In those days we had a ball we made out of string. We chose sides and one group would be on one side of the school building and the others on the other side. We called it ante-over. The group on one side would yell "ante," and the kids on the other side would answer back "over." Then we'd throw the ball over the building, and if anyone from the other side caught it, both teams would exchange sides. But the team that threw the ball wouldn't know if anyone from the other side caught the ball or not until they all come around the end of the building. The whole team would run around to the other side. The person who caught the ball would try to tag someone from the other side while they were trying to get around the building. If someone was tagged, they had to join the other team.

We played baseball with the same ball. We made a bat out of a flat board. It was whittled out of a board with a handle. The batting part was pretty wide—a lot like a two by four. We played a game called town ball. I don't know why it was called town ball. It was similar to baseball except you hold the ball yourself and pitch it up and hit it as far as you can.

I had one boy the year I taught that had the itch. He'd scratch and scratch and scratch. He'd hold up his hand to go the toilet to scratch. He had it a long time, and I don't remember if anyone else had it or not.

There was a lot of information we were able to give those kids at that time. The readers—in going through the old books that we had—I was going through the fifth-grade reader recently, and the classics was the thing that was in those books: inspirational poems and things that were really, really instructive and informative and educational in those readers. They seemed like they were better than they were later when our children came along. There was more information there in those readers.

"But What If Some Kids Use Three Tissues a Day?"
LOUISE STANDARD

During the 1930s things were changing and some schools were providing for the "finer things" of life, such as toilet tissue for the children.

When I was teaching over near Tuscola I attended most of the school board meetings. At one of those meetings the trustees spent the entire evening deciding whether or not to order toilet tissue for the outhouses and, if so, how much they should order. This was quite a new thing, you know. After a long discussion on the merits of tissue and the counter arguments about the extravagance of such, it was finally agreed that toilet tissue should be purchased for the children. Now came the difficult part. Just how much tissue would be needed for forty children?

Well, one of the trustees began the discussion with something like, "We have forty kids, and if each child goes to the privy twice a day, that'll be eighty times. Now if each time a child goes he uses two tissues, then we'll need 160 tissues each day."

Another trustee spoke up and said, "But what if some kids use three tissues at a time? Then, we'll need 240 tissues. I think we'd better count on that." After considerable debate it was agreed that 240 tissues just might be necessary. Then they continued by figuring out how many school days were in a year and multiplied that by 240. So it was finally decided just how much tissue was needed to replace the old catalogs that we'd been using.

Their final admonition to me was to see that the children were not wasteful. They said that there'd be plenty to last the year if I'd see that the kids practiced a little common sense and conservation. To this day, I don't know how they expected me to do that! At the close of the meeting, we all laughed to think that the board of trustees had spent the entire evening on so "weighty" an issue.

It Was a Different Way of Life, Altogether Different
FORRESTER PRICE

There were eight children in my first school, grades one through eight. But there weren't any in some of the grades. I just taught them in the grade they were in. While I was teaching one group, the others were working on their lessons. They were always cooperative. Very cooperative. The fact of the business, the older children—there were three—would help with the others. The Frazier girl was in the eighth grade and would help with the others when her lessons were over. She was nearly as old as I was.

Of course, we had to start the fire every morning when we got there. We were in a pasture down there on a creek, and the trustees would go down and cut a big load of wood and pile it up by the schoolhouse. We had a long stove, a long heater out in the middle of the room. We fed it from the top, you know. Just moved the lid back and put in wood. Everybody carried their own lunch, but we usually kept a pan of water on the stove for washing the kids' hands and faces.

We didn't have school but seven months. I think we started back in September but we'd get out early. We'd just go until we were done.

We didn't turn out for cotton picking at Bitter Creek, but we did in Roby. Bitter Creek was in ranching country, not cotton country.

As far as I know, the building at Bitter Creek was never used for anything but a school. It was out there by itself. It faced the east and it was one room. They had windows on both sides. It had a little stooplike, a little outfit over the door where you came in. And there was a door in the back of the building. There was no platform, but the teacher had a desk. There was a place to hang your coats. We had outdoor toilets, one for the boys and one for the girls. We had maps and all the school equipment they had then, in that day and time. We had books provided by the state. I'd go into Sweetwater and get my books and supplies and things like that. We didn't have teachers' manuals then, and not for several years after that.

On Fridays we'd have spelling bees. Sometimes we'd turn out early. We'd go on home. The trustees and the county superintendent kind of worked together to help make a Friday afternoon schedule. On bad days we'd not have school. There were two or three times we weren't able to all get there. They had telephones, not like the ones we have now, but they had telephones. They had party lines and would spread the word around that we wouldn't have school. If it was too bad for Mr. Frazier to work, he'd hook the mules up to the wagon and take us to school. It was an interesting experience. A different way of life, altogether different.

By the Time We Got Home and Did Our Schoolwork, We Didn't Need Entertainment

LOUISE SMITH CALLAN

I taught the older children, and my twin sister Lois taught the younger ones. Lois taught grades one through three, and I taught four through eight. We had to decide who was going to be the principal. The principal automatically made ten dollars more. I taught the older children so I got the hundred dollars and Lois got the ninety dollars. Then we split that extra ten dollars. Even though I was called principal, we worked together, but I was more or less responsible for getting reports ready and turning them in.

The schoolhouse was up on a hill, and we had to go up the hill from the valley there past the Adairs to get to school. We walked and carried our lunches. We stayed out in the community during the week, but we went back to town for the weekend. We would go out Monday morning and come back to town on Friday, because the trustees said that was all right to do that.

We were about twenty miles from town, but we didn't have to worry about entertainment. I tell you, by the time we got home and did our schoolwork, we didn't need entertainment. Of course, we had a telephone, and our friends would call out. Sometimes they would come out, girlfriends and boyfriends both, and we'd have picnics out there. They loved to come out. Longhorn Valley was beautiful, so we just enjoyed it. Our brother took us out in a car on Monday mornings—we had cars at that time—and then he came for us on Friday afternoons. The trustees said there wasn't much to do out here for a young person; it was all right to spend the weekend in town.

We had to walk about a mile to school. The older boys built the fires; someone was always there and had the fires built. They did all the extra chores and everything for us. There was a cistern. We drew that water out of there with a bucket. We had a happy time out there. I guess the first few years you teach, maybe, are more exciting. Those boys and girls, they had a lot of humor. They liked to have fun, and there was always some kind of little joke, but it was never anything that would cause an accident or injure anybody. We had a nice group of children.

We had a two-room school. They put a partition between the two rooms. At one time it had been just one room. It was a wooden partition and there was a door as an entrance from one room to the other.

School lasted seven months. We must have started the last of October or the first of November, because school was out in May. At Christmas we'd have at least a week for holidays. We got time off for Thanksgiving, too. Any holiday that schools in this area took, we did too. At Christmas we had a tree and one of the girls would do a storytelling, and we had Easter egg hunts in the spring.

Each of those years, we arranged for all of us to have a horse to ride, and we rode over to a neighboring school and played ball. After the game, all of us rode back to the schoolhouse. Then they returned the visit to us, and each time we had a game. It was an all-day adventure. We got home at dusk. Some of the young men in the community would saddle the horses and bring them down to us. They just brought the horses because we liked to ride.

I Taught the Word-Picture Method

FILA CAMPBELL

There were two teachers in our school, and I taught the younger ones. There was twelve girls, all twelve years old in the fourth grade. I had a large class. One of the mothers told me one time, she said, "I didn't think you could teach a child to read with the word-picture method, but you sure have taught mine to read." I've studied about that a lot. How come me to teach that way, I don't know. I didn't learn that way. I learned by phonics—*a b c* s, you know. I had my first-grade pupils sitting over here, my second-grade, then my third-, and my fourth- over there. They studied while I had lessons with each grade.

They had a cistern for water—drew it out with a bucket. They all drank from a dipper, the same one. They'd say, "Give me the dipper. Let me drink next." They all drank together and didn't mind. If we didn't have a dipper, we drank out of the bucket, and when the bucket was empty, we'd let it down in the cistern and draw another one.

Nobody Was Ever Bitten by a Rattler While I Was There

PICOLA FOREMAN

I first taught at Salt Creek near Aspermont in Stonewall County in 1925. I was about twenty-four when I taught there. I was expected to

168

live in the community, because I had no other choice. It was a six- or seven-month school. I'd teach school and then I'd go to Baylor University to school for three months. I wasn't married then. I married a few years later. I was paid seventy-five dollars a month the first year. When I was principal, I'd get eighty, maybe ninety.

I had about twelve students and stayed with a family that was just a half mile from school. At that school sometimes there were two teachers, and sometimes it'd drop down to one. Most of the kids brought their lunch and hung 'em on the old heater to keep them warm. They all had sausage and biscuits and maybe fruit, if they could afford it. Most of the kids would go barefooted in the spring by choice. They had shoes. They were ranch people.

The school building was set on rocks. They just built them that way. Those men didn't close them in around the sides, and lots of times there'd be skunks under there and snakes—rattlesnakes. One time I took the kids down to a little gully for a little picnic, and that very evening, the man I stayed with came back with a big rattler he killed down there. We watched closely, and nobody was ever bitten by a rattler while I was there.

We burned coal in the schoolhouse stove. We had a little coal house near the building. We'd have to get out and rustle our kindling for the next morning. In bad weather, we'd stack it up in the coal house. Every morning I'd have to get down there about an hour before school started and build the fire. The kids would get it all ready the day before, and all I had to do was light a match.

On hot days we'd get out and play mumbly-peg. When we played in couples the loser had to root a peg out of the ground. When the game was over, then you put the peg in the ground and we'd knock it as far down as possible with the knife handle. Then the loser had to root it out of the ground. Boy, they had a time getting it out.

When I taught reading I'd try to find pictures to go with the stories. It was difficult to find them. I'd have to order them from school supplies and *Instructor* or maybe *Grade Teacher*. We'd make things.

Sometimes we'd work up plays. We did Hobo Joe once. We'd bring wagon sheets and make a stage by putting the wagon sheets across a wire stretched across the room, and then we'd have a stage. The parents would come, and we'd have box suppers and night socials. Not for any reason but to have fun. Well, sometimes we'd take a little of that box supper money and buy supplies with it.

169

We'd go to parties on Saturday night and Friday night sometimes. Candy pullings were fun. We'd make taffy candy. The people where I stayed had a big ham supper one night. Sandwiches and all. The other folks would bring stuff. In the spring of the year, we'd have ice cream socials. At the plain ol' parties, we made taffy candy. Most of the older people at the parties would play forty-two, a domino game, you know. Before dark the kids would play flying Dutchman and wolf-over-the-river. Sometime they'd play pop-the-whip. We had to watch that because sometimes they'd put a little kid on the end of the line, and it would be too much. They'd play stiff starch, too. That's where two kids face each other and hold hands and go round and round real fast until one of them lets go.

I didn't go home very often. I'd usually stay out on the ranch on the weekend. I went a whole month once and spent a dime. I sent the dime to town by the people where I was living. They were going in for groceries. I got a dime's worth of something, I don't remember. Room and board was twenty dollars a month. By staying out there, I could save quite a bit of money.

One of the greatest advantages of the one-room school was that you could do individual work, and I guess the biggest disadvantage would be not having all the materials you needed to work with. If I were younger, I'd do it again. Some communities would have one or two bad boys that would try to run the teacher off. I'd hear all those kinds of tales. But my parents that I had were real congenial. They always said, "If you have any trouble, just come to us. We'll settle it." And they would. But I never did have any trouble that way.

We Had a Warm Lunch Supplement
before I Ever Heard of Hot Lunches
INA DINGUS COWAN

The hot lunch program may have been initiated much earlier than is commonly believed. It is true sausages and biscuits were the main fare in the dinner buckets, but in this story, teacher and parents supplemented the meal with jars of warm beans, stew, and other home-canned foods.

When I began teaching, I planned my work so that each grade would get the allotted time allowance for recitation. In the meantime, they had assignments from the board or from charts. This seat work was prepared by the students, graded by the teacher, and returned to the students. It was a good basis for grades. It was not an easy routine, but I thought it very effective. I went to college several summers before they offered education as a course.

The janitor's work was the responsibility of the teacher. It was necessary to get to school early to build the fire. Sometimes you used wood, sometimes coal. The big boys usually brought in the fuel. I rode a horse four miles both ways, eight miles in all. I had to stay after school to sweep and clean the room.

We had a warm lunch supplement before I ever heard of hot lunches at school. Children brought glass jars of soup, turnips and greens, pinto beans, or stew to school. We arranged a wash pot on the top of the jacketed stove. A half gallon or more of water was put into the pot, and the glass jars were set into that until lunchtime. At lunch we handed the warmed food to the owner, and it made a good meal with their sandwich from home. The sandwich was probably a biscuit with sausage. The children brought spoons and forks needed for themselves.

I should explain the pot used to heat the food on the stove. In those days there was an oblong, narrow but deep pot made for boiling clothes. It was of tin or zinc, and it was made to fit over a wood cook stove. You lifted off the two front lids over the fire, and you could boil your clothes in the kitchen in bad weather. It was a necessity to boil our clothes! It was that narrow deep wash pot that we used on the heater at school to heat the food.

We Played a Game Called Wolf-over-the-River

LOUISE STANDARD

There were seven grades that could be taught if they were all represented that year. Some years they were not all represented. There might be only four or five grades represented. The little classes would have drawing while the third and fourth grades would be at the blackboard having their arithmetic. The older classes would be preparing their geography lesson, especially if they had maps to draw. When it was time for the older children to have their geography, the little children could go to the board and draw the things they liked to draw. We had a small library. All of these books came from Tuscola, the larger school. When I saw we needed these things, I went by the big school and picked them up. I'd carry back a load of books and pick up a new load.

One day we had finished lunch and were out playing baseball and I was up at bat. I had to play with them to have enough to play. The superintendent came out to see us, and there I was up at bat. Some of the kids yelled out, "Oh, yonder comes Mr. Bolter." I looked around just as I hit, and of course, I missed my ball. He just laughed and laughed, and his face turned red as fire. He was easily embarrassed. He was our left-handed professor. When he'd get really excited, he'd point at us with his left finger and his face would get redder and redder and redder.

It Didn't Upset Us, All That Going on in the Same Room

MITTIE McKENZIE GEESLIN

Reading the Bible, reciting prayers, and singing religious songs were common practices in rural schools in West Texas during this era.

It just so happened that there was a bigger crop of kids during that time. And the fourth and fifth was the biggest crowd. We had plenty of room for them, and I got through it. And I'll tell you something else that I did, and I'd do it again, as the television commercial says. We had prayer; we opened with prayer. A lot of those country schools did. And we sang, and we read the Bible some but, well, not too much, because I knew the government. I knew the state and the church wasn't supposed to be together. But I encouraged them to go to Sunday school. And most of them did. When we had the prayer, I would do it mostly. Just a morning prayer, and then we'd all repeat the Lord's Prayer. They didn't turn me out for it, nobody objected. That was fairly typical at that time; almost every teacher did that, and I still think it's important.

When I was teaching reading, I just let them read one at a time, you know. One little girl was such a good reader in the third grade, she'd run on. I'd have to stop her. She could outread all the rest of them. It was interesting to hear her rattle it off, but I had to say, "Slow down, Faith, let the next one read." And they were good readers. I usually didn't have kids listen to others read. Maybe I should have. I'd run into trouble toward the end of the day when the bell would ring. Later when I was teaching in a four-teacher school, I'd have to let some of the fifth-graders hear the third-grade spelling lesson, to finish it up—to make everything come out. But I knew they were getting it because I could observe, even though I was teaching another class. I could know what was going on. And it didn't upset us, all that going on in the same room, because we were used to it.

I read stories aloud some. I can't remember what I read. Cinderella, maybe, or all those little interesting tales that children like. The state started to provide textbooks, I guess, in 1921. The first year I taught, the children had to buy them. I believe that was right because it seems like when I went out on the river, and when I was teaching down there in Cedar Knot, the little school that didn't have enough money to run but 'til Christmas, textbooks were provided by the state.

Children didn't start school 'til they were seven. My children started to school at six, and that was the second year that the law had changed to six. Sometimes kids would come to school early just because their parents would let them. Their parents were trustees. I couldn't complain, but they were smart children. They made first grade all right. I got them through it, and they were lovely children.

I Had Fifty-Eight in My Room over at Grasshopper
INA DINGUS COWAN

The school where I first taught was named Grasshopper—Grasshopper School. It was about eight miles out of Munday here in Haskell County. It was in the Grasshopper Community. I don't have any idea how it got its name. Lots of grasshoppers, I guess. In that school we had one hundred and eight children for two teachers, and I had fifty-eight in my class. *One hundred and eight in two rooms, and I had fifty-eight in my room.* Looking at it now, you couldn't get around, but it never did dawn on me except to get busy and grab it.

Teaching four grades in one room is not too difficult, but having fifty-eight students in those four grades is something else again! At first I had no ambition to teach. Well, I changed. I learned to love it. I loved the children. I've made many lasting friendships

173

through teaching. If I had another life to live, I'd like to teach again. Teaching is something to enjoy twice. You enjoy the days with your pupils; then when you are old, you are filled with pleasant memories that make your life happy as you quietly piece quilts to fill the hours.

We had programs all the time, particularly at Lake Creek. At other schools maybe we'd have just one at the end of school. At Lake Creek we had programs for just everything. Miss Weaver bought all the children a harmonica that would learn to play it. We had three teachers at that time, and the middle teacher was able to teach them. We had a harmonica band. There are some people here in town, and when their children get together now—there's three or four of them—they still play the harmonica. They always remind me that Miss Weaver bought their first harmonicas. She bought them out of her own money. We didn't have school money unless we made it up with carnivals or something. She bought those for the children so they could learn. They've had a lifetime of pleasure out of it and they still do it. That's why Miss Weaver was an exceptional teacher. She looked for everything she could do to train children in any way that would be to their advantage. She helped a lot of children.

We took our kids to the circus at Haskell. Everybody would bring nickels. They had to pay a nickel to get in. Of course, some of them didn't have it, but they got to go, too. It didn't matter, we just took them along. Somebody would come in with their cars. There were a few people in the community who had cars. There was no such thing as buses in those days. We'd go to the circus. Then all the next week, the older boys would play clown. Now that was screamingly funny. On the playground somebody would be the clown. They would reenact that whole thing. It was fun.

I had morning exercises, which included Bible reading and prayer. As long as I taught, I did. My brother-in-law kept telling me, "You're breaking the law every day."

I'd tell the superintendent, "If someone comes in to investigate the school, you'd better not bring federal authorities in my room before a certain time." Listen, that was me! That was me! If I could teach a child to worship—I never mentioned church—they had no idea of what church I went to. We'd have something every morning before we'd start. Then if things got busy and something would go

174

wrong, we'd say, "Oh, look what's happened here." Some child would say, "We didn't say our prayers this morning, Miss Cowan." They'd do it every time. Our little prayers were memory gems or poems. We had some beautiful little poems. We just had a stack of these that we'd say. Then there was one for afternoon.

Forgive me if I have this day
Done any wrong in work or play
And help me always to do right
And bless me every day and night.

We said that every time in the afternoon when we started to leave. One day I said, "Children, the bell has rung and everybody's leaving. Let's just not say our prayer this afternoon." And a little girl ran over to the blackboard. They never did kneel, they just stayed where they were. But she knelt down against the blackboard, and folded her hands and said the prayer. I thought it was precious.

In fact, the first year I ever taught school, I came out of high school and taught that year. If I had the money—I think I got sixty-five dollars a month for seven months—if I were to strike oil, I'd try to pay them back. Because, you know, I wasn't worth it. But I learned a lot that year. In our family we were reared with phonics. Our daddy had taught school, and we would play a game where we would take a ship down to Africa and come back loaded with things that started with certain letters. Then we'd make lots of rhymes.

Yes sir, if I had another life to live, I'd teach school again. I most certainly would!

CHAPTER NINE

❧

The Year I Started Teaching Everybody Had the Itch

TEACHING AND THE PUPILS

An experience common to these oral histories is that many of the teachers entered teaching primarily because it was a job, not because they desired to become teachers. Once involved, however, they were "hooked" and remained to become, in the words of Miss Weaver, professionals. Although the strict rules and stern discipline that characterized teaching in this era is off-putting by today's standards, these accounts reflect a sincere warmth and genuine concern for children. Ina Cowan provided food for two needy pupils; Louise Standard included little Mike, who could not walk, on an April Fool's outing; Josie Baird returned to college to take Spanish classes in order to better communicate with her pupils.

Yesterday's teachers may have had large classes, poor facilities, and meager salaries, but this research reveals that their passion and concern were undaunted. One may conclude that the desire to serve the needs of students has always empowered teachers, in early schools as well as present day. Mittie Geeslin summarized what many came to feel, "We had a lot of fun. It was a real joy to teach."

Rudy, What Did You Have for Breakfast?
INA DINGUS COWAN

There was a little girl I had at school that told me they didn't have anything to eat in the house. I got home and told my husband. We had a quarter of a calf hanging up. He cut some steak, and we went over to the house. We were worried about it. They seemed to appreciate it, and I told the girl not to worry about bringing her lunch. I'd bring her lunch. The next day, I brought her a lunch, but she ate so much, it made her sick. Probably wasn't used to having enough food, and it made her sick. I went to the superintendent, and we went down to the grocery store and told the grocery man to let that woman have any groceries she needed. Her husband would take the money and buy liquor. So they wouldn't allow her to have any money—afraid he'd take it away from her. So they allowed her to buy groceries.

In later years, I remember one particular child. I was very observant. I don't hear very well, and I didn't realize that I was hard of hearing as a child, but I do now. I'm very observant of expressions. I read everything. I was having the morning lesson. I was a strict teacher in that, when I gave instructions, I gave it to everybody in the room at once, and they all had to listen. Then they had something to do. They had a paper to do, and then I checked their paper to see if they were moving along with me, but I was watching them just like a hawk. Well, this little boy fell out of his chair. Just fell out of his chair, just like this. I said, "Get up off of that floor and get back in your chair right now," and he did. This child got back in his chair and then he did it again. I hadn't said three words, and he collapsed again. So I walked out the door, and I motioned him to come outside. He got up and came out there, and I said, "Rudy, what did you have for breakfast?"

He said, "I didn't have no breakfast."

I said, "Well, what did you have for supper?"

He said, "I had a little bit of beans, but they wasn't enough, and I didn't have many beans."

You cannot teach a hungry child. If they're hungry, they're thinking about themselves. They can't help it. That's the only two times that I found children needing food. I never did find out why this child didn't have any food. His daddy had a job and worked for somebody. I've decided now that it was child abuse. He was kind of a pushy, messing-around child, and I figured they made him do without food to punish him. Then, I didn't even think of that.

As long as I taught school, child abuse wasn't a big problem. But I did have a child, and my husband told me what was wrong with him. I had a child that pulled down his shirt one day and showed me across his back. It was green stripes across here. And I mean blue-green. Blue, but greenish. I said, "How in the earth did you do that?"

He said, "I fell out of a tree." Well, I didn't argue with that. I went home and told my husband who had a lot better judgment.

He said, "No. Those stripes were put there with a strap." He said, "Somebody beat that child with a strap." In those days, meddling with that would get you in trouble. I look back now, and I didn't even think of child abuse in those days. I didn't even think of that.

I loved to teach, and I loved the kids. I did have one child that I took home with me one summer. I got her because her mother and daddy had had a divorce and her father liked to drink too well. So I got them to let me keep her, and I kept her through the summer, more than one summer. I kinda feel like she's my daughter. She had a hard life. She didn't have a dog's chance. Now she's an RN, and I think it's absolutely a miracle. She had no opportunity to do anything, but she was a bright and beautiful girl. I still keep up with her.

I never stayed out from illness but one day in forty-two years. But sometimes the kids would be sick. I had a little boy that had cancer of the ear. He came to school quite a lot, like six weeks or so, then he wasn't able to come to school anymore. We sent him letters and cards. In the spring when the days were warm and pretty, if it was a holiday, we would go down and play games in his front yard. He would sit in a swing out on the front porch. His mother would wrap him up, and he'd be out watching us. We'd wave at him and sing to him. We'd line up and sing to him, and then we'd play drop-the-handkerchief or something and have a little party. Any time we had an Easter party or Valentine party, we'd always include him. I worried about him. I was afraid he'd die during the school year, but he didn't die until school was over. I was glad not to have that problem to deal with and face with the children. It was up in the summer. He had cancer of the ear. I've thought about him a lot.

I Wish I Could Have Done More

HENRY T. POTEET

In some communities male teachers were paid more than females for doing the same job because they were "breadwinners" and thus, in the eyes of the trustees, needed the extra money. A woman didn't need as much money, it was argued. If married, her husband should be making the living for her; if not married, why would she need more money?

When I got out of college in 1937, I looked at different places for jobs to teach. I finally ended up at County Line. They had two teachers then—Miss Aline Darden and I. I was the principal. I got eighty-five dollars a month. I think Aline got eighty dollars. They gave me an extra five dollars. Of course, Aline had some experience. She had more experience, but I was named principal. I got five dollars more a month.

Some of the kids from Cottonwood School came to me. One was a boy I'll call Neal. He hadn't done well there. I said, "Neal, you can't come here and run over things here. You're going to cooperate with me and do what I say.

"Yeah, I know, Mr. Poteet. I will."

One day the little kids were jumping off a bank into a ditch into the soft dirt. Neal was down there, and the kids came running and said, "When we jump off, Neal sticks his hand up and makes us turn somersaults." It was dangerous. I got Neal and I sat him down and said, "Neal, you know what you promised me? You can't do that."

"Yes sir. I won't do it, Mr. Poteet." People thought I ought to kick him out. Maybe I should have. But he stayed right on with me. I remember talking to Neal outside the schoolhouse once. He said, "Oh, when I get big I'm going to drink and I'm going to get drunk."

I said, "This is not the best. That's not a happy life. That's not good." I've always felt bad about that, but I did the best I could. Neal is dead now, and I wish I could have done more. I guess his life wasn't all that happy.

All of the kids from the valley came in a hack, and the Murphree children came on their horses, except for Betty Jean; she came riding on a mule. I usually came in my brother's old car he used in his trapping. You know, he trapped skunks and coyotes and such and sold their hides.

One of the boys I taught couldn't read a line. He'd read and I'd have to tell him every line.

I said one day, "Son, it's time for you to read."

He said, "I can't read, but I can tell it."

I said, "You can tell it?"

179

"Yes."

"All right, let's hear you tell it." And he told the story just right. I got to where I'd say to him, "You read over this part, and then you can tell it." He could tell it better than any of them, and yet he couldn't read it aloud.

"She's Mean Enough to Step on Little Chickens"

STELLA GIPSON POLK

Lulu was a girl at one of the schools I taught in. She and her mother lived in a little shack with her grandmother, but no one knew anything about her father. Lulu's mother was a big-boned woman with glaring eyes. There were all kinds of tales about Lulu's family. People said her mother could outcuss any man, and it was told that Lulu's grandmother once chased her husband around the house with a red-hot poker from the fireplace.

Well, I wanted to be kind to Lulu, but she wouldn't let me. She never joined in the games, and any time she spoke to any child she used language so vile and filthy that I was just stunned. I tried to talk to her once at recess about her behavior, and Lulu called me a name that I didn't even know and certainly wouldn't repeat. I went outside and cut a little hackberry switch and used it on Lulu, and you know, all the next week she was so sweet that I wondered why I hadn't used a switch before. Well, I thought it was all over between Lulu and me, but I was wrong. A few days after that we were playing basketball at recess when Lulu's mother rode up on a mean-looking mustang pony. I was glad to see her and thought maybe now I could talk to her and she could help me with Lulu.

Lulu's mother never got off her horse; she just rode around and around the ball ground, popping her leather quirt against the leather riding skirt she had on and wouldn't say a word. When the bell rang, I went up to her and told her to come in so she could hear Lulu's lesson. She didn't reply, she just kept wheeling her horse around the ball court and popping her quirt. I went on in with the children and thought maybe she would come in after she tied up her horse. Finally school was dismissed and I forgot all about Lulu and her mother.

Almost immediately after the children were gone, here came a man on horseback as fast as he could. He was Mr. Metz. As he got off his horse, he shouted, "Is she gone?"

I said, "Who?" and then I realized who he meant. "Oh, you mean Lulu's mother. She's gone. I tried to get her to come in and visit, but she wouldn't."

I thought Mr. Metz was going to choke. He said, "Girl, you must have been behind the door when the brains were passed out!"

I was shocked. What in the world did he mean? He had always been so nice and polite, you know. Then he told me what happened. Lulu's mother had come by their garden when Mrs. Metz was picking beans and said she was going to school and horsewhip the teacher. Mrs. Metz ran all the way to the field where Mr. Metz was plowing and told him, and he got here as fast as he could.

Mr. Metz said, "Girl, you just don't know that woman. When she gets her dander riled, she's mean enough to step on little chickens. Don't know what you've got or what saved you from Lulu's ma, but whatever it is, you'd sure better hold on to it." I guess I was just lucky in my ignorance.

I Sat Down and I Felt This Tack

INA DINGUS COWAN

I kept every kid in that room busy all the time except one little boy. He did something naughty one day, and I said, "Get over there and sit on the floor." I forgot what he did. He was sitting up in the corner, right in front of my desk, and I was in the back of the room working. He sat there a long while, and then I went back to the desk later. I told him to go back to his seat and behave himself and not do that anymore. So I sat down, and I felt this tack. I didn't plop down on it. It didn't hurt me. I looked up real quick, and there he was. He had his geography open, and he was watching me. I just looked at him. I knew I had him. He was the only kid watching me. He had the geography book open and was looking around. That's the only time that ever happened.

At that school I opened my desk one morning, and there was a snake coiled up in it. It was dead. I knew immediately it was dead, so I wasn't afraid of it. They thought I was going to scream and run. Somebody had coiled this dead snake up inside my desk. It didn't make that much importance to me because I wasn't afraid of snakes. If it had been alive, I'd have killed it. I wasn't afraid of it, but I never did find out who put it there. I don't know who did that one.

"I Ain't Gonna Undress Here at School!"

FILA CAMPBELL

I had to spank one little boy once; I don't remember why. I thought he wouldn't like me after that, and his mother especially wouldn't like me. I worried about it over the weekend. But on Monday morning, he came in with the most beautiful bouquet of roses you ever saw.

I had one little boy who was just as bright as anyone in lots of ways, but in some ways it was hard for him to do things. He didn't fit in with the rest of the children. Years later I saw him, and we were talking. I didn't know this then, but he told me this. Every day, he said, just as he was leaving school, he hoped and hoped that I would bend down and kiss him. I wish I had. If I'd known to, of course, I would have.

Sometimes in those days, children would bring their little brothers or sisters with them to school. One year there was a certain woman that sent her little boy, about four or five years old, four maybe. He just kept coming with his older brother. I had good discipline, but he disturbed my room and me and everyone else. I asked the trustees about it, and they said to tell his mother I couldn't keep him anymore. So I sent word back with his brother. The biggest weight was lifted when I got rid of him on that Friday afternoon. But on Monday morning I got to school, and there was the little boy. I asked his brother, "Why is Ernest here?" And he said, "Mama said she didn't care if he learned anything or not, just so's he gits out of her way."

We didn't have programs at Christmas but we had programs at the end of school. One time we had a little program, like a skit, and one little girl didn't have any good shoes to wear. She came and asked if she could wear a new pair of white socks. Would that be all right? And I told her it would. I remember her skipping and dancing around in her new white socks. She wanted to be more like the other children, so she wore a new pair of socks.

A most unpleasant thing occurred when I taught out at Moun-

182

tain View, a little one-teacher school north of Rotan. There was a canyon off a little ways from the schoolhouse. We had an outdoor toilet for the girls, but the boys didn't have a restroom. They went down there in the canyon and, of course, they'd play down there. There were two large boys—they were really too large to be going to school. There was another boy down there, and I don't remember just what happened, but anyway they stabbed him somehow with a knife. Well, I didn't know what to do. Of course, I couldn't go down there where they were. I came to the county superintendent with the problem, and he said to expel them—they were too old to be in school—too big anyway—and just causing trouble. He said to expel them. So I did.

One of the boy's daddy was a trustee, and he demanded that I whip them and let them come back to school. I said, "I can't whip those boys. They both are larger than I am." So the trustees came up and sat there and made the boys take a whipping. I started to whip the one whose daddy was a trustee, and I said, "I notice you have on more than one pair of trousers."

One of the trustees said, "Take those top trousers off."

The boy said, "I ain't gonna undress here at school!"

His daddy said, "You get those trousers off right now!" And he did, but he sulked and sulked and tried to give me trouble. However, the other boy, after he married, saw me in town one day and said he was so ashamed of the way they acted.

Why, Mr. Fergus Must Have Been a Sex Maniac!

STELLA GIPSON POLK

Let me tell you about the time Bonnie brought books for every child in the school. She came to school one morning carrying twenty books. She was excited. "Twenty books," she said, "one for every kid in school!"

I said, "Bonnie! Where in the world did you get those books?" I didn't think she came from a family of readers.

"Oh," she said, "they belonged to Mr. Fergus, the man who lived with us for a while. Mama said she reckoned he was a book peddler or something, because all he ever did was read and pay us rent. And when he left, he left all these books and never did send back for them. Mama said he must have died or left the country. Mama wanted to get rid of these books and said I could bring them to school and give them to all the kids."

"My, my," I said, "the kids will be tickled." So I let Bonnie pass them out. It was cold outside and I was anxious to get to the lessons, so I never did get a chance to look at a single book. The weather was bad so I kept the kids in at recess and said I'd give them more time at lunch if the weather cleared. Usually I went out with the kids after lunch to play, but I needed the extra time to straighten out the book closet. While I was busy with that, I happened to glance down at one of the books Bonnie had brought that was sitting on someone's desk. Well, the title just jumped out at me. It was *What Every Man Should Know about Sex.* I was horrified, and I looked around the room at the other books. Most of them were on the top of the desks, but I noticed the older kids had put theirs inside their desks. That meant they had hidden them. I began to search for the books. Every book in the room was about sex! Why, Mr. Fergus must have been a sex maniac!

Well, what was I going to do? The kids were still playing outside. I opened the lid to the stove and began to gather up Bonnie's books. I put in about four at a time, and when they were pretty well consumed, I'd put in four more. I gave the kids extra time for recess that day, but I had all the books in the stove.

When the children got ready to go home, nobody could find his book. Twenty books had disappeared. Somebody accused Bonnie of hiding them to take home again. Somebody else said, "Maybe Santy Claus got them and was gonna bring 'em back Christmas." They finally decided that some traveler had stolen them while I was cleaning out the closet. Well, for them, the mystery never would be cleared up. But some mysteries never are, you know, and I didn't think this one should be either.

The More They Laughed, the Harder I Cried
BARGY FIELDS HARGROVE

The worst thing I had to endure the entire year was when three of my boys trapped skunks on the way to school. They ran their line and would skin their skunks on the way to school. I only had five pupils, so I couldn't send them home. I wanted my job. I was making sixty dollars a month and I needed that job. On a cold day, with a big fire in that room, to sit and smell those three every day was rough. Salaries were low during the depression, but I still needed my job too bad to quit.

My one discipline problem—I was completely unprepared and was only eighteen years old—was a boy, probably fourteen years old. He was bigger than I was. He just had fun. He had made the remark that he was going to run that eighteen-year-old teacher off. He just upset everything. There was no way I could have any kind of discipline in any form. He'd just laugh and stir something else up and keep on. Finally, I said, "Now, I'm not going to put up with this any longer. This is it! You're going to stop it! If you don't, you're going to wish you had."

He said, "Well, what are you going to do?"

Then I realized I'd gone too far. I said, "Do you really want to know?"

He said, "Yes, I do. Show me!"

I told him to take off his belt, and I told the rest of the kids to go on home. I didn't believe he'd do it. I was scared to death he wouldn't do it. And I don't know yet what I'd have done if he said no. But he took it off, and I literally wore him out. I told him that this was just a sample of what he was going to get next time.

The rest of the kids were already home. I started walking toward home that afternoon, and several older boys rode up on horses. One of them was Jim, and he was older and not in school, but he had heard. He said, "I want to know what's going on over there at that school. I saw smoke and heard the loudest womp, womp, and smoke coming up over the hill. What has been going on over there?"

I sat down and started crying. The more I howled, the harder they laughed. The more they laughed, the harder I cried. They swore that, if I ever cried again, they would sit down and cry with me. I thought I had ruined myself completely.

I was so afraid that the boy would come in mad the next morning, but he came in grinning, just as sweet as he could be, and I appreciated his attitude. I never did have any more trouble with him after that. But I never let myself get in that position again. It was him or me! I didn't have much choice.

I did one thing that I have worried for years over, and I still feel bad about it. There was this other boy—the sweetest boy, just as clean and neat and polite and nice, and I loved him. But he did not do well in school. I worried and worried, and I did not know what to do. I knew that he was older than the other kids and would probably go to school only one more year and that was all. I thought if he would stay in the grade he was in one more year he would learn a little more. So I retained him. And he didn't go to school another day! I have regretted it ever since. He might not have learned much, but I think he would have gone to school the next year if I hadn't retained him.

I Knew I Wasn't Teaching Him Much, But I Was Doing the Best I Could

MITTIE McKENZIE GEESLIN

There was one little boy at Star who was in my room two years, fourth and fifth, I believe. He was afflicted, mentally retarded in a sense, but he couldn't talk. I don't know what was wrong with him. He was a really hideous-looking poor little ol' boy. And he couldn't hear very well, and my desk was here, and I had his seat right where the aisle would come up, where he could hear me. I knew I wasn't teaching him much, but I was doing the best I could. When he would answer, in history or whatever, he would hold up his hand, poor little ol' deformed hand, and I'd let him tell what he wanted. I could never tell what he was saying, but he knew what he was saying. So I went ahead and promoted him.

I saw him one time later, several years later. Maybe twenty years later. He was in town. They had sent him to Austin to the state school. I know his father and mother must have passed away because they wouldn't have sent him away to no one. But his brothers and sisters married off, or whatever; I never did know the full story. I met him one day. I said, "Well, hello, Sammy," but he didn't recognize me. Made me feel bad. Evidently he was both handicapped and severely mentally retarded. Now, I'll cry again. One time his older sister, Hattie, came to me and said, "Miss Mittie, some of the boys have been saying bad things about my brother." I sure gave them a raking over about it. I just gave them a strong talk. And we never heard any more about it. I was pretty strict, but still I was generous with them. We had a lot of fun. It was a real joy to teach.

"We Can't Take Little Mike Because He's Crippled!"

LOUISE STANDARD

Many good teachers, years before public law 94-142 mandated, were including children with physical and mental limitations in their regular class activities.

One year on the day before April Fool's Day, some of the students told me that one of the boys was going to run off the next day and play hooky from school. So to get ahead of him, I announced that afternoon before school closed for everybody to bring a sack lunch tomorrow and that we were going to have a surprise for all of us.

They begged, "Oh, Miss Louise, what are we going to do?"

Finally, I thought I'd best just tell them. I said, "We're going to run off from school. We're going to hike to the top of that mountain behind the Joneses'." Mr. Elmo Jones was one of the trustees. I had three of the Jones children in school at that time.

They said, "But we can't take little Mike because he's crippled, and how can he go to the top of the mountain?"

I said, "Well, we're going to borrow the little boy's red wagon who lives across the road from here, and we're going to take turns pulling Mike in the wagon."

So we left the school and passed the Jones home and waved to Mr. and Mrs. Jones. Of course, they knew where we were going because the children had to tell them to prepare that sack lunch and a jug of water that we'd pick up at their house. Mike held the water in the wagon with him. When we got up to the top of the mountain, there was nothing much to do but eat our lunch and see how far we could throw rocks and sticks or whatever we wanted to throw. We managed to get back at three thirty and take a rest break before we dismissed school at four o'clock.

To the big boy that suggested that he was going to run away from school on April Fool's Day, I said, "Henry, did you have a good time today?"

He said, "Oh, Miss Louise, I had the best time I've ever had in school."

187

I said, "Don't you wish April Fool's Day came more often? Why don't we try to get the calendar rearranged and have April Fool's Day on the first of every month instead of once a year?"

All the children said, "Yes, why don't we just take that up with the school board and get that done!"

It Was Customary for Teachers to Visit in Their Pupils' Homes
OPAL WATSON NANNY

When I was teaching out at this ranch over at Douglas, I had eleven pupils. It was customary for the teachers to go out and visit in their pupils' homes some time or another during the term. These little kids lived seven miles from school. They had a horse named Thunder and a buggy that they came in—three of them. And they had a donkey. If they couldn't catch Thunder, then they would put the first-grader on the donkey and bring him. Well, they told me they would be there in the buggy the next day, and they would get me to come back with them. Well, they couldn't catch Thunder that day. So they got there and they had such long faces and said, "Miss Opal, we couldn't catch ol' Thunder this morning."

I said, "Well, is your mother looking for me?"

They said, "Well, she made a cake!"

I didn't want to disappoint the children, so I said, "Okay!" So we left at four o'clock, and we walked seven miles. It was dark when we got there. I spent the night and prayed they'd catch ol' Thunder the next morning!

I boarded at the Baldwin Ranch. My parents lived eleven miles away from the school, and the road was not paved out of Throckmorton in those days. The mud got so deep in 1932, they couldn't come for me. My brother had a little mare—she was the greatest thing in the world. I loved to ride her. I went home on Friday and would ride her back on Sunday afternoon.

He Was Arrogant and He Tested Me and I Showed Him
VICTOR WOMACK

You take little ones and big ones all in one room; discipline is a problem, too. The year before I went to teach at Carmel out in Pecos

County, the teacher lost control of the school and had to resign. The teacher had to be let go. I had been told about her and been warned about it. The boy that caused the trouble was fifteen and I was seventeen. I watched him very carefully the first week or two, and he began to give me trouble, and so I talked to him. I told him we had to have discipline. I gave him a chance, but the next week he was worse than ever. So when I went by the corral on my way to school, I picked up a bridle rein—a strip of leather about an inch wide— and rolled it up and put it in my pocket and put it in my desk.

That day he was disruptive sure enough. So I kept him in. He got a little bit arrogant with me, and I guess I lost my temper. I just beat the hell out of him. A few days later, his brother come over and said, "You must have whipped my brother pretty hard with that bridle rein. You broke the skin in several places."

So that worried me. About a week later, his father rode up to the ranch house one afternoon. I think it was on Saturday. So I said to myself, well here my trouble starts. He came in and introduced himself to me and told me how he appreciated what I had done for his son. He said the boy's mother had died several years before, and they hadn't had much control over him. He told me what the boy had done the previous year at the school. He said what I did was the very thing and he appreciated it very much.

Several years later I met that boy, and he said I'd done a good thing. It changed his life around. Of course, what I did was a little extreme. I lost my temper. I got mad, I suppose. I was seventeen years old and I was pretty strong, pretty much of a man physically. He was arrogant and he tested me and I showed him.

Tell Sister to Take Those Clothes and Bury Them

PICOLA FOREMAN

One of these little ranch boys up at Salt Creek came to school one morning. He had his mouth full of something, and I said, "Burris, what are you eating?"

And he said, "Cow cake." He had gone to the barn that morning, and he had a tobacco can and he filled it full of cow cake. Little cottonseed cakes. Kids would often eat it, not because they were hungry, but because it tasted pretty good and because it was there, I guess.

I never will forget that. That was so funny. Kids would eat any-thing in those days. We'd go out there and snip off those ol' ripe berries off the cactus. Prickly pears. We'd get those little stickers all off, and we'd peel them and eat them. Kids would sometimes chew cedar wax. On those ranches, they had a lot of cedar trees. There would be a little glob on the trees, like sweet gum, and they would chew it. Mix it with your own chewing gum and it'd go a long way. We'd take tow sacks and lay under an algerita bush and thrash them. Then we'd take the berries and make jelly.

I had kids from about six families. The farthest anybody lived from school was about two miles. One morning, oh, did I smell a polecat! One of these little stinkers had roused some skunks up by chunking them with rocks and got the smell on his clothes.

I said, "Listen here, you're going to have to go home and change those clothes." The boy's mother and father were dead, and an older brother and sister took care of him. They were grown.

I said, "You go home and tell sister to take these clothes and bury them a little while—two or three days and then wash them." They say that will work.

She Said, "Well, We've Got the Itch"

MAUD ARNOLD BAILEY

When I was teaching at Willow Grove I always tried to spend one night with each family. These little children had been asking me every day since school started if I was going home with them to spend the night. So I got my work up enough so I could spare the time to go home with them that night. It was out in the county, you know, on a ranch. When we walked up, the lady that lived there—the mother of these children—met me at the gate. She seemed sur-prised to see me! She said, "Miss Maud, what did you come for?"

I said, "Well, I promised the children all year that I would come, and this is it."

She said, "Well, we've got the itch." She said, "But if you will stay, we'll put on fresh linens and everything so you won't get it."

I said, "Ma'am, I think I'd better not stay because people in the

190

community might think I was bringing the germ to school." So I started back to my uncle's where I lived.

I had to go by another trustee's home. The wife was out in the yard and she said, "Miss Maud, where are you going? Are you going back home?"

I told her yes and laughed and told her why. She said," Well, stay all night with us." It was getting kind of late, and I had to go around this mountain to get to my boarding place. So I decided to stay with them. Her husband, being a trustee, called the other trust-ees, and they called a meeting that night and decided that these children that was exposed to the itch shouldn't come to school. Of course, that made it kind of hard on me. It made me look like a tattletale!

The Year I Started Teaching Everybody Had the Itch

CARL HENDRIX

The year I started teaching everybody had the itch. I'll never forget that. It was during the war and everybody had the itch. Those little kids wanted to put their arms around my neck. I had two little neph-ews and they and the other little kids wanted to sit on my lap. I said, "No, you can't sit on my lap. I don't like that. I'll put my arm around you, and you can put your arm around my neck, but you can't sit on my lap."

I must have had twenty or thirty kids. There was one little girl and I think her daddy was dead, because the mother was the only person I met. She was a cute little girl, but she was independent. I think it was because she had been mothered all her life, and she wasn't used to a man. Well, I had to paddle her. She was pretty sassy with the other kids and would knock the food out of their hands and things like that.

I said, "Here, you can't do that. We've got to treat each other right."

Finally one day, I sent word to her mother to please show me how to get along with this little girl. Her mother sent word to me. "You're the teacher. You're doing all right. If you have to paddle her, you can paddle her." That's when I decided to paddle her. But it didn't do any good. One day she was real sassy to me or some of the other students, I don't remember which, and I said, "Hey, come here."

And I said, "Right here and now, before all these children, I want to be friends with you, and I want you as my friend. I'm getting tired of this paddling stuff. I don't know whether you are or not. I don't want to paddle you another time."

She said, "Well, how do we work it?"

I said, "You just go on and be a nice little girl, and I'll never paddle you another time, and let's be friends."

She said, "Okay, when do we start?"

I said, "Right now!" And that was the end of it. That was the end of it.

"Miss Mittie, Pa Told Me to Take My Whuppin'"
MITTIE McKENZIE GEESLIN

The second year I taught, I didn't want to go back to my first school. I got along all right, and they invited me back, but there was some tough boys. I controlled them, I got through, but I felt that there might be a little resentment some way, and I didn't go back to that school. There were some tough boys, and I would have to give them a spanking. They were pretty good size, some of them. They were third-grade boys and fifth-grade. I'm a crybaby. I tear up if I get excited. Well, one day, they played hooky. They just took off at lunch and didn't turn up 'til nearly the end of the day. And so I just gave them what they had coming. That was what I was brought up to do. That was what other teachers did.

So one boy said, "Miss Mittie, I ain't goin' to take no whuppin'."

So I said, "Okay, Aubrey."

He had his books, and so the next morning, here he came and said, "Miss Mittie, Pa told me to take my whuppin'."

You know, I hadn't taught them long enough to speak correct English, or no one else had taught them to say "whipping" for punishment, but "whuppin." I was a greenhorn. Anyway, we got through it fine, and that worked out. But once, another fellow, another man, resented it enough that he took his boy out of school. It wasn't too long before school was out. You see, they had spring fever, which was all right. Now, I wouldn't do it. I wouldn't do what I did. But then, that was the way it was done. So that was the reason I didn't want to go back to that school.

"You're the Spittin' Image of Leon's Ma. Now, Git!"

STELLA GIPSON POLK

During another year I had an interesting experience with Leon and his father. Leon was a new boy in our school, small for his age. Leon was defiant—wouldn't play with the other children. There wasn't much I could get Leon to do. Around Thanksgiving time we made paper posters for the children to take home. I noticed Leon wasn't making his, and I asked him why. "No need to make it," he said. "Pa would just laugh at me."

While Leon was not very cooperative, I did notice that he seemed to stare at me a lot. People had said that Leon's mother had run off with a salesman when Leon was a baby. Perhaps he just missed his mother and that's why he kept looking at me. Leon seemed to grow increasingly fond of me, but he never studied, and as a result, his work was never done very well.

Well, I decided to have a talk with Leon's father to see if he could help Leon do better in school. So one day I got in my car, and I drove Leon out to his little shack. Leon's father was standing in the door. He couldn't have been very old, but he looked old. When I got out of the car, his father said, "Don't bother to come in. Talk where you are."

Well, I was taken aback but managed to say, "I wanted to see you about Leon's grades."

Before I could say another word, he stopped me, "You're his teacher. Don't you know enough to teach a seventh-grade boy?"

I said, "But Leon is failing, and he shouldn't be. It's as if a spark has gone out of him. He needs someone to care about his grades at home and somebody to love him."

He just scoffed at me. His laugh was like a bray—somewhere between hate and scorn. "Love," he shouted. "Huh! His ma used to cuddle him before she run off with that sugar-talking peddler." By now I was getting a little frightened. His eyes were terrifying. Then he said to me with such hatred in his voice, "You're the spittin' image of Leon's ma." And then he shouted, "Now, git!"

Well, *I got!* But I drove home with such a heavy heart. Leon had been taught to hate his mother's memory. Yet something had lived on within him. My resemblance of his mother had brought it out.

Several years later when World War II was on, Leon came by

the house to see me. He had on a uniform and looked quite manly, and I recognized him instantly. He said, "Leaving Fort Hood next week. Going overseas. Just dropped by to say hello and good-bye."

I said, "Leon, you're so young to be going off to war."

"Wanna go," he said. "Gonna be fun stabbing Nazis."

I tried not to show my shock. I said, "Do you have to hate them so much?"

With the same tone of voice his father had used, he said, "What do you want me to do, kiss 'em before I stab 'em?"

I heard from Leon twice after that—I got a valentine from him from somewhere in France. It read, "For my teacher who was more like a mother to me." Well, you know it just brought tears to my eyes. Then his next letter said something like "Gunning them down like hell. Haven't had my shoes off in ten days." Later I read that Leon had been killed in France, still manning his machine gun.

You know, when I hear today's kids complaining about the inequalities of life, I think about Leon. If only I could have done more. There was a little spark of love in his heart when he was in my class, but I didn't do much for it. If only I could had helped him to rekindle that flame!

CHAPTER TEN

❧

The Preacher's Sermon Was
"The Younger Generation
Is Going to the Dogs"

LIVING IN THE COMMUNITY

Teachers who taught in rural schools were usually local men or women who had obtained teaching certificates, or they were from a neighboring locale. In the latter case, they customarily lived in the community during the school term. They may have chosen to board locally because it was too far to commute from home, but in many cases, living in the community was a requirement of the school board. Some trustees felt teachers should also be required to attend all community functions—Sunday school, parties, picnics, funerals, and as Bargy Hargrove pointed out, nightly revival services. "You were expected to go to everything every night in the community."

Boarding among strangers could be an ordeal for teachers. They were expected to eat without complaint what the family ate—no matter that the wife was a poor cook or the diet tedious and monotonous. Sometimes one had a private room, but all too often one did not and would be asked to share a bed with a member of the family. Frequently the teacher was expected to assist with cooking, child tending, and general household chores. Victor Womack even served as the resident barber: "I don't know how good their haircuts were, but they were satisfied." It was a lucky teacher that had both private quarters and the freedom to leave the community on weekends to pursue personal interests.

Teachers who boarded some distance from school found travel to school as difficult as did the children. Walking, riding horseback, or driving a hack were the only means of transportation until later years when some would drive a Model A Ford. Wind, rain, cold, and the occasional blizzard were all elements with which to deal. They did whatever was necessary to arrive at school on time—in good weather and in bad.

"Oh, No, You're Not Going to Live in Will's Room"
ALINE DARDEN NORTHRUP

When I was teaching one year, I lived with Oscar Gray and his mother, Aunt Lindy. I had what was called Will's room—he was the married son who had moved away. There wasn't a door from it into the rest of the house. It was outside on the porch. You had to go outside on the porch from his room to enter the rest of the house. At first Aunt Lindy wouldn't hear to it. She said, "Oh, no, you're not going to live in Will's room."

I don't know whether Oscar talked to her or what, but she said I could move in. I had a half-bed and one chair and a little two-burner oil stove that set on a box. I made me a closet by tying a string across the corner. I paid rent, but I cooked my own meals. Well, Aunt Lindy got sick. She was a sweet person when you got to know her. Lots of afternoons I would go in her kitchen and cook supper for the three of us.

While she was sick, I didn't know how Oscar was handling the linens. So I sneaked around—I forget who came after me that Friday to take me into town—but I gathered up all the sheets and things and took them to town and washed them there at the laundry. Oh, I thought Oscar was going to beat me to death. I said, "Now, you just hush. It's all right for me to do this. Your mother needed clean linens."

It was a great experience for me when we put on a community play. We had to go to the church tabernacle because it was larger and had a stage or platform, but it was several miles from the schoolhouse. In my mind I was wondering what are we going to use for curtains. Well, some of the men brought wagon sheets. We strung them up there and we had a big play. Just a Christmas-type play. Fun things. Somebody was Santa Claus. And boy, he was funny. Someone said he must have had a bottle because he was so funny. All of our programs were done at the tabernacle.

Merle Made Me a Riding Skirt with Great Big Legs
INA DINGUS COWAN

When I taught at Lake Creek School, which was in Haskell County, we lived four miles from school on a farm. I rode a horse four miles to school, four miles there and four miles back. Eight miles in all. We had a car but we bought only the gas we had to. In those days gas must have been eleven or twelve cents a gallon, so we didn't buy much gas. We rode a horse if we had to go short distances. Once in a while, I'd use the car. I rode the horse for four years, but I enjoyed it.

I had a big, long-legged, gray horse. Gray mare. She was a good ol' horse, Dolly. One time she threw me. She was skittish. I was coming down the road, and I was running in a fast lope because I wanted to get home. A paper of some sort blew across from the pasture right in front of her and she whirled just like that, and I went over the fence. The fence was there and I got caught on it. It was wintertime, and I had a heavy coat on. And there I lay across that fence. It caught me at the waist, but it didn't hurt me one bit. I pulled myself up and unhooked that barbed wire and then got back on the horse. The horse had stopped nearby. Ever'time something like that would happen, she'd stop right there.

The kids had a lot of fun about me riding the horse. I couldn't wear pants, but my sister Merle made me a riding skirt, we called it, with great big legs. And we wore starched dresses. You can imagine how my starched dresses looked when I got to school. The skirt was made out of a heavy-type denim. I pulled my dress up to make it work. We called it a riding skirt. I just put it over my clothes and just pulled it off when I got to the schoolroom, but my dress was just wadded, you know. We starched and ironed our clothes. We didn't have very nice clothes to wear. We just wore what we had. Homemade.

The Preacher's Sermon Was
"The Younger Generation Is Going to the Dogs"

BARGY FIELDS HARGROVE

Sometimes I went home on the weekends and sometimes I didn't. I went to church in the community when I stayed over the weekend, or to the goat ropings, or whatever event they had. You were expected to go to everything every night in the community.

Once there was this revival meeting at church. If there was anything going on, everybody went. I went to church every night during the revival and was offended and insulted regularly, but I went. One night my boyfriend Tom came up to see me, and we went into town to see the show. Tom always bought cigarettes to smoke on his dates, but he rolled Bull Durham to smoke for everyday. You know, Bull Durham was a type of "roll your own" tobacco. Tom usually bought "ready-rolls" to smoke with me.

On the way home from the show, we went home by the canyon road, but he had forgotten to buy cigarettes. So he said he wanted to smoke and pulled over beside the road to roll a cigarette. I looked back and said, "Here comes the preacher." Tom had the lights on so he could see to roll his cigarette. Headlights, dome light, and everything. The preacher had a floodlight. He came on by, and that was all there was to it. I didn't think any more about it.

The next Sunday morning, I was sitting in church, half asleep. The preacher's sermon was "The Younger Generation Is Going to the Dogs." He said, "And just last Wednesday night, as I was coming in from church, across those seven canyons, just as I topped the hill, there was a car, and I narrowly averted a wreck. I had to turn to the ditch to miss it, and there were two people in that car, but they were so closely embraced, they looked like one." Everybody turned and looked at me. I could have died. If we had been sitting there smooching, it would have been different. If it had been the truth, I wouldn't have felt so bad. I hated him as long as he lived.

They Sent to Town for Five Pounds of Cheese

BARGY FIELDS HARGROVE

One man in the community was a character. I boarded with them. He'd sit and talk and advise me. I got all kinds of advice. He didn't believe in life insurance. He thought that was a form of gambling. You were just betting the devil a certain amount of money that you wouldn't die, and you were going to lose it anyway because you were going to die anyhow. He would sit and talk about the first time he saw his wife. He said he thought she was the cutest little thing he ever saw in his life, and he just knew he had to have her.

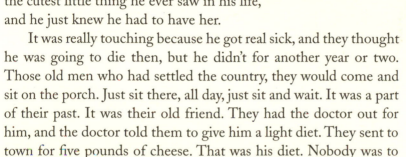

It was really touching because he got real sick, and they thought he was going to die then, but he didn't for another year or two. Those old men who had settled the country, they would come and sit on the porch. Just sit there, all day, just sit and wait. It was a part of their past. It was their old friend. They had the doctor out for him, and the doctor told them to give him a light diet. They sent to town for five pounds of cheese. That was his diet. Nobody was to touch that cheese but this man. The doctor said he was to have a light diet—and the cheese was their idea of a light diet!

When I was staying with the same family, right at the foot of my bed, in a place of honor, was a picture of "Papa's first wife's little dead baby." There was a picture of a baby, life-size picture of a baby, just propped upon a pillow. A dead baby, very dead. I got the impression it was a baby about several months old. It was the last thing I saw at night and the first thing I saw in the morning. That picture did haunt me. It was in a place of honor.

"Mrs. Robinson, Get Me to a Doctor Quick. I Think I'm Dying"

NARCISSA CLEGG

In the twenties I was teaching across the river. A teacher at a neighboring school was named Miss Flora Ball [all names changed], and she was secretly married to Curtis Harris, a young man in our community. She was a nice, pretty girl. She boarded with Mrs. Robinson.

We didn't know it then, but we found out later that she was married to Curtis. The way it was, they married secretly. In those days if you were married you lost your job. They wouldn't give a married woman a job teaching. There were two reasons. One was because you might get pregnant and have to quit, but the main reason was that jobs were scarce, and a man should make the living. If a woman was married, the husband was supposed to make a living for his wife. If you were a married woman, you weren't supposed to be teaching. You needed to give up your job so somebody else could have one. Jobs were scarce.

When Miss Flora got sick, she said she had appendicitis, and she was out of school a whole week. I don't know how she knew she had appendicitis unless she was sick before and the doctor told her. As far as I know, she didn't have any doctor at that time. Some folks were suspicious about that. I heard later that she might have been pregnant. But of course, we didn't know she was married.

My father was a trustee, and he went by where she was boarding to see her on Friday. He said, "Are you going to be able to teach on Monday?"

She said, "If I can climb that hill, I will." There was a big hill on the road between the Robinsons and the schoolhouse. He said he just thought she wouldn't be able to climb that hill from the way she looked when he saw her.

He told us later, "If I'd have known she and Curtis were married, I'd have got him word right then." But it wouldn't have done any good, because Saturday morning Curtis did come over there, and he found her sick. He was living at that time over in another part of the county about fifteen miles south.

Mrs. Robinson said that when Curtis came and found her sick, he came to her and told her that they were married. He then showed her the license, which was proof, of course. She said, "All right, you can stay in the room with her." So he did. He stayed all night. On Sunday morning, he left and went back to his place, and after he left she took a bad spell. Mrs. Robinson said Flora called out to her, "Mrs. Robinson, get me to a doctor quick. I feel like I'm dying." So Mrs. Robinson called the doctor, and he came out, and he was scared. He knew she certainly needed help right away.

He said, "I'm going to call the ambulance." The ambulance had to come from Stamford, which was sixty miles away. There wasn't a hospital closer. It was in the afternoon after church, and they called my brother Jim and asked him to come with his car and start Miss Flora to meet that ambulance. That was the doctor's orders: *Somebody take her to meet that ambulance.* So Jim went and he didn't get very far before they met the ambulance. The ambulance took her, and when they got to Stamford, they wouldn't operate, because they said it wasn't any use.

They called her family who lived somewhere down toward Fort Worth, and when her sister called the hospital back to see about her, she asked for Miss Flora by name and nobody knew where she was. Finally, somebody came on the line and told her, "She's too sick to be in the hospital." Later they found her at the funeral home. She was dead. And I think that was the end of that school year.

When We Got Ready to Go Home, That River Had Come Down

JEWELL BRANCH

When I taught at Red Bluff, I stayed on one side of the river and the school was on the other. The school was on the Double Mountain Fork of the Brazos River, you know. We usually didn't have any trouble getting across. Unless it rained pretty big, it never had much water in it. We'd walk across or sometimes ride a horse. One time we went to school in the morning, and the sun was shining as pretty as could be, but when we got ready to go home, that river had come down from way up yonder, and it was bank to bank—rolling on.

Mr. Whatley came out there with his horse and would swim across the river on his horse. He took one or two of the kids across at a time. The horse was getting tired, and my time was coming, and I was afraid of that thing. So I just told Mr. Whatley to go ahead that I would stay with some people on this side of the river. Mr. Whatley said, "Oh, I'll just put William on the horse with you. He don't weigh much. He's lighter'n I am." William was his young son. I said, "You just let him go on with that horse, and I'll stay over here on this side of the river tonight." So I stayed.

I Had to Room with Their Youngest Girl
FORRESTER PRICE

Someone in the community would volunteer to board the teacher. I stayed with the Fraziers. They lived about three miles back northeast of the school. I think I paid about twenty-five dollars a month for room and board. There were three children in their family and two were in school. The girl was in eighth and the little boy was in the second or third grade. I had to room with their youngest girl. She was six years old but didn't go to school. I had to sleep with her. We walked to school. I went home nearly every weekend. That helped me and them too.

I Cut the Hair of a Lot of Men and Boys out There
VICTOR WOMACK

I boarded with a man who had a son about my age. For entertainment I'd ride out on the range over here, there, and yonder. I didn't go to town from the time my school started until Christmas, and from Christmas until time it was out. It was too far. Fifty miles.

I cut the hair of a lot of men and boys out there. The ranch hands, men from the different ranches around, would come in. I don't know how I got started, but anyway I cut the hair on them. I don't know how good their haircuts were, but they were satisfied.

Occasionally they'd have dances out there and invite everybody in. They'd dance all day and spend the night a lot of times. It'd be too far to go home after dark. I didn't have a girl, but I attended some of those dances—square dancing. The whole family would go in the hack or the wagon. They'd bring quilts for them to sleep on when they spent the night. Some of them would come for twenty-five miles. I didn't have a date with a girl until school was out.

I knew my wife for eight years before we were married. I had just been discharged from the army and I began to court her in earnest. She was still in SMU then, and I'd go see her pretty often. I wanted to be sure she wasn't ashamed of me so I would hire a Packard limousine to go out to see her. That was some automobile in those days. I used the Aldophus Rent-a-Car Company. It was pretty expensive. I didn't drive the car—I had a driver. They didn't rent them without a chauffeur. It really impressed the girls. They had a big living room when I would come and would have to wait. My wife

202

says that the girls would flirt with me until she came down the stairs. Maybe they did.

When Somebody Wanted Entertainment, We'd Have a Kangaroo Court

BARGY FIELDS HARGROVE

In those days we usually had to invent our own fun, so out at County Line, when somebody wanted entertainment, they'd say, "Let's have a kangaroo court." That's a mock trial, you know, usually done for fun, and most of the time, I was the one on trial. When I was there, they didn't have to figure around about who the victim would be. I was the victim. You had to be a good sport and go along with it or it would be worse. They'd pick out something to try me over. Somebody would be the defense attorney, and somebody else would be the prosecuting attorney. They would go at it just like a real trial. They'd bring up witnesses and everything.

I remember one that I just cringed over. I would have done anything if I could have gotten out of that kangaroo court. They decided to try some ol' boy for breaking my heart. I don't remember his name, but I'll call him Sam. He wasn't too bright. He would come down to where I was boarding in his little old red car, and I'd see him coming, and I'd just disappear and wouldn't come back until he was gone.

One Sunday afternoon we were all sitting on the porch, and Sam told me that I had a head like a striped watermelon. That was his compliment. I thanked him kindly. Sometimes I wouldn't see him coming and would get caught. Once he just appeared, and it was at night. I just got up and took the lamp into the next room and shut the door. Other times when I would see his car coming, I'd head for the canyons.

Well, one time Sam had gone to Oklahoma and came back with a little bride. Before they had married, the girl's daddy phoned Sam to get up there right now because his daughter was pregnant, and they were going to get married or else. Sam comes back with this little old girl. So they tried Sam in the kangaroo court for breaking my heart—for going off and getting married. And here sits this little pregnant bride on the front seat in the middle of it. There was nothing I could do. There was no way I could get out of any of it. She never spoke to me again, but I couldn't blame her for that, either. I wanted to kill a few people around there, too.

They got me up on the witness stand and said, "Is it true or not true that when Sam came to your house that you took the lamp and went into the bedroom?"

I'd say, "Wait, let me explain." I couldn't say that I was running from him, and there sits his little wife.

They'd say, "Yes or no? Answer yes or no."

So I said, "Yes, I did go to the bedroom." Someone else would testify that they saw me break into a run when I saw Sam's car coming toward the house.

They'd say, "Is that true? Yes or no?"

Well, it would be true, only I was running in the opposite direction. That was how they would conduct their kangaroo court. It was more fun than anything they had in the community. But I was the goat. There wasn't a thing to do but grin and bear it.

A Big Rattlesnake Got under the Schoolhouse during Church
BARGY FIELDS HARGROVE

The church at Lloyd Mountain met in the schoolhouse. That was the only church they had there. One Sunday, a big rattlesnake got under the schoolhouse during church. They knew there would be school the next day, and they all had kids there in school, so they had to get that snake out. There was just one opening to go under the schoolhouse. Mozelle Rubenstien, who didn't have any children in school, went under the house with a fishing pole with a hook on the end of it. He crawled under there with a flashlight, not knowing how many snakes he was going to find. They just knew that big one went under there, and he eventually brought it out. I was impressed by his bravery. I just couldn't feature it. The last house I went under, I met a snake, so I've never been under another one.

I got really upset when we began to bring up mice in the water from the school cistern. I just pitched a fit. The mice got in by going down the drain pipe and falling into the water where they would drown. I carried on and argued with the trustees until finally they went over and emptied all the water out and refilled it. When I found out that they had filled it from out of the stock tank where the cows and everybody in the county was wading in and out, I knew I hadn't helped myself any.

They Had Never Seen Me Show Such Anger Before
STELLA GIPSON POLK

Another year when I was teaching—it was about noon—I looked out the window and saw a woman coming down the road toward the school as fast as she could come. She looked like she was carrying something, and as she got closer I realized it was a baby. I put down my books and went out to meet her. It was Mrs. Hart carrying her year-old baby boy with her two little children running along behind her. The Harts were a family of poor renters. I thought the baby was dead, but Mrs. Hart was finally able to quit babbling enough for me to realize the baby had drunk some kerosene.

There was no telephone around, so I got one of the older girls to take over the lessons while I took Mrs. Hart into town to the doctor. I didn't know if it was too late for help or not, but I had to try. I drove my rattletrap of a car too fast and prayed for my threadbare tires to hold out. Mrs. Hart couldn't climb the stairs to the doctor's office with the baby, so I took him. He was making bubbles with each breath, and he smelled like kerosene. It was all so frightening and nauseating that I was afraid I was going to be sick right there on the stairs.

The doctor started to work right then with a stomach pump, and the terror of it all—the smell of kerosene as it come up—was too much for me. I ran to the window and was sick as I could be. After the baby was revived, I drove Mrs. Hart and her babies home to the hovel they lived in. I had paid the doctor bill and I was concerned about that, because I knew my husband and I didn't really have money to spare. I went on back to school wondering what my husband would say. I knew he would say I had done the right thing, but I couldn't help but worry.

A little while before this happened, I'd been having trouble with some snotty kids when we were playing games because they didn't want to hold hands with some of the poorer, dirty kids from the sharecroppers' families. Instead of holding hands with them, they'd place a stick between them and make the poorer kids hold on to one end while they held on to the other. That way they didn't have to touch each other, don't you see. I had been doing my best to keep this from happening, but sometimes they did it without my noticing. Well, that afternoon when we went out for recess, we were playing "Squat, Little Josie," and I saw that there was a stick between one of the girls and the oldest Hart girl. After what I had been through, the revulsion of it all just hit me. I grabbed that stick and threw it as far as I could. The children were shocked. They had never seen me show such temper before. Then I let them have it. I laid down the law as I should have done when I first noticed the sticks. I told them if I ever saw any child hold a stick between him and some other child, I would switch him good—and that rule was for the girls as well as the boys.

The Empty Schoolhouse

Epilogue

Rural schools continued to flourish until the advent of automobiles and mechanized farming. With improved transportation and the development of larger farms, the small rural district was no longer necessary, and the move toward consolidation began. All-weather roads, fast-moving buses and cars, and dwindling rural populations enabled school districts to assemble large numbers of children together in one place. It was no longer necessary to teach all of the children in a community in one building with one or two teachers. The consolidation of several small districts into one larger unit meant classes could be arranged by grade level, teachers could be more specialized, a secondary school program could be developed, and funds for additional supplies and resources were available from state financing.

Major population shifts, which began to occur shortly before and soon after World War II, brought great influxes of people into urban centers. African American families seeking a less hostile environment and improved economic conditions migrated from the rural South to Chicago, Newark, and Philadelphia. Poor sharecroppers and drought-stricken farmers left Oklahoma, Texas, and other dust bowl states for the "promised land" of California. Soldiers and sailors returning from the war were less willing to remain on the farm; more favorable economic opportunities awaited in the cities.

As more and more people moved into urban areas, competition for housing became more intense. In the heart of the cities, diverse ethnic groups were crowded into adjacent and often overlapping neighborhoods, leaving little room for new arrivals. What had been small communities of families sharing common interests and goals (and often a common heritage, including the same religious background) evolved into a conglomerate of people and too frequently a clash of cultures.

Postwar years saw large numbers of American women joining the workforce for the first time. As they began punching time clocks, there was less time for nurturing and rearing children. Societal problems relating to adequate day care, latchkey children, and overstressed moms became common. Additionally, the rising rate of divorce became a phenomenon that threatened the traditional family structure.

The 1960s produced dramatic changes in the composition of schools in the South as the Supreme Court outlawed segregation and mandated racial integration. Busing to schools outside one's neighborhood became commonplace as efforts were made to achieve racially mixed schools.

The schools that evolved after World War II reflected the changes in society and were different establishments from the rural schools of the 1920s and 1930s. Instead of the children in a family "taking lessons" together in one room with a common teacher, it was unlikely they would see one another during the school day. They were not only in different rooms but were often in separate buildings, sometimes on separate campuses. As individual schools moved from the traditional calendar toward a year-round school, siblings might start and end the school year at different times and have different holiday recesses.

While the goal of education has remained constant—to imbue pupils with knowledge and skills that would enable them to lead happy, productive lives in a democratic society—materials, methodology, and philosophy have been in continual flux. Educators have torn down walls to create open-concept classrooms, put up walls to create a more conducive environment, abandoned phonics in favor of whole language, abandoned whole language in favor of phonics, advocated teachers be specialists teaching one discipline, advocated

208

teachers be generalists teaching multilevel, multidiscipline classes. In spite of this "much ado," educators have yet to find the illusive formula that would ensure that all children learn to read, think critically, or for that matter, stay in school until graduation. Critics decry the problems facing today's schools, citing falling test scores, disciplinary problems, drugs in the schools, lack of safety for children, and time spent on controversial subjects as opposed to basic learning, for example, reading, mathematics, and science.

The criticism surrounding today's schools has spawned new movements as parents and school districts have sought alternative means of educating their children. There is a growing trend toward home schooling, a renewed interest in private and parochial schools, and an increased emphasis on specialized schools, such as accelerated schools, magnet programs, applied learning centers, schools-within-a-school, and Montessori programs.

Amidst the controversy that defines present-day schools, there is a mystique that surrounds the schools of yesteryear. It is not uncommon to hear people lamenting the loss of the good old days, when children were taught to obey their elders and study their lessons, when they could parse their verbs and one could read their handwriting, and when they knew a spanking at school meant an additional one at home. There are those who clamor for a return to the basics and those who lay the ills of test scores on a failure to teach as they did "when I was in school." There are even those who would advocate a return to the one-room school. The implication is that those schools succeeded in ways today's schools have not.

Although the great debate as to what constitutes an "effective school" is not likely to be settled in this century, there are lessons to be learned from looking at the past. It is hoped this research will add to the growing body of educational knowledge and will, in some way, help serve the ends of education.

ɞ And so my project is ended. I have held a mirror to the face of rural West Texas, and it has reflected to me a slice of life of the early days of this century. We have learned much of the one-room school. We know how pupils were taught, what games they played, what they carried for lunch. More important, we know something of their value system, of their indomitable spirit, of the sense of playfulness that alleviated the harshness of their environment. It is all here—

Lizzie Underwood's mother's fried pies, Buddy Burnett's clandestine cigarettes, Dorothy Head's hand-me-down clothes, Jim Poteet's games of mumbly-peg, Ina Cowan's joy of teaching.

While my research was intended for the enrichment of future generations, it is my own life that has been most enriched. When I read portions of these accounts aloud in gatherings, the audience is universally pleased, but it is I who derives the most pleasure from the reading. Like Ina Cowan, I have enjoyed this project twice—once in the collecting and writing, now in the reading and sharing. Thank you, Maud Bailey and Leo Clegg. Thank you, Fila Campbell and Stella Polk. Thank you, all of you. Now let us shut the gate and get on home!

Selected Bibliography

Books and Articles

Blanton, Annie Webb. "The Child of the Texas One-Teacher School." *University of Texas Bulletin* 3613 (1936).

———. "A Hand Book of Instruction As to Education in Texas: Scholastic Years, 1918–1922." *Department of Education Bulletin* 157 (January, 1923).

Boyer, Ernest L. *The Basic School: A Community for Learning.* Princeton, N.J.: Carnegie Foundation, 1995.

Butterworth, Julian Edward, and Howard A. Dawson. *The Modern Rural School.* New York: McGraw-Hill, 1952.

Charyk, John C. *Syrup Pails and Gopher Tails: Memories of the One-Room School.* Saskatoon, Saskatchewan: Western Producers Prairie Books, 1983.

Cordier, Mary Hurlbut. *Schoolwomen of the Prairies and Plains: Personal Narratives from Iowa, Kansas, and Nebraska, 1860s–1920s.* Albuquerque: University of New Mexico Press, 1992.

Cubanz, Larry. *How Teachers Taught: Constancy and Change in American Classrooms, 1880–1990.* 2nd ed. New York: Teachers College Press, 1993.

Cubberley, Ellwood Patterson. *The Improvement of Rural Schools.* Boston: Houghton Mifflin, 1912.

Eby, Frederick. "Education in Texas: Source Materials." *University of Texas Bulletin* 1824 (April 25, 1918).

Eells, Harry L. *Rural School Management.* New York: Scribner's Sons. 1924.

Eggleston, Joseph Dupuy. *The Work of the Rural School.* New York: Harper and Brothers, 1913.

Evans, C. E. *The Story of Texas Schools.* Austin: Steck, 1955.

Foght, Harold Waldstein. *The American Rural School: Its Characteristics, Its Future, and Its Problems.* New York: Macmillan, 1918.

Fuller, Wayne. *The Old Country School: The Story of Rural Education in the Middle West.* Chicago: University of Chicago Press, 1982.

Gordon, Julia Weber. *My Country School Diary: An Adventure in Creative Teaching.* New York: Harper and Brothers, 1946.

Graves, Frank Pierrepont. *A History of Education in Modern Times.* New York: Macmillan, 1920.

Grumet, Madeleine R. *Bitter Milk: Women and Teaching.* Amherst: University of Massachusetts Press, 1988.

Gulliford, Andrew. *America's Country Schools.* Washington, D.C.: Preservation Press, 1984.

Hilton, Ernest. *Rural School Management.* New York: American Book Company, 1949.

Johnson, Clifton. *Old-Time Schools and School-Books.* New York: Dover, 1963.

Kirkpatrick, Marion Greenleaf. *The Rural School from Within.* Philadelphia: Lippincott, 1917.

Lewis, Charles Dickens. *The Rural Community and Its Schools.* New York: American Book Company, 1937.

Lowth, Frank J. *Everyday Problems of the Country Teacher: A Textbook and a Handbook of Country-School Practice.* New York: Macmillan, 1926.

Manning, Diane. *Hill Country Teacher: Oral Histories from the One-Room School and Beyond.* Boston: Twayne Publishers, 1990.

Polk, Stella Gipson. *For All Those Pupils Whose Lives Touched Mine.* College Station: Texas A&M University Press, 1989.

Power, Edward J. *Main Currents in the History of Education.* New York: McGraw-Hill, 1962.

Prentice, Alison, and Marjorie R. Theobald, eds. *Women Who Taught: Perspectives on the History of Women and Teaching.* Toronto: University of Toronto Press, 1991.

Rowold, Milam C. "The Texas Rural Schools Revisited, 1900–1929." Ph.D. diss., University of Texas at Austin, 1983.

Schatzmann, Iman. *The Country School at Home and Abroad.* Chicago: University of Chicago Press, 1942.

Sitton, Thad, and Milam C. Rowold. *Ringing the Children In: Texas Country Schools.* College Station: Texas A&M University Press, 1987.

Smallwood, James, ed. *And Gladly Teach: Reminiscences of Teachers from Frontier Dugout to Modern Module.* Norman: University of Oklahoma Press, 1976.

Stokes, L. D. *Report of the Results of the Texas Statewide School Adequacy Survey.* Austin: State Board of Education, 1936.

Thomas, Roy Edwin. *Come Go with Me: Old-Timer Stories from the Southern Mountains.* New York: Farrar, Straus, Giroux, 1994.

Waldstein, Harold. *The Rural Teacher and His Work: In Community Leadership, in School Administration, and in Mastery of the School Subjects.* New York: Macmillan, 1918.

Woofter, Thomas Jackson. *Teaching in Rural Schools*. Boston: Houghton Mifflin, 1917.

Works, George Alan, and Simon O. Lesser. *Rural America Today, Its Schools and Community Life*. Chicago: University of Chicago Press, 1942.

Interviewees

FANNIE WILLINGHAM ALBERT
> Born 1900, interviewed October, 1986
> Attended Old Hobbs School, Fisher County, 1907–14

MAUD ARNOLD BAILEY
> Born 1890, interviewed November, 1986
> Taught at Mitchell and Willow Grove Schools, Hamilton and Eastland Counties, 1912–16

JOSIE MAE BAIRD
> Born 1905, interviewed September, 1986
> Attended Riverdale and Perkel Schools, Kent County, 1916–20
> Taught at County Line, Cottonwood Flat, and Harmony Schools; Fisher, Kent, and Scurry Counties, 1924–30

JO MATTHEWS BLACKSHEAR
> Born 1933, interviewed October, 1986
> Attended Wright School, Stonewall County, 1939–40

MARY THOMSON BOYDSTUN
> Born 1920, interviewed September, 1986
> Attended County Line School, Fisher County, 1927–34

JEWELL BRANCH
> Born c. 1906, interviewed October, 1986
> Taught at Red Bluff School, Stonewall County

FRED BROWN
> Born 1909, interviewed November, 1986
> Attended Bunker Hill and Flattop Schools, Haskell County, 1916–?

THELMA THOMSON BURK
> Born 1927, interviewed October, 1986
> Attended County Line School, Fisher County, 1933–38

PRENTICE MERRILL [BUDDY] BURNETT
> Born 1914, interviewed October, 1986
> Attended Camp Springs School, Scurry County, c. 1920–22

LOUISE SMITH CALLAN
Born 1910, interviewed September, 1986
Taught at County Line School, Fisher County, 1929–30

FILA CAMPBELL
Born 1898, interviewed October, 1986
Taught at Center, Mountain View, and Dowell Schools; Fisher County,
c. 1916–24

COMER CLAY
Born 1910, interviewed March, 1996
Attended Hawley School, Taylor County, 1916–19
Taught at Wylie, Taylor County, 1931–32

OVESTA McCLESKEY CLAY
Born 1910, interviewed March, 1996
Attended Veale and Frankell Schools, Stephens County 1916–24
Taught at Frankell School, Stephens County, 1931–35, 1945

ERNEST CLIFFORD CLEGG
Born 1910, interviewed October, 1986
Attended County Line and Riverdale Schools, Fisher and Kent Counties,
1917–25

JAMES PAUL CLEGG
Born 1928, interviewed October, 1986
Attended County Line School, Fisher County, 1935–38

LEO EARL CLEGG
Born 1907, interviewed September, 1986
Attended County Line and Riverdale Schools, Fisher and Kent Counties,
1915–22

LEWIS HILLIARD CLEGG
Born 1901, interviewed October, 1986
Attended County Line and Riverdale Schools, Fisher and Kent Counties,
1909–18

NARCISSA POTEET CLEGG
Born 1902, interviewed July, 1983
Attended County Line School, Fisher County, 1909–17
Taught at Riverdale School, Kent County, 1924–25

BESSIE CLEVELAND
Born 1914, interviewed October, 1986
Attended Pleasant Valley School, Fisher County, 1924–29
Taught at Pleasant Valley School, Fisher County, 1942–44

BILL CLEVELAND
Born 1909, interviewed October, 1986
Attended Pleasant Valley School, Fisher County, 1925–?

WALTER CLEVELAND
Born 1906, interviewed October, 1986
Attended Pleasant Valley School, Fisher County, 1913–20

INA DINGUS COWAN
Born 1906, interviewed December, 1986
Attended Van Dyke School, Comanche County, 1913–20
Taught at Bowman, Grasshopper, and Lake Creek Schools; Comanche and
    Haskell Counties, 1924–38

DONO DARDEN
Born 1903, interviewed October, 1986
Attended Hitson and Pleasant Valley Schools, Fisher County, 1909–17

BESSIE FORD DAVIDSON
Born 1903, interviewed February, 1987
Attended Kelly School, Collingsworth County, c. 1912
Taught at Kelly and Kessler Schools, Collingsworth County, c. 1923

PICOLA CAMPBELL FOREMAN
Born c. 1901, interviewed February, 1987
Taught at Salt Creek School, Stonewall County, 1925

MITTIE McKENZIE GEESLIN
Born 1898, interviewed November, 1986
Taught at Chapel Hill, Cedar Knob, Hannah Valley, Regency, and Star Schools;
    Mills County, 1918–24

H. GOVAN
Born 1898, interviewed October, 1986
Attended Crockett Colored School, Crockett County, 1906–14

ADDIE BOSTICK GREEN
Born 1900, interviewed September, 1986
Attended Riverdale School, Kent County, 1906–15

DELIA THOMSON HARDIN
Born 1922, interviewed October, 1986
Attended County Line School, Fisher County, 1929–36

MARGUERITE [BARGY] FIELDS HARGROVE
Born 1916, interviewed September, 1986
Taught at County Line and Lloyd Mountain Schools, Fisher and Scurry
    Counties, 1932–36

VIRGINIA PATE HAYES

Born 1923, interviewed January, 1995
Attended Northwest Ward and Southwest Ward, Lubbock County,
   c. 1930–36

DOROTHY THOMSON HEAD

Born 1924, interviewed October, 1986
Attended County Line School, Fisher County, 1930–38

LORENE RUCKER HENDERSON

Born 1906, interviewed October, 1986
Attended school in Erath County, 1912–16

CARL HENDRIX

Born 1894, interviewed October, 1986
Taught at Grady School, Fisher County, c. 1920

ERNESTINE COX HERREN

Born 1915, interviewed November, 1986
Attended Corinth School, Haskell County, 1924–26
Taught at Tanner Paint and Tonk Creek Schools, Haskell County,
   1934–37

IRA HESTER

Born c. 1906, interviewed December, 1986
Attended Mid and New Mid Schools, Haskell County, 1920–23

CLYDE HODGES

Born c. 1900, interviewed November, 1986
Attended Pound School, Comanche County, c. 1907–14

EUNICE POTEET HUCKABY

Born 1918, interviewed July, 1994
Attended County Line School, Fisher County, 1924–32

J. D. [BUDDY] HUDNALL

Born 1916, interviewed October, 1986
Attended Cottonwood School, Scurry County, c. 1923–30

MOLLIE CLEGG HUDNALL

Born 1908, interviewed September, 1986
Attended County Line and Riverdale Schools, Fisher and Kent Counties,
   1915–23

A. B. LAMPKIN

Born 1934, interviewed December, 1994
Attended Anson Colored School, Jones County, 1940–47

ABBIE WILLINGHAM MARTIN
Born c. 1898, interviewed November, 1986
Attended Old Hobbs School, Fisher County, c. 1905–13

ROBERT MARTINEZ
Born 1912, interviewed October, 1986
Attended Riverdale and Harmony Schools, Kent County, 1917, 1925–29

NAOMI ANDRESS MAYFIELD
Born 1914, interviewed October, 1986
Attended County Line, Fisher County, 1923–25

OPAL WATSON NANNY
Born 1907, interviewed November, 1986
Taught at Douglas School, Haskell County, 1932

ALINE DARDEN NORTHRUP
Born c. 1913, interviewed November, 1986
Taught at County Line School, Fisher County, 1936–38

JOE NORTON
Born 1910, interviewed October, 1986
Attended Prairie Valley School, Alfalfa County, Oklahoma, c. 1916

CORDELIA PATTERSON
Born c. 1905, interviewed November, 1986
Attended Dry Ridge School, Runnels County, c. 1911

MELVIN PATTERSON
Born 1903, interviewed November, 1986
Attended Pierce School, Runnels County, c. 1917–20

GRACE POTEET PHILLIPS
Born 1921, interviewed July, 1994
Attended County Line School, Fisher County, 1927–35

MARTHA HUDNALL PIKE
Born c. 1910, interviewed September, 1986
Attended Cottonwood Flat School, Scurry County, 1917–24

STELLA GIPSON POLK
Born c. 1901, interviewed November, 1986
Taught in Mason County and surrounding counties, 1917–44

HENRY THEODORE POTEET
Born 1911, interviewed October, 1986
Attended County Line School, Fisher County, 1919–25
Taught at County Line School, Fisher County, 1937–38

JAMES [JIM] POTEET
Born 1906, interviewed November, 1986
Attended County Line School, Fisher County, 1914–21

WILLIAM IVA POTEET
Born 1908, interviewed July, 1994
Attended County Line School, Fisher County, 1916–24

FORRESTER PRICE
Born 1909, interviewed September, 1986
Taught at Bitter Creek School, Taylor County, 1928–29

JUNA CLEGG REYNOLDS
Born 1932, interviewed October, 1986
Attended County Line School, Fisher County, 1937–38

CECIL A. SINGLETON
Born 1908, interviewed October, 1986
Attended Eureka School, Navarro County, 1915–22

EVA WALL SINGLETON
Born 1908, interviewed October, 1986
Attended Shady Grove School, Tarrant County, 1915–20

LOUISE STANDARD
Born c. 1906, interviewed October, 1986
Taught at Mountain View, Taylor County, c. 1926–30

BERTIE CLEGG THOMSON
Born 1903, interviewed September, 1986
Attended County Line and Riverdale Schools, Fisher and Kent Counties,
   1911–19

CONNIE HAYTER TUTT
Born 1901, interviewed October, 1986
Attended Hobbs School, Fisher County, 1908–16
Taught at Hobbs School, Fisher County, 1925–27

LIZZIE HELMS UNDERWOOD
Born 1898, interviewed September, 1986
Attended County Line School, Fisher County, c. 1906–14

JUANITA VINSON
Born 1933, interviewed November, 1986
Attended Oak Grove, Stephens County, 1940

NAOMI CLEGG VINYARD
Born 1912, interviewed October, 1986
Attended County Line School, Fisher County, 1918–25

MARJORIE SMITH WHITFIELD

Born 1913, interviewed November, 1986

Taught at County Line School, Fisher County, 1933–36

CLARA HAYTER WOMACK

Born 1898, interviewed February, 1987

Taught at Hobbs School, Fisher County, 1920–21

W. VICTOR WOMACK

Born 1898, interviewed February, 1987

Taught at Carmel, Lone Star, and Guinn Schools; Pecos and Fisher Counties,
1914–21

Index

Geeslin, Mittie McKenzie, 151, 172, 176, 186, 192, 215
Gilmer-Aikin Bill, 135
Goldthwaite, Tex., 151
Govan, H., 29, 215
Grady School, 7–8, 12, 149
Grasshopper School, 173
Grayson School, 8
Green, Addie Bostick, 85, 115, 215

Haliburton Readers, 66
Hamilton, Tex., 155
Hamlin, Tex., 39, 138
Hardin, Delia, 36, 37, 75, 96, 215
Hardin-Simmons College, 140
handicaps: as mental, 88–89, 186; as physical, 186, 187
Hankins Normal College, 160
Hannah Valley School, 152
Hargrove, Marguerite (Bargy) Fields, 146, 184, 195, 198, 199, 203, 205, 215
Harmony School, 9, 10, 96
Haskell, Tex., 174
Haskell County, xx, 22, 197
Hayes, Virginia, 32, 50, 216
Head, Dorothy, 41, 97, 210, 216
heating, providing for, 3, 5, 15, 16, 167
Henderson, Lorene, 132, 216
Hendrix, Carl, 149, 191, 216,
Herren, Ernestine Cox, 216,
Hester, Ira, 5, 21, 88, 109, 128, 216
Hitson School, 39
Hobbs School, 6–8, 11, 12, 67, 132, 154
Hodges, Clyde, 6, 10, 34, 66, 80, 110, 115, 119, 216
home visits, 188, 190–91
Huckaby, Eunice, 56, 81, 95, 136, 216
Hudnall, Buddy, 89, 123, 216
Hudnall, Mollie Clegg, 42, 47, 136, 216

illnesses, 53–54, 128–29, 141, 152, 176–78, 199–201, 205–206
itch (scabies) 163, 190–91
kangaroo court, 203
Keller School, 31
Kelley School, 148

Kent County, 9, 116
Kessler School, 148

Lake Creek School, 174, 197
Lampkin, A. B., 61, 75, 124, 216
library books, per capita expenditures, xx
lice, head, 131
literacy society (literaries), 14, 45, 58, 113
Lloyd Mountain School, 205
Lubbock, Tex., 50
lunches, providing for, 13, 27–28, 29, 110–12, 170–71
lunch time, 91–92, 104–12

McCauley, Tex., 153
McMurry College, 141
McWilliams School, 142
Martin, Abbie Willingham, 27, 45, 62, 70, 127, 129, 217
Martinez, Robert, 9, 55, 96, 217
Mason, Tex., 155
May Day, 104
Mayfield, Naomi, 26, 29, 30, 34, 77, 94, 118, 217
Merkel School, 155
Mid School, 5
Mills County, 9, 151
Mitchell School, 160
Mountain View School, 150, 182
Munday, Tex., 173
Murphree, Betty Jean, 36

Nanny, Opal Watson, 118, 188, 217
New Mid School, 5
Nolan County, 147
Northrup, Aline Darden, 36, 142, 159, 179, 196, 217
Norton, Joe, 25, 217

Oak Grove School, 13

Palava School, 137
parties. *See* social activities
Patterson, Cordelia, 64, 217
Patterson, Melvin, 217

223

Tuscola, Tex., 164
Tutt, Connie Hayter, 11, 120, 218

Underwood, Lizzie, xxiii, 32, 49, 101,
  125, 131, 218

Vinson, Juanita, 13, 95, 218
Vinyard, Naomi, 60, 72, 109, 136, 218
vouchers, payment with, 144, 154

water, drinking, providing for, 3, 22–25
weather: as blue northers 39–40; as bliz-
  zards 41, 42
Wellington, Tex., 148

Wesleyan College, 141
West Texas Normal School, 136
whippings. *See* discipline and punish-
  ment
Whitfield, Marjorie Smith, 158, 219
Will and May readers. *See Haliburton
  Readers*
Willow Grove School, 190
Womack, Clara Hayter, 163, 219
Womack, Victor, 153, 162, 188, 195, 202,
  219
Wright School, 19
Wylie School, 155